Worn

Worn

Footwear, Attachment and the Affects of Wear

Ellen Sampson

BLOOMSBURY VISUAL ARTS
LONDON • NEW YORK • OXFORD • NEW DELHI • SYDNEY

BLOOMSBURY VISUAL ARTS
Bloomsbury Publishing Plc
50 Bedford Square, London, WC1B 3DP, UK
1385 Broadway, New York, NY 10018, USA
29 Earlsfort Terrace, Dublin 2, Ireland

BLOOMSBURY, BLOOMSBURY VISUAL ARTS and the Diana logo are
trademarks of Bloomsbury Publishing Plc

First published in Great Britain 2020
This edition published 2022

Cover design by Adriana Brioso
Cover image: Black copper flip-flop: wear 1, 2015. © Ellen Sampson

A catalogue record for this book is available from the British Library.

A catalogue record for this book is available from the Library of Congress.

ISBN: HB: 978-1-3500-8718-7
         PB: 978-1-3502-9454-7
         ePDF: 978-1-3500-8720-0
         eBook: 978-1-3500-8719-4

Typeset by Integra Software Services Pvt. Ltd.
Printed and bound in Great Britain

To find out more about our authors and books visit www.bloomsbury.com
and sign up for our newsletters.

For Tim Stelfox-Griffin (1979–2007) who understood the magic of the everyday things.

Contents

List of Figures

Chapter 3

Chapter 4

Chapter 5

Afterword

Acknowledgements

This book would not have possible without the advice and support of my PhD supervisors Claire Pajzckowska and Flora Mclean: my work has been enriched immeasurably by their insight and guidance. Without their questions, kindness and conversation, it would not have been possible. I also thank my PhD examiners Carol Mavor and Jonathan Faiers, whose feedback and encouragement helped develop my doctoral thesis into this book, and my editor Frances Arnold who guided me through that process with kindness and wisdom.

Fellow researchers, Angela Maddock, Yeseung Lee, Elaine Igoe, Hilary Davidson, Yana Melkumova-Reynolds, Colleen Hill and Alexis Romano, who read and commented on aspects of the text at different stages of its development; your suggestions and critiques helped shape both this research and my thinking. I also thank my colleagues at the Fashion Research Network, for their collaboration and companionship on this journey.

A huge thank you to the numerous staff at Royal College of Art (RCA) who facilitated and advised on this project throughout. Beyond the RCA, I received invaluable technical support from Jessica Outred, Weronika Lesniak, Andrew Olley, Robyn Smith, Virginia Roundling and Sarah Cunningham.

To my wonderful husband Andrew Olley for all of his advice, kindness and love, always, my parents Nick and Daphne, for continually going beyond what is expected, and my dear friends, Judith Bovenscipen and Tara Blake-Harbord, who have been there throughout.

Lastly, I thank the Arts and Humanities Research Council, which provided funding for this research.

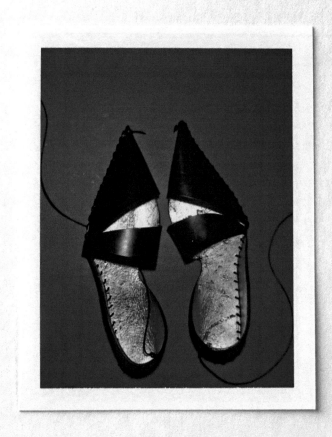

Preface

This is a book about the material culture of clothing, about the artefacts we hold closest to our bodily selves. It is an examination of our relationship with the things we wear, through a focus on a single group of garments: shoes. It examines the intimacies of our relationships with the things we wear: how they may work with us, for us and upon us. Analyses of clothing form an increasingly large part of material culture research. Often, however, these works address garments as objects of commerce, consumption and exchange, focusing on the points where clothing is distributed or acquired; new garments, ready to be bought and worn or those at the end of their useful life. Though the choices and processes through which we acquire and dispose of our clothes are important, a far greater part of these relationships is of wearing, of habitual tactile contact, maintenance and repair.

This book is about practices of wearing and the materiality of wornness; the experience of the body enveloped in clothes and the resultant imprints upon the garment. It brings to the fore the sensory and psychic processes of wearing; the intimate and unarticulated relationships with clothing that constitute a part of our daily lives. Locating itself within a psychoanalytic and phenomenological approach to material culture, it asks how these relationships can be interpreted. It investigates the unspoken intimacies we have with the things we wear and how their materiality makes these tactile relationships manifest. This book brings into focus the processes of wearing and the materiality of wornness – the experience of the body enveloped in clothes and the resultant imprints upon the garment. It addresses the reciprocal touch and counter-touch of the body and the shoe, the ways that they may cleave.

This book is about the self, about the surfaces and substances that bind us; the ways that we intermingle with the material world. It is an exploration of how material artefacts can come to hold a place within our psyche, how the tangible and intangible may interact within our interior and exterior worlds. Instead of addressing them as symbolic or historical objects it addresses them as everyday, as habitual material artefacts. It asks how shoes may afford us certain behaviours and what they might take in return; the materials that are sacrificed – and the bodies that are altered – through wear. It investigates the unspoken intimacies we have with the things we wear and how garments make these tactile relationships manifest. This is research about the trace of the body upon the garment, about the presence of absence, about things left behind.

This book is about wornness, about the particular affect of viewing worn clothing, about the way that used artefacts may act upon us as viewers. It explores the experience of an object outside of verbal narratives, the impact of these seemingly unintelligible markings made by the body over time. How does the empty shoe impact upon us, not as a symbol, but as a materialization, as trace? This research suggests that, in their wornness, our shoes are not simply signifiers of absence but indices of the gestures performed within them.

Opposite

Figure 0.1 *Black copper pointed shoe - Polaroid 1, 2015. Ellen Sampson.*

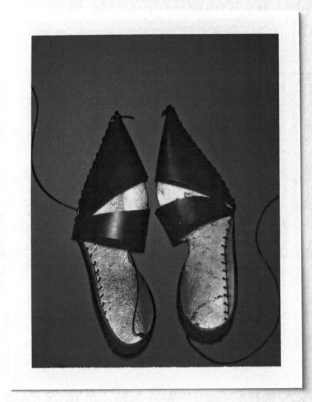
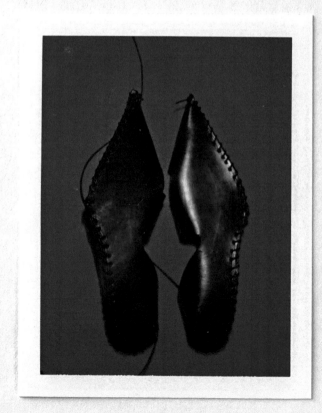

Introduction

I will start by asking you to look down at your feet, to inspect the garments in which they are clothed, your shoes. How does it feel to consider them? A shiver of disgust? A puff of pride? Are they scuffed and worn? Are there creases where toes have flexed, stains from rainy streets? Or are they new and shiny – manifestations of a fantasy of a self you have yet to become? 'You can tell a lot about someone by their shoes', people say, and there is some truth in this, though perhaps not quite in the way that they mean. Shoes are so often task-specific (wellingtons, ballet slippers, steel-toe-capped boots) and gendered (stilettos, wing-tipped city brogues), indicative of wealth (£1,000 designer heels and bespoke shoes) or poverty (flip-flops worn by labourers across the globe), of employment or leisure. Yet, they are also records: of the steps you have taken and the paths you have walked. They are imprinted with the weight of your body, the shape of your feet or the traces of those who wore them before you. More than almost any other garment, shoes tell our stories: where we have come from, where we have been.

Looking down at my own feet, I feel a rush of shame at my battered leather plimsolls (a footwear researcher should be better shod, I think). These shoes are shoes at the edge; almost – but not completely – destroyed. I have mended them many times – bought new laces, washed and bleached out stains, polished leather and carefully painted in scuffs – and yet they are explicitly and visibly worn. The vulcanized sole has spilt away from the leather and curls up towards my ankle at the heel, the mid-section is irreversibly creased by the perpetual rocking of my feet as I write. On the left-hand side the sole is nearly sheared, revealing a mess of composite layers within. 'Well-loved', someone might say kindly, but the truth is they are ruined – worn out, broken and old. These shoes, bland and neutral, have travelled with me for years, across continents, between jobs and archives, through interviews and exams. These shoes, which, through daily wear, have moulded so closely to the shape of my feet, are almost gone.

The battered shoe both connotes and denotes: it is layered with meanings and significations. Whilst new shoes may correlate more directly to a symbolic language of fashion (cf. Barthes 1980), wornness renders the shoe ambiguous: worn shoes are simultaneously object-like – inanimate and motionless away from the body – and bodily; inescapably corporeal relics shaped by the body that has worn them. In this ambiguity, wornness – the marks we inflict upon our clothes – confuses subject/object distinctions – the line between person and thing. At the centre of this book is a discussion of these

Opposite

Figure 0.2 *Black copper pointed shoe - Polaroids 1 and 2, 2015. Ellen Sampson.*

transitions, the shifts from new to used, from commodity to inalienable possession, from thingness to personhood and back again: transitions which typify our relationships with the things we wear. It explores how, in the progressive alteration of garments through use, they come to embody both internal and external experience. In doing so it raises questions about our relationship with imperfect garments, asking how imperfect garments act upon us as both viewers and wearers of clothes.

Opposite
Figure 0.3 *Author's trainers, 2017. Ellen Sampson.*

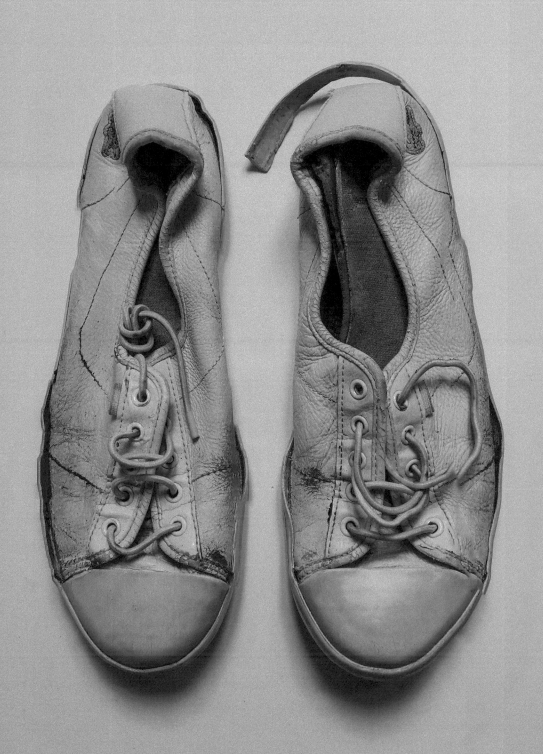

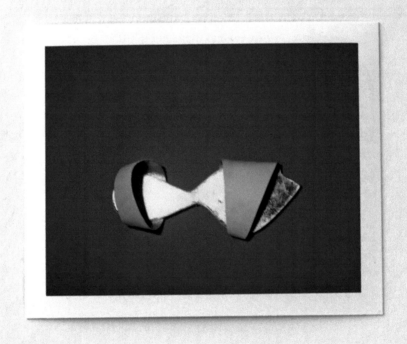

Wearing and wornness

Imperfect garments sit at the peripheries of fashion research, perhaps because used and imperfect garments are often on the peripheries of fashion itself. The fashion system – as both a cycle of commerce and of representation – is concerned with newness, with reinvention and transformation through the acquisition of goods. Fashion exists for an audience, it is a process of image making performed on the body and through its representations: films, photographs, illustrations and exhibitions. Fashion and fashioning are visual and performative acts – of identities and outfits constructed and composed through practice and things. Whilst clothing may be manipulated into fashion, often everyday garments are simply worn; wearing clothes is mundane practice. Clothes are active objects, busy agents in our networks of things: most garments are neither static in shops and showrooms nor preserved in archives and museums. Clothing is worn, used, laundered, mended, discarded and exchanged outside the formal cycles of the fashion system. Though the decisions and discourses which structure the purchase and disposal of our clothing are important, a far greater part of our relationship with our own clothes is of wearing (and not wearing); of the bodily experience of becoming and being clothed. These acts of wearing are both performative – the 'fashioning' of garments and selves – and habitual daily practice.

Over the past two decades there has been an increased interest in the embodied experience of wearing; the way clothes 'feel' as opposed to how they 'look'. Entwistle's seminal book *The Fashioned Body* (2000) led a broader move towards a more embodied understanding of wearing clothes. More recently, Sophie Woodward's (2007, 2015) research highlights the material agency of the garment: its capacity through form – rather than signification – to impact on bodily and embodied experience. Her work is part of a broader shift away from the structuralist and linguistic model of fashion, typified by Barthes' assertion that 'the tendency of every bodily covering [is] to insert itself into an organized, formal, and normative system that is recognized by society' (Barthes 2006: 7). This is an assertion which Carter, writing of the problematic nature of structuralist readings of fashion, critiques, highlighting that 'one of the problems attendant on placing garments into neat, definitional boxes, for instance protection, modesty, or communication, is that neither the category nor the garment seems to fit easily with one another. Only very rarely will clothing assume a form that is congruent with its designated use' (Carter 2012: 347). That is to say that, though we may attempt to taxonomize the garment, users do not abide by these taxonomies; they appropriate, subvert and alter garments to fit within their lives. Wearing is an active process of appropriation, alteration and compromise.

Opposite
Figure 0.4 *Tan copper sandal – wear 1. Polaroid 1, 2015. Ellen Sampson.*

If the greater part of our relationship with clothing is of wearing, then the majority of the clothing that we interact with is in a state of 'wornness'. That is to say, the majority of clothes we own are neither pristine and new, nor destroyed, preserved or archived. Wornness is a state of impermanence; the worn garment is always in flux. If we are to understand wornness as an intermediate state – an expanse between new and old – then we must also understand it as transitory, impermanent and unstable; unless a worn garment has been expertly preserved, it rarely stays in the same state for long: decay and use are intrinsically interlinked. Through use, the gradual inevitable destruction of an artefact (its entropy) is accelerated. This wornness is the outcome of wearing; it is the result of the sensual and embodied experience of wear. Transitory bodily experience is made manifest and material in the things we wear.[1] As we use clothes, they become records of our experiences, archives of the experience of wearing. Worn things are the outcome of our 'being in the world'; they are a mediating layer at the confluence of environment and bodily self. As such, our used garments hold a particular place in our networks of things, at once intimate (steeped in sweat, stretched by the girth of our thighs) and public, visible and on display.

This book suggests that, in researching clothing cultures and practices of dressing, we must turn our attention to wornness, to the ways our bodies affect our clothes. Wornness, the intermediate state between new and destroyed, is, in reality, the state of most of our clothes; most garments are on a spectrum between pristine and destroyed. Thus, worn and used clothes are a worthy topic of study; beyond ethical, philosophical or psychoanalytic concerns with wornness, worn things matter through sheer volume alone. Within fashion theory – as within much of the arts and social sciences – there has been a turn towards more materially focused research. This 'material turn' directly engages with the materiality of artefacts and the means of their production. Perhaps most famous is Stallybrass's haunting essay 'Worn Worlds' (1993), in which he explores the personal and historical materiality of mourning. De la Haye, Taylor and Thompson's book *A Family of Fashion: The Messel Dress Collection* (2005) and Evan's beautiful essay on stains and damage in Isabella Blow's clothing archive, 'Materiality, Memory and History: Adventures in the Archive' (2014), address accidental damage as evidence of lives well-lived. Similarly, both Davidson (2013) and Crooke (2012) have examined damaged and decaying garments as sources of affect; as powerful signifiers of violence, absence and grief. More recently, papers by Bide (2017) and Mida (2016) have addressed the traces of wear, in relation to social histories and the role of the researcher in the archive. These studies unpick the complex and entangled relationships we have with the materials we wear, bringing the garment's materiality into focus. Despite this increasing interest in imperfection, the materiality of garments and the material culture of the everyday, our relationship with used garments merits further exploration.

Opposite

Figure 0.5 *Tan copper sandal – unworn. Polaroid 21, 2015. Ellen Sampson.*

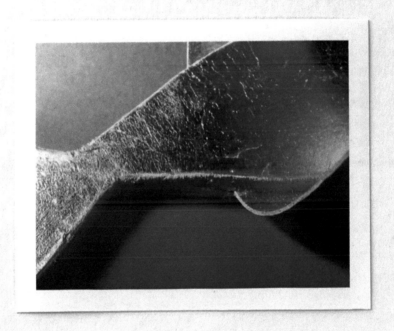

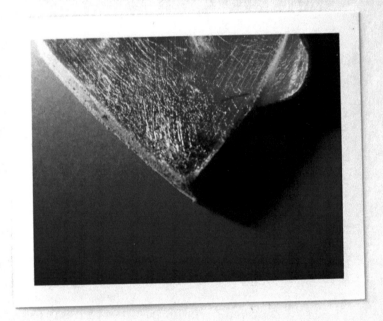

In examining our attachment to our own garments and response to the used garments of others, this book attempts to uncover the ways that, through use, garments and wearers become entwined. Through a focus upon a single garment – the shoe – it seeks to address broader questions about the embodied experience of wearing and the affect of worn and used clothes. Fusing anthropological and psychoanalytic theories of attachment, value and exchange, this book investigates wearing as a reciprocal relationship between two agents – the wearer and the worn. In doing so, it explores the ways that, through tactile engagement, they become incorporated into our bodily and psychic selves. It explores how through use the mass-produced is made unique and powerful; the particular affect of the marks of use and wear. This book seeks to put use and the user at its centre, addressing shoes not only as objects of desire or as commodities for consumption, but as objects of wear.[2] It is a shift in focus away from the point of acquisition and towards the material, tactile, habitual and bodily. In use the commodity is subverted, personalized and made active. It is no longer an object of exchange but something 'inalienable' which becomes 'entangled'[3] with the self. This 'entanglement', the transition of experience from material to immaterial and back again, is at the centre of this book; the ways that persons and artefacts may entwine over time.

This book is concerned with object relations in both a literal and a psychoanalytic sense. In addressing our relationships with our clothing as a form of object relations, it draws upon both psychoanalytic and anthropological theory, examining the sites where internal experience and material culture intersect. In particular, it draws upon the work of psychologist Donald Winnicott (1953) and anthropologist Alfred Gell (1998). Winnicott introduces the concept of the transitional object, an artefact – such as a soft toy or blanket for an infant – capable of mediating and maintaining the boundaries of the psychic (and physical) self. This idea of an object which is both 'me' and 'not-me' is applied both to the relationship between wearer and garment and between artist and artwork. This book is equally indebted to the work of anthropologist Alfred Gell. Gell's formulation of an 'art nexus',[4] which mapped the agent–patient relationships embodied in artworks, has been fundamental to this research. Here I suggest that one could easily apply Gell's art nexus (1998), in which he outlines the multiple agencies at play within the art object, to the complex agent–patient relation embodied in a garment and to the particular affective properties of the worn and used. Finally, this book is deeply informed by the works of phenomenologists Paul Schilder (1935) and Maurice Merleau-Ponty (1962), in particular their development of the ideas of a 'bodily schema', a conceptualization of the bodily self which included not just the body or mind, but the habitual material culture of the self: glasses, garments, furniture and tools.

Opposite

Figure 0.6 *Tan copper sandal – unworn. Polaroid 3, 2015. Ellen Sampson.*

The shoe as subject

Shoes are among the most ubiquitous items of material culture, and among the most symbolically and culturally loaded. Across multiple cultures and societies shoes are used as metaphors for behaviours, moralities and lives, becoming signifiers of social status, rites of passage and different forms of enfranchisement. Shoes and their representations are pervasive, from the shoes on our feet, to those standing empty in shops, museums and memorials. From fairy tales to advertisements, the image of the shoe has multiple iterations and forms. The shoe is, to borrow Freud's (1900) term, an 'over-determined' object, the bearer of a multiplicity of meanings. Yet in spite of its ubiquity, the everyday and used shoe is under-represented in current writing on clothing and the body.

This book explores our relationship with and attachment to shoes. Focusing upon the shoe as an everyday object, and on the embodied experience of wearing, it examines how through use we become entangled with the things we wear. Though it focuses on footwear, this book asks broader questions about the garments we wear, calling upon the reader to consider wearing as a transactional relationship and to reconsider the value of things which are marked and worn. It asks, in a culture preoccupied with – and a fashion system predicated upon – newness, what is the significance of the worn and used garment? What is our attachment to clothes which are marked through wear and why do they have the power to affect us so deeply? How are our relationships to clothing produced and maintained through the embodied and bodily practices of wearing, cleaning and repair? With the dominance of fast fashion, and the prevalence of semi-disposable garments, this book asks the timely and important questions: Why do we hold on to a well-worn sweater, or a pair of shoes we no longer wear? Why might the abandoned shoes of a stranger evoke such pathos or an infant's shoe compel us to reminisce? What, in a culture of mass consumption, is the affective power and value of the worn and used?

Frequently the shoe is framed as both everyday (and therefore either vulgar or mundane) and superficial (a site of spurious feminine desire or of capitalism gone mad). When the shoe is addressed, it is usually interpreted as a signifier of identity, or as a marker of cultural or social capital.[5] In fashion studies, footwear is often addressed in terms of its symbolic function or the narratives ascribed to it: for what it represents rather than for what it is. Whilst no artefact is ever free of its role as a signifier, this focus on the shoe as metaphor, signifier or symbol obfuscates the shoe's material presence. Though shoes undoubtedly do function as symbols in the language of fashion, they warrant further study as material objects in themselves. Frequently, there is a confusion between representations of shoes and shoes as material artefacts; literary or pictorial images of shoes are often discussed interchangeably with real shoes. Footwear has multiple representations within literature and the visual arts, from fairy tales and folklore to painting, sculpture and film. However, it is important to make a distinction between representations of shoes and the shoe as a material artefact (and, I would extrapolate, between representations of clothing and garments themselves more generally). The shoe described within a fairy tale or painting has no material form; it is an image of a thing rather than a 'thing' itself. This image may allude or refer to the real or material shoe, but equally it may not. Though our interactions with the material may be mediated by the symbolic, and the symbolic may create a framework through which we read or interpret artefacts, the material shoe and its representations should not be confused.

Opposite

Figure 0.7 *Tan copper sandal – wear 1. Polaroid 7, 2015. Ellen Sampson.*

As garments, shoes are unusual in that the same pair is often worn day after day for extended periods of time. The shoe, unlike a shirt, a dress or a pair of trousers, is not laundered between wears, but instead becomes increasingly bodily and individualized with each wear. The shoe as a structured garment does not enfold and wrap the foot, as a softer fabric garment might,[6] but, over an extended period of time, stretches and alters to accommodate the foot. One has only to think of blisters and bloody heels from wearing-in new shoes to know that the shoe is not always an altogether accommodating artefact. Importantly, shoes impact upon – and occasionally determine – their wearer's ability to walk. The shoes we wear often impact upon our mobility and motility, the experience of our bodies in motion. Footwear affords us the ability to walk, just as a chair affords us the chance to sit. This book seeks to address the shoe as a material and bodily object, as a garment that mediates the boundaries between the self and the world. It explores the relationship between the wearer and the worn, between the shoe and the foot – footwear as a vessel for the body, and also as a vessel for the self, carrying the wearer through the world.

The research process

This book draws upon my doctoral practice-based research undertaken at the Royal College of Art, London. The research sought to examine the embodied experience of wearing and how the material outcomes of wear – the marks of use – embody experience. In doing this it sought to make explicit our intimate, and at times uncomfortable, relationship with the material and worn shoe, and to highlight the materiality of our relationships with the things we wear. In doing so, this research sought to position our relationships with clothing, the ways we acquire, wear and dispose of it, as a form of social relations, suggesting that clothing should be understood as an active agent (rather than as a conduit for other agencies) in our entanglements with it. It asked what methodologies could be employed to examine a commonplace but over-determined artefact – a thing which is simultaneously fetishized and mundane. How might one bring into focus the experience of artefacts, which are obfuscated by their everyday nature, and what, in turn, might that focus reveal? Rather than drawing on a social science methodology of object-based interviews or participant observation, or historical research into archival objects, this research utilized processes of wearing and performance to examine our attachments to, and relationships with, our shoes (see Chapter 1 for a lengthier discussion of my research methodology).

This research interrogated our bodily and embodied experience of shoes through the act of wearing. In selecting wearing as a research methodology, I sought to untangle the way we, through touch and use, become attached to our clothes. It utilized walking both as a way of being in the world and of meeting the other bodies (human and non-human) which affect us and that we, in turn, affect: exploring the ways we are changed in our encounters, as are our clothes. By placing myself at the centre of my research, making my body the means through which it was enacted, it sought to emphasize the enagled nature of our relationships with the things we wear. These experiences were recorded both in 'wearing diaries' and in the marks of wear, marks which were then photographed[7] and filmed.

Opposite
Figure 0.8 *Tan copper sandal – wear 1. Polaroids 9 and 10, 2015. Ellen Sampson.*

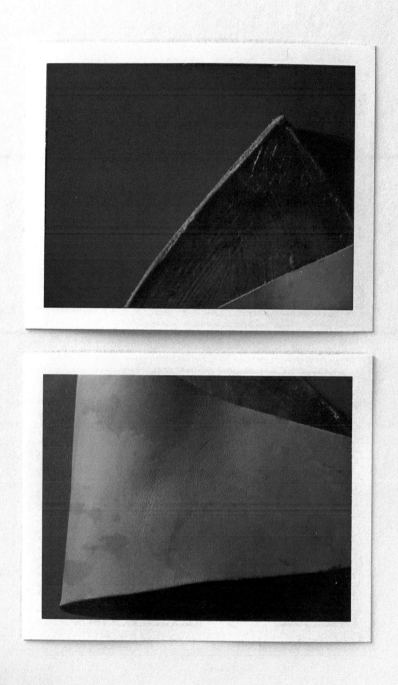

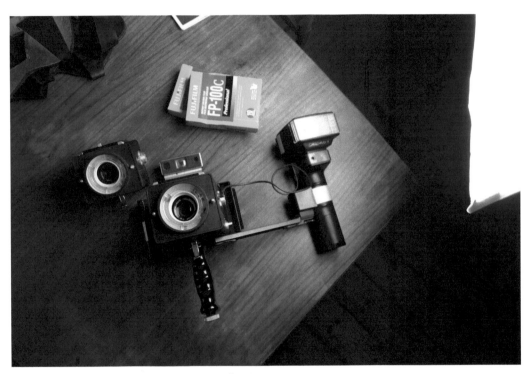

Figure 0.9 *Polaroid CU-5 macro camera, 2014. Ellen Sampson.*

My research – like the object of its study, the shoe – was paired, resulting in two distinct but interdependent manifestations of knowledge – the written and the bodily material. Though the text and the artefacts were designed to sit alongside one another, they are not analogous. These different forms of knowing informed each other, each building upon the knowledge developed by the other. The two bodies of knowledge may complement and contextualize each other but do not attempt to describe one another. Goett, writing of the relationship between text and artefact in her research practice, articulates a similar position: 'Its task is neither to describe … nor to explain the artwork and thereby reduce its meaning, taking away from the receiver a multitude of potential links to be made beyond the stated and verbalised intentions of the artist' (Goett 2009: 82). The artefacts are auto-ethnographic objects, objects which directly embody experience. This writing does not describe their making through wear, because it is manifest within them, visible in the marks imprinted upon their form. These non-verbal records, embedded in the artworks, do not require translation into words, because they themselves embody a form of knowledge, which is apparent and available for those who view them. The text here is not a theoretical framework designed to shore up ambiguous artefacts, but is an alternative manifestation of the same ideas and processes. Neither are the artefacts and images designed as illustrations to the text. Word and object complement one another, each saying something the other may not.

Book structure

The book's structure follows a relationship with a pair of shoes: leading the reader from acquisition through walking and wearing to maintenance and repair. It then explores the material outcomes of wear, the creases and scuffs which are records of use. Finally, it explores the shoe away from the body, the empty shoe in archives, galleries or memorials. The eight chapters start with a methodological discussion which foregrounds wearing as a means of doing material culture research.[8] Next 'Objects of desire' – a chapter which presents the shoe as an over-determined object, one capable of conveying many meanings. This chapter first seeks to contextualize this discussion within the multiple ways footwear has been interpreted and read. It gives a brief overview of some of these approaches to footwear, to think about the shoe as an object of fantasy and desire. It looks at the ways that the shoe is presented as an object of desire both in everyday life and in literature and the arts – with a particular focus on footwear in fairy tales. The chapter also provides an overview of current literature about shoes, looking at the way schools of both fashion and folklore studies and psychoanalysis have interrogated and interpreted footwear. Finally, it highlights the power of empty shoes, the capacity to function as both symbolic and material stand-ins for absent bodies. The next chapter, 'Wearing', addresses the experience of new shoes, of the foot encased in the shoe and the tactile experience of wearing. The chapter commences with the purchase of new shoes and a brief overview of the cultural significations frequently assigned to footwear. It positions the maintenance of clothing both as an act of restitution, of making amends for the damage done to garments, and as a form of self-care, of tending to the distributed parts of the self which constitute the 'bodily schema'. Next, it considers the experience of wearing shoes, the tactile and reciprocal relationship of touch and counter-touch between the shoe and the foot. The third chapter, 'Walking', examines footwear's ability to mediate our relationships with the world: to help or hinder the way we walk, move and interact. Walking holds a particular place in culture; not only are our movements learned, but they are also socially and culturally specific. Walking,

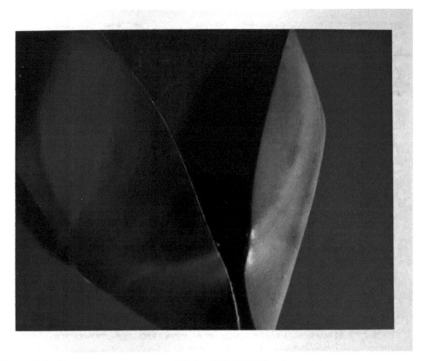

Figure 0.10 *Tan copper sandal – wear 2. Polaroid 3, 2015. Ellen Sampson.*

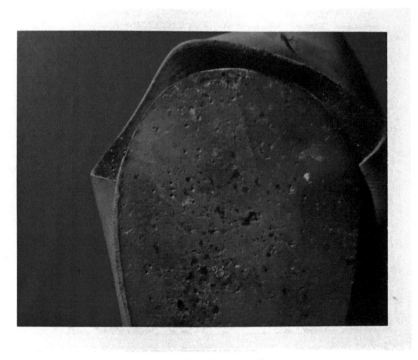

Figure 0.11 *Tan copper sandal – wear 2. Polaroid 4, 2015. Ellen Sampson.*

almost more than any other activity, renders us social beings. Taking a phenomenological approach to our relationships with clothing and the environment, this chapter positions our interactions with the material world as meetings of bodies, encounters with other agencies than our own. In walking, the body, the self and the personal accoutrements that make up our material culture are placed on display.

'The Cleaved Garment' interrogates the intimacies of these relationships,[9] exploring the ways that the self and the garment may become entwined – the processes of entanglement and intermingling that occur through making and wearing clothes. How through making and wearing clothes, the garment and the self become cleaved, to and from one another. It presents the processes of making and of using garments as both a negotiation with the garment's materiality and the projection of the user's fantasy on to their material form – a process through which the maker or user's agency becomes entangled with the material agency of the garment. It draws upon the work of anthropologists Strathern (1988) and Weiner (1992) to present wearing and making clothes as interlinked forms of entanglement – the displacement and distribution of persons into things and things into persons.[10] Next, 'The Empty Shoe: Imprint, memory and the marks of experience', examines the material traces of this relationship, the ways they are embodied within the materiality of artefacts themselves. This chapter considers the manifestations of wear: the scuffs, wrinkles and creases which make apparent the relationships of wearing. Over time, garments become records of lived experience, covered with the marks of use. Our garments are simultaneously signifiers of identity, participants in and witnesses to our embodied experience. How do these traces of use become manifestations of the passage of time, and how they might be viewed and read? It asks, if cleaning garments is an attempt to restore the symbolic order (cf. Douglas 1966), what might the erasure or reduction of the marks of experience mean?

'Encounters and affects: Garments and the memory nexus' maps the multiple relationships between memory and the things we wear. This chapter shifts the focus onto the encounter with the worn and used garment away from the body, exploring the different ways these bodiless things may affect us as viewers. The mnemonic functions of clothing have become an increasingly important strand of research in fashion and dress. Many different mnemonic and recollective processes and experiences are grouped under the umbrella term of 'clothing and memory': from those that relate to our own clothing to those that involve the clothing of others. This chapter seeks to identify the different means through which clothing acts upon us as viewer, through the construction of a 'memory nexus' of the ways that clothing, experience and affect intersect. The final chapter 'Worn: Imprint, attachment and affect' seeks to untangle the particular affect of the worn shoe as a record of lives lived and paths walked. It begins to unravel the web of connections and affordances that produce our relationships to our own clothing and that of others; it uncovers the ways that the worn garment may act upon us, to explore how garments and people may become entwined. This chapter seeks to highlight the particular affect of viewing the used and worn shoe; to examine how the traces of intermingling might impact upon the viewer– how are the marks of an absent body understood? What is the affect of this absence of presence, this trace? Interspersed between the chapters are extracts from the wearing diary that I kept as I wore and walked in the shoes I made. These notes are auto-ethnographic field-notes on the experience of the body in clothes: a reminder that this research was performed and lived, as well as thought, written and made.

Overleaf

Figure 0.12 *Tan copper sandal – wear 2. Polaroid 5, 2015. Ellen Sampson.*

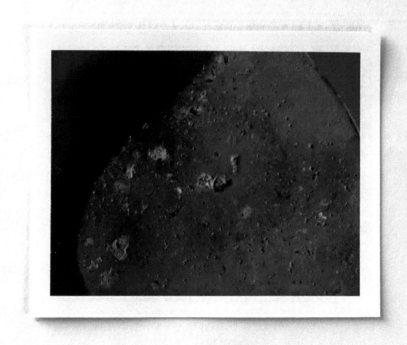

Wearing Diary 1

I have flattened the back of my shoe, unthinkingly pressing my heel into it as I walk around the flat. My gentle morning routine, the shuffling from kettle to fridge to table has damaged my shoe. Conscious of the damage and unsure of whether to repair it, I am suddenly aware that this unconscious behaviour is not new but a regression. That throughout my childhood I did exactly this; flattened the heel of my left shoe while the right remained intact. At some point I grew out of it, I left this bodily tic behind. I had forgotten the familiar feeling of the compressed leather beneath my heel but now it is there for me. I am flooded with familiarity and loss. My past selves have re-emerged.

(Wearing Diary, August 2015)

Entanglement, Affect and Experience: Walking and wearing (shoes) as experimental research methodology

1

The experience of wearing is fundamental to our relationship with cloth and with clothing. Though we engage with our clothes through all of our senses, wearing is a relationship grounded in touch: it is through the tactile experience of garments that we come to know them. Understandings of clothing are both sensory and cumulative: our knowledge of a garment is predicated on both our experience of it and of all the garments we have worn before. This chapter explores the methodology utilized throughout this research; presenting wearing-based research as an addendum or adjunct to more widely utilized practice-based and performance-based research methodologies in fashion and dress. It asks how wearing as research practice might open up new avenues in fashion and textile knowledge, producing different perspectives on the spaces and situations where body, cloth and psyche meet. In doing so it presents a methodology of entanglement, or of blurred subject-object relations, which draws upon the works of phenomenologists Schilder (1935) and Merleau-Ponty (1962), psychologist Winnicott (1971) and sensory ethnographer Pink (2015). In exploring my methodology of 'wearing-based research', this chapter does the following: first, it addresses approaches to wearing as both a subject and methodology. Second, it asks what a 'wearing-based' research methodology might look like and what types of knowledge such a methodology might produce. Finally, it explores the theories of entanglement and blurred subject/object divides that have informed my research practice.

Practice-based research and tactile knowledge

I have flattened the back of my shoe, unthinkingly pressing my heel into it as I walk around the flat. My gentle morning routine, the shuffling from kettle to fridge to table has damaged my shoe. Conscious of the damage and unsure of whether to repair it, I am suddenly aware that this unconscious behaviour is not new but a regression. That throughout my childhood I did exactly this; flattened the heel of my left shoe while the right remained intact. At some point I grew out of it, I left this bodily tic behind. I had forgotten the familiar feeling of the compressed leather beneath my heel but now it is there for me. I am flooded with familiarity and loss. My past selves have re-emerged.
(excerpt from wearing diary, August 2015)

This chapter commences with an excerpt from the wearing diaries written[1] as I walked in shoes I had made. Recording the re-emergence of forgotten habits and bodily memories, which resurfaced through my sensory engagement with the material world, it seems an apposite place to start a discussion of the tacit and sensory knowledge, which are central to practice-based research. Practice-based research occupies an increasingly large space in the growing field of fashion studies from research into making processes and design techniques (Lee 2016; Valle-Noronha 2017) or technologies and materials (Petreca et al. 2013), to historical and archival research (Rossi Camus 2019), and research into methodologies themselves (Igoe 2010). Within the context of a burgeoning culture of fashion research through doing, this chapter therefore presents wearing as a tool for practice-based research.

The term 'practice-based research' encompasses many practices in diverse disciplines, from ethnography, to international relations, to architecture, to the arts. Since Frayling's seminal 1993 paper

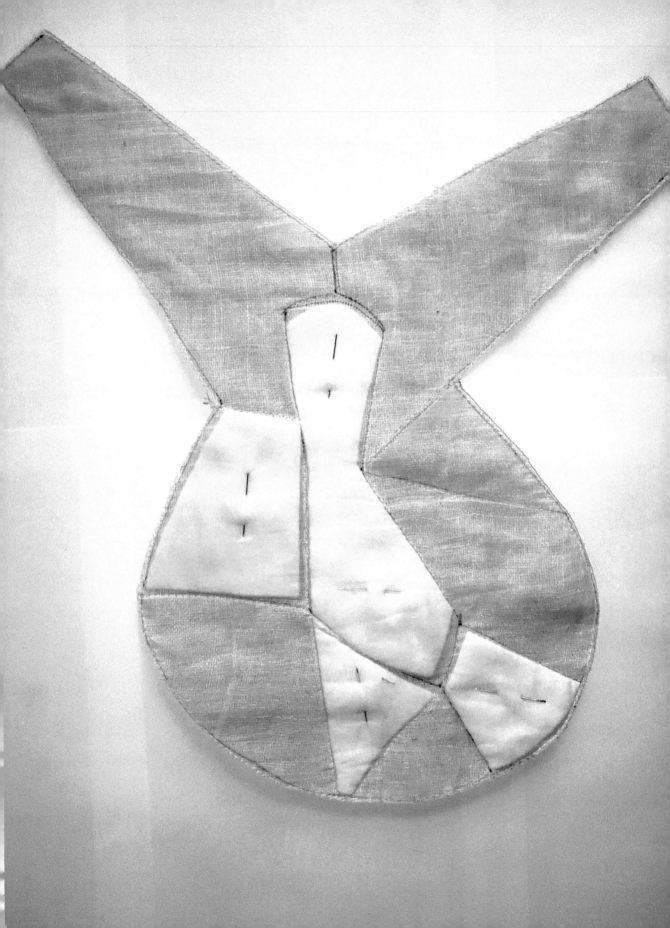

on research in the arts and Candlin's (2000) insightful review of the 1997 UKCGE report into 'Practice and Performance Based Research', practice-based research in the arts has become an established and accepted methodology. It is widely understood that knowledge may be produced through 'doing' as well as observing. In the arts, the predominant utilization of practice-based research has been self-reflexive: practice-based methodologies are used to examine the practice itself. However, throughout this book, the term 'practice' refers to my research methodology as a whole, or the practice of conceiving, producing and displaying artworks as research; however, the practice itself can be split into three distinct yet inter-related facets: making artefacts and images, wearing them and processes of recording, writing and display. Though this chapter addresses the practice of wearing, it should be noted that these processes were not and cannot be neatly separated. The shoes, and thus the work, were 'made' through wearing, so that wearing became simultaneously a mundane and creative act.

What is distinct about research by, through or into practice, is that it often examines those things that are unspoken: knowledges and experiences that sit outside words. As Polyani famously stated, 'We can know more than we can tell' (1967: 4) and, to paraphrase him, we, as researchers, sense more than we can write. The knowledge produced in fashion practice-based research is not always articulated or articulable in text. Wearing is often a tacit and tactile experience: from the tacit knowledge embodied in acts of dressing, to the sensory experience of garments and skin, to the complex relationships between memory, experience and garments. Indeed, wearing clothes is a form of what Ingold (2013) terms 'friction': a meeting of materials and intentions, not as a seamless convergence, but instead as a practice which is constituted in the ways that these disparate things, garments, bodies and thoughts, fail to fit.

Over the past two decades there has been a resurgence in interrogations of materiality and the material, which have engaged both with concepts of materiality, and the nature of the artefact itself (Ingold 2011a: 26; Hodder 2012). This material turn has led to a renewed emphasis on the tacit and tactile, and on the experiential nature of our relationships with things. Within the context of the material turn, the unspoken and un-verbalized practices of doing and knowing by hand and by eye, and the role of knowledge beyond or outside language, are increasingly understood as central aspects of how we encounter and navigate the world (Ingold 2013; Sennett 2008). In the context of this interest in inarticulable and embodied knowledge, what might be the nature of knowledge produced through practice-based research, and in turn through wearing? Macleod, writing of the artwork as a form of knowledge, suggests:

> This is theory which is not written; it is made or realized through artwork. This theory is the result of ideas worked through matter. It might be appropriate to see this as a matrixial theory, a complex of ideas/matter/form and theory which is external to practice.
>
> (2000: 5)

Opposite
Figure 1.1 Fold 1, *2013. Ellen Sampson.*

Similarly for Scrivener (2002), the role of the artist-as-researcher is in uncovering knowledge through its manifestation as a material form. That is to say, the artist-as-researcher's role (and the role of the artwork as research output) is not to present explanations but to produce or enable the encounter, or to create an affective experience. For Scrivener, art-based research is concerned with producing apprehensions or abductions, so that the experience of viewing the artwork must create a new way of knowing for the viewer.

Frequently recurring in discussions of practice-based research are questions about the relationships between object (or artwork) and text. Returning to Macleod:

> The written text was instrumental to the conception of the art projects but the art projects themselves exacted a radical rethinking of what had been constructed in written form because the process of realizing or making artwork altered what had been defined in written form.
>
> (2000, 3)

In exploring wearing-based research, what I suggest is that the knowledge produced and embodied in wearing is not just tacit but tactile. To begin to address this, one must locate knowledge as material and bodily. This is not to say that this knowledge should not be articulated but that its verbalization may not, in itself, be necessary. It might be experienced and understood by interaction with artwork rather than read. The works I produced attempted to create and contain body knowledge, to make body experience apparent in material form. The manifestations of this knowledge are dual, both the marks made through wearing (both on the garment and on my body) and the knowledge within my body, or the memory of sensation, the understandings of fit, restriction and comfort.

While fashion and fashioning are predominantly visual practices – practices of image making, of looking and of mimicry – dressing, or the day-to-day 'fleshy practice' of covering the body is tactile: we feel our clothes (Entwistle 2000). Garments produce a multi-sensory experience, which both mediate and create our experience of the world. This tactile experience of our garments binds us to them. If as Pink (2015) states the auto-ethnographer's task is to participate with the world, then it is through these participations that we become bound to the things we wear. In his development of the idea of 'bodily schema', Merleau-Ponty expresses this particularly well: 'To get used to a hat, a car or a stick is to be transplanted into them or conversely to incorporate them into the bulk of our own body' (Merleau-Ponty 1962: 166). Thus, a wearing-based research into clothing is research into and within the 'body schema'.

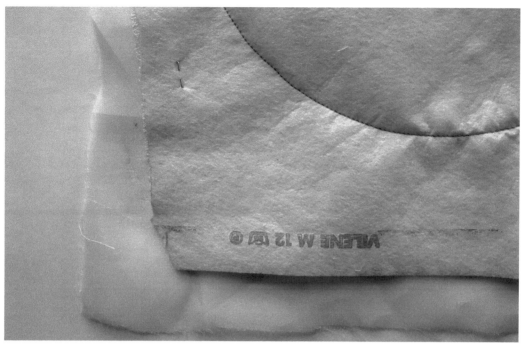

Figure 1.2 Fold 2, *2013. Ellen Sampson.*

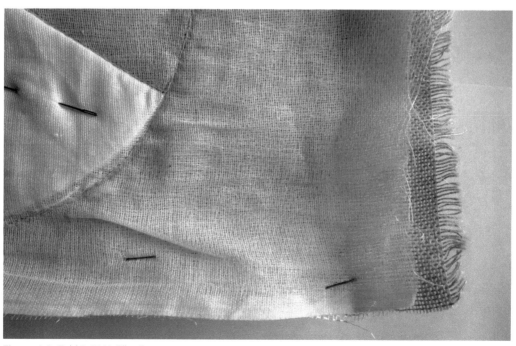

Figure 1.3 Fold 3, *2013. Ellen Sampson.*

The maker as researcher

As research into (and through) the 'body schema', this research addressed the dual themes of transmissions and of transformation – the ways that persons and artefacts entwine over time. This blurring of subject and object is common to much practice-based research. Ideas of entanglement were central to this project, which is concerned with object relations in both a literal and psychoanalytic sense. In viewing our relationships with clothing as a form of object relations, this research positioned the work of Winnicott (1953, 1971) as central. Winnicott's theory of the transitional object (1953), an object capable of mediating and maintaining the boundaries of the psychic self, was applied both to the relationship between wearer and garment, between artist and artwork, between ideas of touching and holding, and of the capacity to contain. Winnicott's ideas are further present in this work both in relation to ideas of touching and holding and of the capacity to contain (1953, 1971). For Winnicott the 'transitional object is not an internal object (which is a mental concept) – it is a possession. Yet it is not (for the infant) an external object either' (1953: 3). Transitional phenomena are intermediary spaces, spaces which allow inside and outside worlds to meet. It is this capacity for a possession (or in the case of the artist an artwork or performance) to become an intermediary between psychic and external realities, which this research aimed to both explore and embody. It was the shifts from me to not me, from new to used and from commodity to inalienable possession, that my work explored.

It is the nature of practice-based research that the researcher is also often the creator of the object of enquiry – a fact that sets practice-based research apart from more traditional research practices that fashion studies typically employ. Making gives the researcher the ability to alter or enhance their experience of the research subject in a manner that would not be possible through observation alone. Maker-researchers come to know their subject through touch and often the material manipulation of its form. For the maker, the capacity to look, the self-reflexive ability to spot a problem or error and acknowledge it, is an intrinsic tool in the production of the artefact. Indeed, as Scrivener writes, 'Like qualitative researcher, the artist and designer is central to the sense that is made and is engaged in a process in which reflexivity dominates. Hence, reflexivity must be seen as a central feature of research-in-design' (Scrivener 2000: 15). Said differently, the practice of making is one of charting the dissonances between intention and actuality. Making as auto-ethnographic process is self-reflexive so that in my work I was both the producer and the product of this research.[2] The shifts in my research were mirrored by shifts in my own capacity to contain and articulate knowledge.

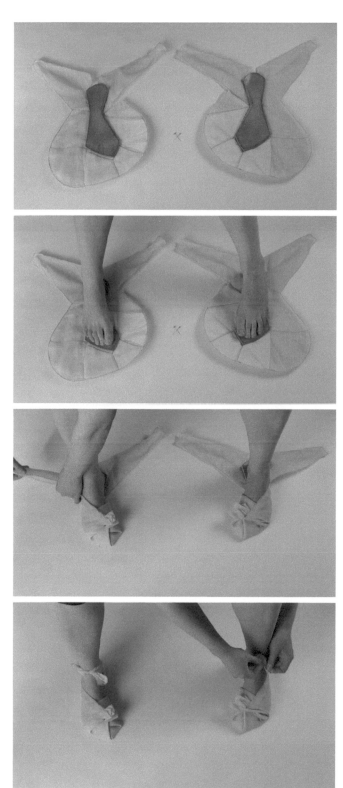

Figure 1.4 *Stills from film* Fold, *2013. Ellen Sampson.*

Making and wearing as practice-based research

Though the methodology of my research was the creation of artworks, the subject was the wearer's relationships with clothing, specifically shoes. The project was research 'through practice', or practice as a way of uncovering knowledge about another distinct subject. Practice was the means through which the research was conducted, making (and wearing) as a means of uncovering embodied and bodily knowledge. It was research into an artefact via that artefact's production and use, so that the researcher held the position of maker, user and observer.

This research aimed to examine the attachments that wearers have to their garments; the ways that, through tactile engagement, they become incorporated into our bodily and psychic selves. Locating itself within the new materialism and materiality studies that have dominated social science and humanities research over the last decade, it asked if, by addressing the material outcomes of wear and the experiences of wearing, we might develop a greater understanding of the relationships we experience with our shoes. In doing so it suggested that attachment to footwear derives not simply from consumption, status or desire, but from the sustained tactile relationship that develops through wear. When the shoe is addressed in fashion literature it is often interpreted as a signifier of identity, or as a marker of cultural or social capital, so that the real shoe, the shoe as a habitual, worn and bodily object, is missing from these discussions. Here, however, rather than drawing on a social science methodology of object-based interviews (Woodward 2015 and Chong-Kwan 2017), participant observation (Clarke and Miller 2002) or on historical research into archival objects, this research utilized processes of wearing and performance to examine our attachments to and relationships with our shoes: it was material culture research enacted through the production of artworks. As practice-based research its outputs were artefacts, images (installation, film and photographs) and writing.

The project was developed in two parts: a thesis was written to accompany an exhibition of installation work, photography and film: text to be read alongside artworks and vice versa. The material outputs explore both the experience of wearing and the affect of the worn and used shoe. The practice aims to speak to the viewer in an embodied language of tacit and tactile knowledge, knowledge produced through making, wearing and watching. This embodied and sensory knowledge informed the writing, which in turn was further developed through the written research itself, so that the processes of making and writing became iterative and self-reflexive. Together, the thesis and the artworks produced a whole: the outcomes of the research in objects and in word. It is presented as separate chapters of text and of images, each new chapter building upon the ideas explored in the last. The images are not illustrations but outputs of research in themselves, equivalent but not analogous to the written work.

This research employed shoe and image making as its primary practices, constructing objects and making images of them as they were used and worn. However, central to the research was the practice of wearing, of using these handmade shoes and altering their material form through use: leather stretching and heels wearing away. As such, it positioned wearing as another form of 'making', as the shoes themselves are transformed through use. This wear 'activated' the objects as they became resonant with experience. They were made affective not only through design or production but through the process of bodily imprint. These were objects which were 'made' through wear.

Over the course of this research I made, walked in and wore multiple pairs of shoes, a repeated practice of production, use and wear. These shoes, as objects 'made' through wear, were designed to amplify and increase the wearer's interaction with the world, both through their maker's choice of materials and the design of their form. Many of the shoes produced and worn throughout this research had pronounced pointed or extended toes. The choice of these shapes was, to some extent, aesthetic (or influenced by my own taste); however, these decisions were also conceptual, pertaining both to a desired visual outcome of the works and the manner in which the shoes might behave during their wearing. By extending and lengthening the foot, and thus the bodily schema, and the boundaries of the body, I, as wearer and performer, was more 'in the world'. The toes of the shoes scuffed more easily and the soles had a greater surface area to press into the dirt of the ground. My dressed body moved forward before me, my shoes jutting out beyond my feet. The shoes became degraded or abject more quickly; they hastened and amplified my interactions with the world. The curled toes and scuffs that are the outcomes of wear are the indexical imprints of my research, they are the traces of the research performed. The empty shoes are records of an absent performance, of gestures that are lost to the viewer, so that only their traces, the marks upon the shoe, remain. This extension of the bodily schema, the pushing of myself into space, became a means of research, a way of pushing up against boundaries and at times of pushing through them.

These shoes broke down more readily than 'normal' shoes and were open, so that the imprints of the body were revealed. The shoes made the traces of the embodied and bodily relationship between wearer and worn more apparent to the viewer and, in doing so, shifted the focus from the shoe as a commodity to the shoe as a record. In doing this, I abstracted the shoe, taking it apart and simplifying its construction. I emphasized certain qualities such as the capacity of the insole to bear an imprint of the wearer's foot, the soft enfolding nature of a slipper, the solidity and echoing resonance of wooden soles. I made shoes whose insides are explicit and open and which demanded that the viewer engages with the intimate materiality of wear. In abstracting the shoe, I drew upon two traditions of shoe making: the soft and the hard shoe. The soft shoes were simply constructed with pieces of material, cut, folded and tied in order to envelop the foot. The shoes broke down quickly, moulding to the foot as they stretched and wore. Their simple folded structure allows them to be opened and laid flat after wearing, making the marks of use apparent. Eventually the softest shoes, those made only of silks and leather, broke down completely, disintegrating under the weight of my body. Simultaneously I made clogs and pattens, or hard wooden and metal over-shoes, which chipped, scratched and bent, rather than stretching or fraying. Hard shoes pushed back against my body, jarring my knees and stubbing my toes. In creating these abstracted shoes, this research drew upon Shklovskij's ([1917] 1998) concept of 'making strange', or the defamiliarization of the shoe and of wearing as an everyday practice. the shoe was made strange both in the abstraction of its form – so that it is not 'read' as an everyday shoe – and by placing it, an everyday and potentially abject artefact, in the gallery space.

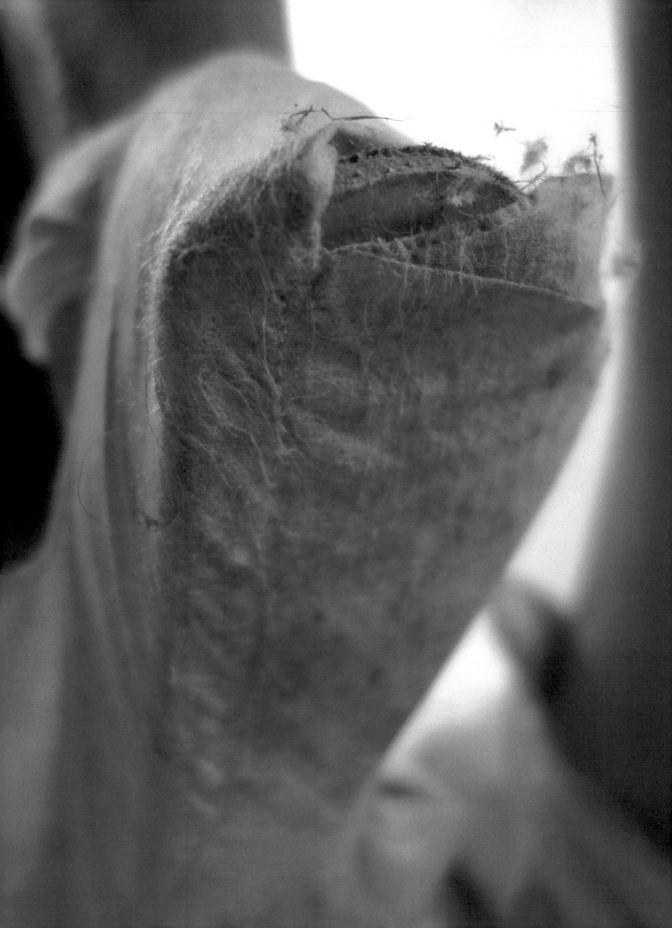

Walking as practice-based research

Walking – a process of imprint through movement – was the primary means of mark making for much of this research. Shoes were designed to mark through wear and in turn to make marks on my body. The shoes were worn for varying periods, which ranged from hours to days, weeks and months. These acts of walking crossed and re-crossed lines between the habitual, the routine and performative. As I performed my research, the work of making art in turn became daily practice. In 'Techniques of the Body' (1935), Mauss writes of his ability to identify people by their walks, not only in situations where walking is fundamentally performative, but in non-performative settings like walking down the street. As Mauss explains, 'For example I think I can recognize a girl who has been raised in a convent. In general, she will walk with her fists closed […]. Thus there is an education to walking too' (1935: 458). The practices of everyday life are the mastery of these 'techniques of the body' – that is, learning to walk, move and interact towards and in context of others (see De Certeau [1980] 1984).

Though these techniques are acquired in the transmission of tradition, in acquisition and performance they become individuated, movements are both cultural and personal, our gestures

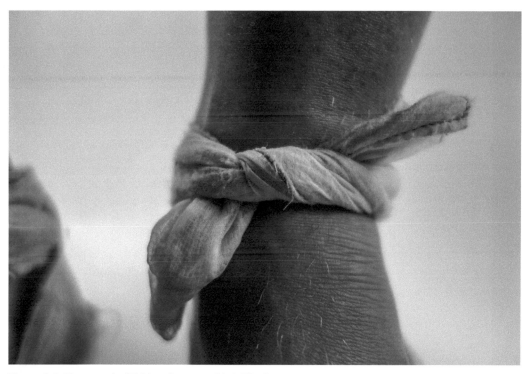

Figure 1.6 *Photograph of* Fold *performance, 2013. Ellen Sampson.*

Opposite

Figure 1.5 *Photograph of* Fold *performance, 2013. Ellen Sampson.*

simultaneously culturally specific and only ever our own. Our movements are a form of skilled work, a bringing together of social and bodily knowledge in the performance of the everyday. The worn and used garment, and in particular the worn and used shoe, is made unique through these techniques of the body, the individual's assimilation and interpretation of bodily cultural practices. In the performance of dressing and the practice of everyday life, we are marking and altering our clothes. Just as the line of a pen or paintbrush is fundamentally gestural, informed by the techniques of the body, the marks upon our clothes are the output of our bodily techniques. It was these marks that this research sought to augment and make apparent. Walking is an act of being present in the world. It is a means of 'presencing' the self, the conflation of intention and existence in the public sphere. As Ahmed writes:

> I have always been struck by the phrase 'a path well trodden'. A path is made by the repetition of the event of the ground 'being trodden' upon. We can see the path as a trace of past journeys. The path is made out of footprints – traces of feet that 'tread' and that in 'treading' create a line on the ground. […] A paradox of the footprint emerges. Lines are both created by being followed and are followed by being created.
>
> (2006: xix–xx)

In the context of this research, these ideas of reciprocal modification and interdependencies are particularly relevant – the behaviour of the wearer/researcher (their research practice) is the negotiation of multiple relationships; both material and bodily.

Wearing clothes as social relations

Though the particular methodology of this research may be unconventional, the topic of enquiry, the wearing of clothes as embodied experience, is not. Wearing, as the embodied relationship between garment and user forms a distinct and increasingly important strand of fashion studies. Commodity theory (i.e. clothing as a commodity within a network of transactions, rather than a vessel of lived experience), gifting and exchange underlie much of our thinking about clothing.[3] The relationship between garment and person is reciprocal. This reciprocity is both physical and psychic. Garments are active agents who may act upon us as users in a multiplicity of ways. In understanding the garment as active agent in our networks of things I return to Gell's words:

> The immediate 'other' in a social relationship does not have to be another 'human being' […]. Social agency can be exercised relative to 'things' and social agency can be exercised by 'things' […]. It just happens to be patently the case that persons form what are evidently social relations with 'things'.
>
> (1998: 17)

So that, in studying wearing, one is studying the social relations between people and their clothes. Clothing has both the capacity to affect deeply and to effect change. Garments are active and at times unruly agents.

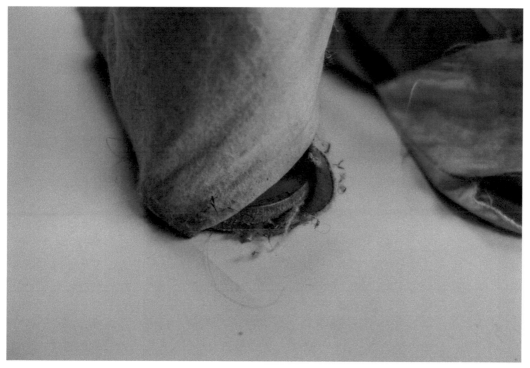

Figure 1.7 *Photograph of* Fold *performance, 2013. Ellen Sampson.*

Within fashion studies, Entwistle's book *The Fashioned Body* (2000) was at the forefront of a move towards a more embodied understanding of wear. Situating fashion as a 'fleshy practice', she suggests,

> understanding the body in culture requires understanding both how the textual body (the body articulated in discourses produced by texts, such as the fashion magazine) relates to the experience of embodiment (the body articulated in everyday life through experiences and practices of dress).
>
> (Entwistle 2000: 239)

As Entwistle outlines, wearing is an active process of appropriation, alteration and compromise. In exploring the modifying and mediating capacity of garments, practice-based costume and performance researcher Sally E. Dean articulates (and utilizes) this particularly well:

> In our daily-life observations, we see how what we wear affects the way we move and how we are perceived. If I wear high heels, for example, I walk in an entirely different way than if I wear boots. My experience of my feet, and indeed of my whole body, is different; I create a quite different 'character', and the basis for my interactions with my environment and with others around me also changes.
>
> (2012: 168)

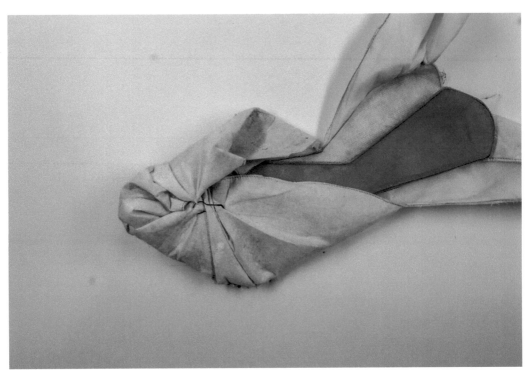

Figure 1.8 Fold 4, *2013. Ellen Sampson.*

This affect – the particular capacity of garments to affect us – is both symbolic and bodily/material. Clothes are both loci and agents of affect, while at the same time being affected themselves. To borrow from Ahmed, 'We are moved by things, and in being moved, we make things' (2010: 33), which is to say, the body and the garment are in a constant reiterative cycle of affecting one another. The body-self is affected physically and emotionally through wearing and simultaneously the material of the garment, its meanings and value are changed through wear: 'Matter feels, converses, suffers, desires, yearns and remembers' (Barad in Dolphijn and Tuin 2012: 60). This cycle of affects moulds both bodily selves, identities and garments. As Ahmed (2006), building on the works of Husserl and Merleau-Ponty, writes, 'I have suggested that the orientation of objects is shaped by what objects allow me to do. In this way, an object is what an action is directed toward' (Ahmed 2006: 27). Our garments (both part of our 'body-schemas' and other to them) afford us the capacity (both physically, psychically and socially) to traverse spaces and perform acts: our garments (and perhaps because of their capacity to alter our motility and mobility, particularly our shoes) orientate us in the world.

In the context of these orientations, Woodward and Fisher (2014) explore the garment's capacity to affect bodily and emotional experience. They address the garment as an agent in complex sensory interaction with the body-self, suggesting that, 'whilst there has been a shift towards looking at embodied fashion phenomenologically […] there has been a lack of focus upon ways of wearing and making fashionable things is multi-sensory, and where the material is central' (Woodward and

Fisher 2014: 12). They write of the sensory and material nature of clothing, or the ways that garments help and hinder intention. Writing of fashion failures, they observe that the tactile experience of 'not feeling good' in something can lead a garment to be relegated to the back of the wardrobe. Woodward and Fisher's research highlights the material agency of the garment, or its capacity through form, rather than signification, to impact on bodily and embodied experience. As they observe,

> The clothes in a successful outfit that a woman wears and feels comfortable wearing effectively externalize that person's intentions through their materiality. Conversely when outfits go wrong, the materiality of clothing can thwart women's intentionality – the leather skirt that they hoped would make them look sexy can make them look hot and sweaty instead.
>
> (Woodward and Fisher 2014: 4–5)

This discomforting potential, be it mental or physical, is central both to clothing choices and the tactile experience of wear – we often seek the right 'fit', be it stylistically or physically (see Eco 1986).

Woodward's work utilizes a number of methodologies to presence the sensory and material aspects of wearing clothes. In particular object-based interviews in which the garment is present and examined or held as it is discussed, a tactile engagement with the garment stimulates discussion, reminiscence and reflection. Similarly, sensory fashion researcher Chong-Kwan (2017) attempts to map the multiple sensory and emotional affects of dress. Drawing on Woodward's (2015) object-based interviews, and Pink's (2005, 2015) sensory ethnography, Chong-Kwan explores 'how sensory engagement with dress affected both the materiality of the dress items and the participants by triggering behaviour, thoughts, memories and emotions' (2017: 2). In a turn away from the visual, Chong-Kwan seeks to capture how garments make wearers and non-wearers feel in examining how textures and scents affect them.

Chong-Kwan highlights the difficulty in capturing these experiences in language, the ways that her interviewees struggled to articulate what they had experienced:

> The interviews hinted at a lack of appropriate language to clearly articulate certain types of sensory experience. There were often times when participants found it tricky to explain their experience. This could be when multiple sensory modalities were implicated, and as a result they struggled to define individual sensory modalities, describing instead a more holistic overall 'sense', 'feeling' or 'essence'.
>
> (2017: 25)

It was in the context of this failure of language, the difficulty of articulating to another how the overlapping sensory experiences of wearing 'feels', that I chose to explore wearing as a research methodology – a methodology which sought to privilege, embody and materialize the affects of wear. In selecting wearing as a method of doing research I sought to enact a shift, a shift from observer to participant much in the way that maker-researchers have made that same leap. This shift both allowed me greater access to my bodily experience of wear and simultaneously intensified the agency of the shoes I wore. By positioning myself as wearer/researcher I made myself, my body and my garments the subject of the research. I experienced the garments – my sensory knowing was at the centre of the research. This sensory knowing, as the output of my auto-ethnographic practice, was recorded in writing (the wearing diaries and thesis), images and film.

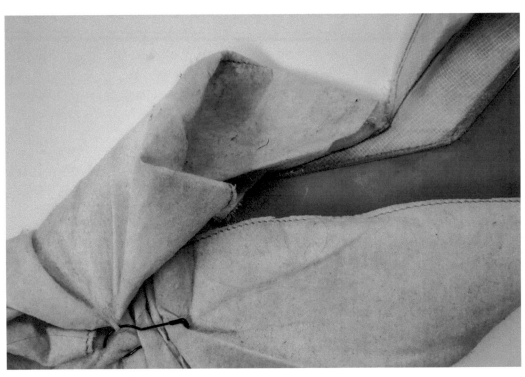

Figure 1.9 Fold 5, *2013. Ellen Sampson.*

Woodward and Chong-Kwan both predominately discuss the clothing of others rather than their own sartorial choices and experiences. Both researchers' work relies upon the mnemonic power of garments (and for Chong-Kwan's the particular affect of the marks of use and wear) and require the research subject to reminisce while touching or holding and item of dress. While Woodward briefly discusses feeling overdressed for one interview and thereafter thinking twice about her wardrobe choices, we are rarely aware of her embodied and bodily experience of 'doing' research. Nor do we understand how (or if) Woodward as researcher experienced the garments her subjects held and discuss: she writes of listening and looking but not of touch. This is not to say that either of these (excellent) methodologies is less valid, only that in positioning myself as 'wearer-researcher' I sought to overcome this 'gap', or the space of unknowing that writing of another's experience requires.

Feeling and knowing

While the experience of wear and the practice of wearing are both frequent subjects of fashion research, wearing itself is rarely used as a methodology. If the act of wearing is to be a method for research, one must ask what is the embodied experience of wearing: the daily and habitual interactions of body and garment, of cloth and skin? More than that, however, what does wearing do? What are the relationships and affects which are produced and maintained through the tactile experience of wearing? And what is made manifest and apparent through the acts of wear?

Here I return to my own methodology and to the works of psychoanalyst Bick (1968) and psychologist Winnicott (1953) who suggest that attachment to others and self-identification are, from the outset, located in touch. The process of giving and taking, of touch and counter-touch which underlies much of our relationship with clothing, has echoes of the reciprocal, touch-based relationship between mother and infant. Although touch may mediate internal desire, Marks suggests that its manifestations occur not within the interior-self but at the peripheries of the body: the skin, the hands, the feet, the eyes (2000). Touch is the foundation of our attachment to others and our sense of self; touch positions us within the world. Pioneer of infant observation, psychoanalyst Bick observed that this idea of being held or enveloped in skin is central to the development of a sense of self. She suggests that, 'in its most primitive form the parts of the personality are felt to have no binding force amongst themselves and must therefore be held together in a way that is experienced by them passively, by the skin functioning as a boundary' (Bick 1968: 56). If touch creates and maintains attachment, then it follows that wearing, as an experience located in touch, does as well. The tactile experience of wearing both binds subject and object (or to use Winnicott's phrase 'me and not me' [1953]) and at the same time stimulates and produces sensory knowledge: wearing as a form of thinking. To return to Ingold, 'this is a knowledge born of sensory perception and practical engagement, not of the mind with the material world […] but of the skilled practitioner participating in a world of materials' (2011: 30).

If wearing and knowing may coalesce, then how might this experience be expressed, quantified and explored and what might wearing as a research practice tell us about people and their clothes? To return to the start of the chapter, what might this methodology of entanglement look like? If we reframe wearing not as a passive process but an active engagement of two agents, how might we view

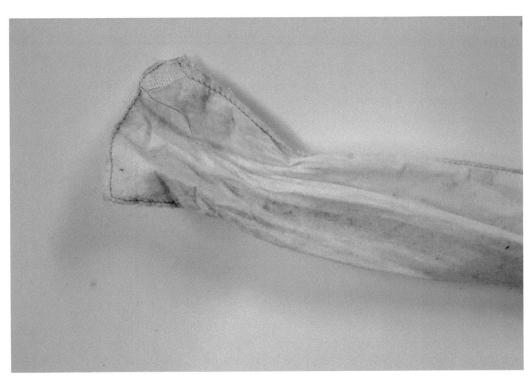

Figure 1.10 Fold 6, *2013. Ellen Sampson.*

our attachment to our clothes? Ingold's (2007) call to look at the transformations of materials can here be utilized to view wearing as 'process', or wearing as a shifting and transformative dynamic between wearer and worn (cf. Ingold 2013: 31). If we understand wearing as process, a process continuously updated and mediated by the wearer's and the garment's changing forms, then wearing-knowledge is changeable too: iterative, tactile, cumulative and potentially complex to articulate. To borrow from (and paraphrase) Sennett's work on making, could it be that wearing 'establishes a realm of skill and knowledge perhaps beyond human verbal capacities to explain; […] language is not an adequate "mirror- tool" for the physical movements of the human body' (Sennett 2008: 95)?

Entanglement as research methodology

My research adopted a methodology based around theories of entanglement: of the enmeshed and indivisible relationship between artefact and user. Hodder (2012) writes of people and things being 'entangled' or as inseparable from their environments. The user, artefact and environment are in a continuous reiterative dialogue, each change impacting the next. Drawing upon Gibson's (1979) theory of affordances, he interprets the world as one in which artefacts afford or allow human behaviours. A shoe, for example, may permit a user to walk longer, while a chair may allow them to sit or a path to cross space. Material things facilitate and produce our relationships with the external world. In this research, the shoes were positioned as active agents themselves; they were both research subject and collaborator. In their interactions with my body-self they shifted and altered the course of the research – from one which initially explored memory to one which focused on tactile experiences of wearing and the material evidences of wear. It was this shift, instigated by the shoe as both locus and agent of research, a thing made by me, which in turn co-made and co-constituted the research. As such, my research practice became a material negotiation between body and shoe.

Within this context, the terms 'entanglement', 'intermingling' and 'incorporation' are afforded dual meaning, referring both to the physical cleaving of garments and body through touch and wear and to the psychic mingling as the garment becomes a repository for bodily experience and is simultaneously incorporated into the wearer's psyche or body ego. Instead of attempting to lessen this entanglement in hope of an elusive objectivity, my research practice embraced the entangled position of maker and wearer as researcher. It placed this enmeshed nature of our relationship with the material world at its centre, as both the subject and the research methodology. Borrowing from the terminology of Merleau-Ponty (1962), it used a methodology of 'being in the world' particularly in relation to motility, moving and walking. Ingold, in writing on ethnography and anthropology, writes of the idea of 'observing from the inside' (2014) as central to fieldwork practice. In this way, the anthropologist must be 'along with' their subject. This 'being with' is the act of acknowledging and embracing one's enmeshed relationship with the research subject. In my research, I was 'along with' my subject; I made, I walked, I wore.

Touch is central to our capacity both to self-identify and to relate to others, for it is through touching that we come to know ourselves and the world. For Pink (2015), 'sensory knowing is produced through participation with the world' and it was through these participations (walking to the shops, meeting friends, going to college) that my knowing was made. It follows that as wearers we know

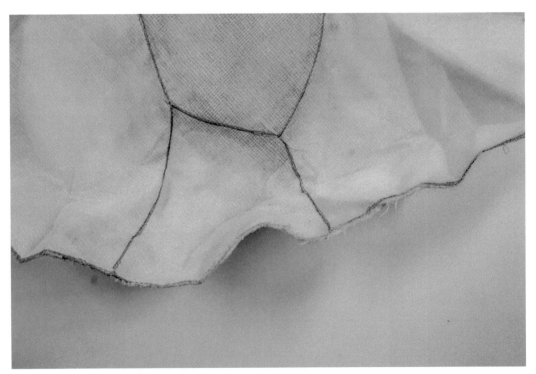

Figure 1.11 Fold 7, *2013. Ellen Sampson.*

our own clothing through touch, and that for the researcher touch may produce a form of knowing. However, for the auto-ethnographer, knowledge produced through touch may be problematic; it raises questions about how the sensory and non-verbal can be articulated, recorded and quantified.

By acknowledging my position at the centre of this research, I used techniques borrowed from auto-ethnographers such as Taussig (1983), acknowledging and embracing my subjective position within this work. My own subjectivity and sensory experience became inseparable from the research: seeing, sensing and knowing became entwined. In locating myself as subject and researcher, I utilized Pink's formulation:

> (Auto)ethnography is a process of creating and representing knowledge (about society, culture and individuals) that is based on ethnographers' own experiences. It does not claim to produce an objective or truthful account of reality, but should aim to offer versions of ethnographers' experiences of reality that are as loyal as possible to the context, negotiations and inter-subjectivities through which the knowledge was produced.
>
> (2015: 22)

Wearing, as the extended sensory interaction of the garment and the skin, was at the centre of my research methodology. As I read and wrote, carved and sewed, I also walked in the shoes that I had made. This wearing was a performance enacted over many months and recorded in the objects themselves. They travelled with me and became records of my movements and experiences. As such my 'field' was not geographical but instead was bodily and psychic. My body-schema (Schilder 1935: 7) was the site both on and through which this research was conducted. As such my 'field notes' were multiple: the diaries I wrote as I wore and walked in the shoes, the images I made as they altered and broke down through use, but also the shoes and my body themselves as they as the imprinted and changed, becoming records of the research practice I performed. As a whole these 'notes', the records of my research performance, became a cumulative and ever-changing record of my experience of wear. In layering different kinds of 'notes', I attempted to produce for the reader/viewer a fuller and more embodied understanding of my experiences of wear; so that what could be said (or written) was enveloped in what could be sensed and seen.

Auto-ethnographic methods are perhaps more frequently used in arts-based practice-based research than in fashion studies, a frequency that perhaps highlights the blurring of subject and object, which is so central to research through doing. While within fashion studies auto-ethnographic works such as 'Urban field-notes: An auto-ethnography of street style blogging', by Brent Luvaas (Luvaas in Jenns 2016) have been critiqued for his 'co-creation' of his field, in much practice-based research the co-creation of the field (through making) is both explicit and necessary. In wearing as research practice, the role of the garment as agent became more apparent – not only in a theoretical manner (through reading and writing about agency), or through listening to participants describe their experiences, but in a habitual and embodied way – these shoes could offer new sensory experiences or stop me in my tracks; causing blisters or preventing me from walking through their material form.

This discomfort resonated with Pink's assertion that:

anthropological practice is a corporeal process that involves the ethnographer engaging not only with the ideas of others, but in learning about their understandings through her or his own physical and sensorial experiences, such as tastes or pain and illness.

(Pink 2015: 13)

Wearing made it impossible for me to ignore the importance of my shoes in my lived experience. In denying myself the comfort of my usual everyday footwear, my embodied and sensory experiences were brought to the fore: my gait was changed, my pace, my experience of navigating spaces and social situations shifted – my body and the material of the shoe were altered and marked. Similarly, the function of the garment (and the shoe in particular) as records of experience, bearers of material memory, was made evident in the ways that the materials moulded to my body or were altered by the environment.

It became clear that what I wore was integral to my lived experiences, that each change in footwear constituted a shift in the practices of the body. That the ways I navigated the world, the complex negotiations of dressing, and acquiring clothes, are, without doubt, negotiations of ideals, imageries and agencies, but that wearing itself was predominantly a material negotiation, one constituted in and by tactile bodily engagement. Wearing as practice forced me to engage with the garments' agency by extending or altering their form. In doing so, their power to impact upon and alter my embodied experience was increased; their agency made materially manifest. In wearing as research, I pushed and orientated my body in ways I might otherwise not have done. I chose shoes which were uncomfortable in order to problematize wearing. In wearing as a research method, both I and the shoes I made became subject and object of this research; together, we became records of the experience of doing, wearing and of being together in the world.

Being in the world

The breakdown of subject/object dualism, which underlies the material turn and is immanent in much of the development of practice-based research in fashion, is brought to an unconventional if logical conclusion in wearing as research. In wearing, one is creating a 'fleshy practice' of research, a practice which is embodied and bodily. It suggests that both sensory ethnography and auto-ethnography might come together in fashion research practice, just as they have in the writings and outputs of craft-person researchers (Lee 2016; Harrod 2015; Marchand 2015) to communicate and make present embodied and bodily knowledge. It is apparent that most, if not all, fashion and dress research is concerned with wearing (or not wearing) clothes: that wearing clothes is what we do. However, while wearing, alongside buying, making and disposing of clothing is an aspect of clothing research, the experience of wearing is still relatively under-explored. In this chapter, I put forward the idea that wearing need not only be a topic for fashion research but might also be a methodology. Much in the way that making has shifted from being the subject of craft/design research to the methodology through which it is enacted, I asked if wearing too may make the leap from subject to method.

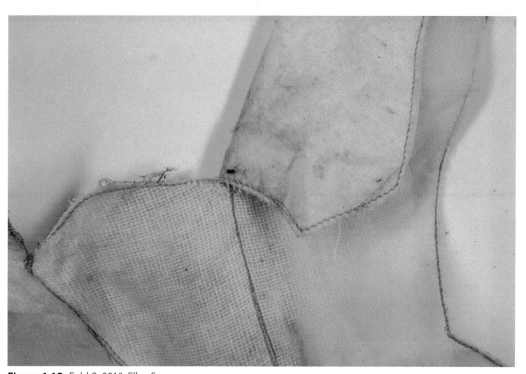

Figure 1.12 Fold 8, *2013. Ellen Sampson.*

Wearing Diary 2

Although I walk for several miles the shoes do not appear to loosen at all, they still grip my feet tightly, pressing my toes together and biting at my heels. They are cool and faintly sticky inside, I can feel the copper adhering to my soles.

When I reach home, I peel off the shoes, letting them fall to the kitchen floor. I look down at my feet to see perfect imprints of the stitching; the shoe mirrored on my foot. The dye has bled, leaving stitch marks where the sole and upper meet. The marks are uncanny and unsettling, like something from a horror film. Stigmata of the path I walked.

(Wearing Diary, July 2015)

New Shoes: Objects of fantasy, objects of desire

2

Shoes are over-determined objects, bearers of multiple meanings. The focus of this book is the embodied experience of wearing and the outcomes of wear: the way that, through use, we and the things we wear are changed. Though this book takes a psychoanalytic and phenomenological approach to the materiality of clothing and the embodied experience of wearing, this chapter first seeks to contextualize this discussion within the multiple ways footwear has been interpreted and read. No artefact is ever free from the symbolic meanings it is layered with. That is to say, we cannot help but engage with material culture in the context of the meanings that we and others have ascribed to them. These processes of meaning making and symbolization are continually evolving: our understandings of ourselves and the world are constantly being remade. As both interpreters and makers of meaning, we continuously move between subject and object. With an over-determined artefact like the shoe, these symbolic meanings are so prominent that they dominate the shoe's interpretation. Symbolic interpretations are both ubiquitous and seductive.

Shoes are often interpreted as symbols or metonyms: either as standing for something else or as a part that is representative of the whole. These semiotic and structuralist analyses of fashion (cf. Barthes (1967) and Bourdieu (1977)), understand the shoe as a referent, a thing which demarcates another, be that a body part, behaviour or social position. As with all garments, shoes function simultaneously as a form of cultural capital, a marker of taste and an expression of identity; they are part of the 'habitus' (Bourdieu 1977). Semiotic readings of fashion suggest that one can quite literally read someone's shoes, from the 'limo' shoes of a footballer's wife to the wellington boots of a farmer, so that certain types of footwear demarcate certain types of person: their taste, class, behaviour, employment and education. Footwear, so often task-specific (steel-toe-capped work boots, chef's plastic clogs, stripper's Perspex-heeled platforms), affords excellent potential for this type of categorization. Though the layers of meaning and signification may have become more complex (e.g. work boots on a fashion model, the multiple meanings afforded to training shoes, complex re-appropriations and subversions of a signifier over time), these highly semiotic interpretations are still the predominant way by which footwear is addressed in popular culture, fiction and film. These processes of signification, the understanding of fashion as a language, which may be 'read', often obscure the material agency of the artefact: the garment is understood as a sign rather than a material agent in its own right. It could be suggested that this preoccupation with what shoes represent obscures their material agency.

However, for many it is precisely this capacity of the shoe to become symbolically overloaded which is of interest – the idea that a single item of clothing might become representative of the wearer as a whole; see, for example, Riello and McNeil's (2006) exploration of how shoes were used to demarcate shifting queer identities in the twentieth century, or McNeil's (2009) discussion of eighteenth-century men's footwear and the foot, which compares the structured form of the shoe, its precision and neatness, with the disciplining of the post-Enlightenment body through the scientific and analytical gaze (McNeil 2009). Similarly Breward (2006), writing on nineteenth-century men's footwear, outlines how 'good' shoe design (simple, elegant and functional) became analogous with the desirable masculine traits of rationality, control and healthfulness: the shoe as a symbol of the body, mind and ethics of its wearer. For Hovey (2001) writing of Du Maurier's *Rebecca* (1938) and

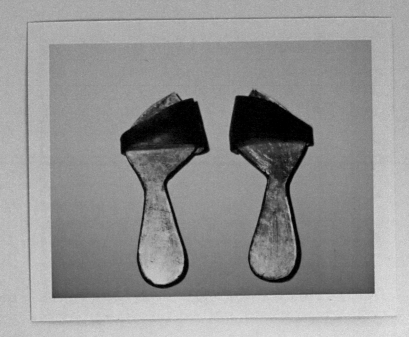

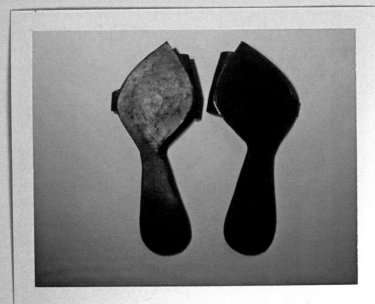

its film adaptation (Hitchcock 1940), the shoe serves as both metaphor for the body of the first Mrs De Winter and as a symbol of feminine desire: the deceased woman's shoes become her substitute, standing in for her as an object of obsessive love and rage. Powerfully, Barthelemy (2001) examines the capacity of a garment to become analogous, not with individual identity, but with that of a whole culture or group. For Barthelemy, the brogan, a roughly made and often uncomfortable boot, is a powerful metaphor for the subjugation inflicted upon enslaved African-American bodies by both their owners and the state. He writes of how the 'awesome and infallible signifying power of the shoes' (ibid.: 195) was internalized by their wearers, an inescapable symbol (and bodily reminder) of their subjugation.

Opposite

Figure 2.1 *Black copper flip-flop – unworn. Polaroids 4 and 5, 2015. Ellen Sampson.*

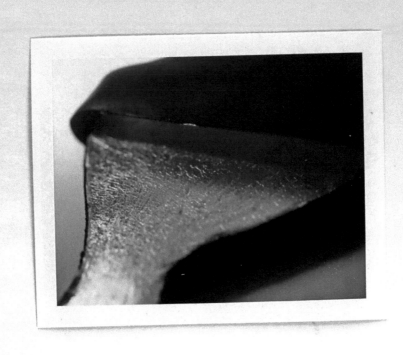

Consumption and desire

Much of the symbolic meaning ascribed to footwear, in the west, has its roots in folklore and fairy tale – in stories of magical powers, transformation and change. The symbolism of materials is of huge importance in European folklore: fairy-tale shoes are frequently described as being made of improbable materials which highlight their impossibility in the material world. In Cinderella-type tales, 'slippers are always splendid. Some are red … Others are of silk, satin, spangled with jewels, matchless, or like the sun. Overall, though, the cinder-girl's shoes are golden' (Davidson 2015: 26).

Though Cinderella's glass slipper (Perrault 1697; Grimm Brothers 1812a) is the most famous example, there are many other improbable materials: red-hot iron shoes in *Snow White* (Grimm Brothers 1812b), copper shoes in a Finnish folktale. The materials which fairy-tale shoes are made of are often valuable and outlandish, in direct contrast to everyday shoes in their role as protectors of the feet. This contrast makes the shoe 'strange', highlighting its role as a magical or transformative object. As I write elsewhere:

> In fairy tales, shoes frequently represent a shift in status, from Cinderella's upward trajectory, to Puss in Boots' anthropomorphic shift. The acquisition of finer and more delicate shoes indicates the ability to eschew 'sensible' shoes designed for manual labour or traversing long distances. In this context, 'impossible shoes' such as Cinderella's glass slippers – shoes that one could never walk in – are particularly telling. Her shift from sabots to slippers, even without the attendant transformation of clothing, pumpkin and mice, would be enough to indicate her upward social shift.
>
> (Sampson 2016: 239)

Both within and outside fairy tale, the shoe is frequently presented as an object of desire. In women's magazines, 'chick lit'[1] and television, the shoe is positioned as an artefact to be lusted over, fantasized about and ultimately acquired. Desire is the predominant theme in contemporary representations of footwear: shoes not as functional objects, but as 'fetish commodities'. The shoe, in many ways one of our most functional of garments, has become synonymous with conspicuous consumption: delicate, vertiginous or highly decorated shoes stripped of their function as aids to walking[2] make perfect Veblen goods. Much media discussion and representation of footwear perpetuates this idea: women's shoes as the epitome of conspicuous consumption, artefacts acquired solely for their capacity to convey status and wealth. Shoes, and particularly their purchase, have become metaphors for qualities that patriarchal hegemony assigns to women: compulsivity, hysteria, greed and superficiality.[3] The shoe is a site of uncontrollable and pernicious female desire.[4] Nowhere is this more evident than in descriptions of Imelda Marcos's shoe collection, where the purchasing of numerous unnecessary shoes is interpreted as representative of extreme moral corruption, akin even to the crimes committed by her husband.[5]

Opposite

Figure 2.2 *Black copper flip-flop – unworn. Polaroid 1, 2015. Ellen Sampson.*

Fairy tale and fetish

Nowhere is the compulsivity ascribed to shoes more apparent than in the representation of fairy-tale shoes in literature and film. In *Cinderella*, *The Red Shoes* (Andersen 1845) and *The Twelve Dancing Princesses*, the shoe is an agent of change. In putting on shoes, the heroine in each of these tales is transformed. For Davidson, 'Shoes punish and reward, elevate and entrap, speed and hinder through their own powers or their transformative possibilities' (Davidson 2015: 1). The shoe, with its capacity to transform rich to poor, ugly to beautiful and girl to woman, is a recurrent symbol in fairy tales, a trigger for uncontrollable and covetous longing. Within fairy tales the shoe is also often used as a metaphor for the moral or social transformation of the wearer, and is simultaneously the site on which change takes place; to put on shoes is to be transformed. From Cinderella's transformation from scullery maid to princess to the anthropomorphic transformation afforded by the boots in *Puss in Boots*, shoes in fairy tales are magical or transformative artefacts, the object through which change or transformation is facilitated.

In both *Cinderella* and *The Red Shoes* the quest for shoes pushes women to the edge. They are compelled to sacrifice their feet, their mobility, freedom and independence for the status that shoes represent.[6] Elsewhere, I suggest:

> Shoes represent both a shift in bodily experience and a giving in to their allure – a loss of self-control. These shoes, with their magical or malevolent qualities, compel the characters to act. There is an obvious ambiguity about who is in control: do the wearers or the shoes perform the dance? For Karen, leaping in agony, the shoes are steadfastly in control. She is overtaken by them.
>
> (Sampson 2016: 245–6)

The image of the glass slipper in Cinderella, an impenetrable, impossible shoe (whether a material mistranslation or not[7]) has captured our collective imagination, so that the term 'Cinderella' has become analogous with many forms of positive transformation. Like the glass slipper, the red shoe has become a 'meta-symbol' in the language of fashion. Red shoes have become a trope within feminist theory, folklore studies and, perhaps most significantly, film. The red shoe (as a metaphor for sexuality, power and desire) has a particular valency, most notably in Powell and Pressburger's post-war film *The Red Shoes* (1945).[8] Similarly, Dorothy's 'ruby slippers' in *The Wizard of Oz* (Flemming 1939) become a literal agent of life and death. In more recent films, red shoes remain a trope; in *The Red Shoes* (2005), a Korean horror version of the Andersen fairy tale, the covetousness brought on by shoes is the trigger for a series of terrible events. Davidson presents this film as a conflation of all the previous red-shoe tales: 'Bunhongsin prioritises the violence implicit in the earlier texts to enhance the potency of the red shoes symbol as a vehicle for impassioned, destructive "self-fashioning"' (Davidson 2008: 143).

Opposite

Figure 2.3 *Black copper flip-flop – unworn. Polaroid 2, 2015. Ellen Sampson.*

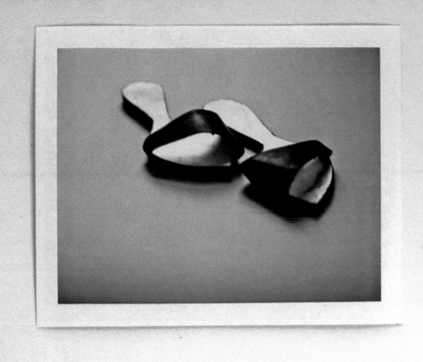

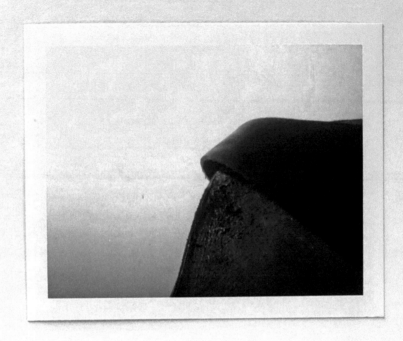

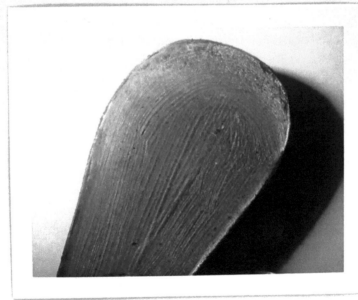

Perhaps the most pronounced and frequently reiterated interpretations of footwear are those that emerge from Freudian literary and film theory: the shoe as a vaginal symbol.[9] For Freud, in dreams, the shoe, like many vessels, could be interpreted as 'a corresponding symbol of the female genitals' (Freud 1905: 299). Drawing on Freud, Bruno Bettelheim sees Cinderella's glass slipper 'as a symbol of the vagina' and asserts that 'Cinderella's running away from this situation could be seen as her effort to protect her virginity' (Bettelheim 1976: 265).[10] This interpretation of the shoe is reductive; any and all container-like vessels could symbolize, and in dreams stand in for, female genitalia. Bettelheim's focus on the shoe as a vaginal symbol obscures what the glass slipper actually is: a shoe too fragile to walk or move in, a shoe that renders the wearer immobile – an impossible shoe. This focus on the shoe as metaphor relegates it to the realm of the symbolic, distancing it from the materiality of everyday shoe. Like all fetishizations the interpretation of the shoe as a symbolic object dematerializes it, rendering it an object of fantasy, an object without form. Stallybrass writes of Freud, dematerialization and the fetish:

> For what is it that Freud discovers in the fetish? Not a shoe, but a system of displacement. Freud, in this at least, is the true heir of Protestantism. The fetish cannot be a real presence; rather, it symbolizes an absence…. In front of a shoe, Freud finds meaning; in front of a painting of tulips, an art critic finds a memento mori.

> (Stallybrass 2014: 278)

The symbolic dematerializes things.

Opposite
Figure 2.4 *Black copper flip-flop – wear 1. Polaroids 4 and 11, 2015. Ellen Sampson.*

Overleaf
Figure 2.5 *Black copper flip-flop – wear 1. Polaroids 7 and 8, 2015. Ellen Sampson.*

Figure 2.6 *Black copper flip-flop – unworn. Polaroids 2 and 3, 2015. Ellen Sampson.*

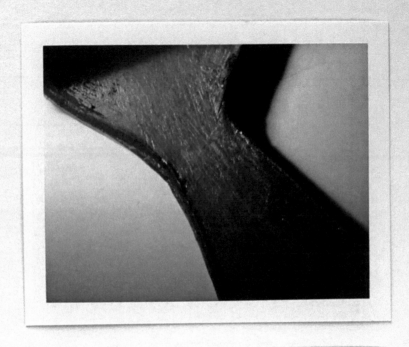

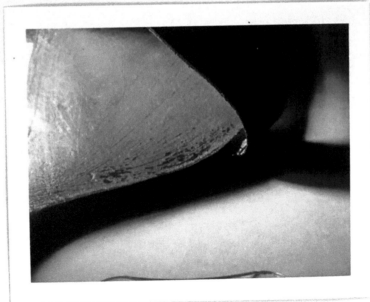

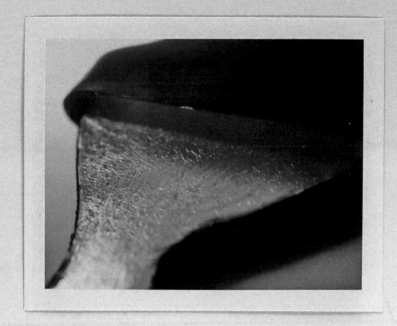
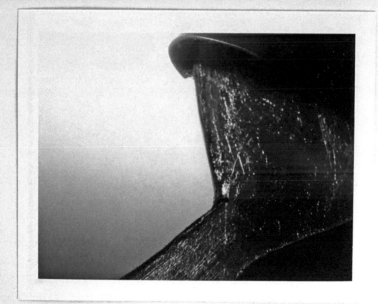

New shoes

We shall start with a new pair of shoes …

When one circumvents the discourse around consumption and fantasy that often dominates discussions of footwear, a new pair of shoes is a good place to start. The acquisition of new shoes is, in part, significant because it is often the start of the longer embodied relationship of day-to-day wear. As footwear is frequently task- or time-specific, the acquisition of new shoes often represents a juncture or shift in the wearer's embodied experience.[11] Whether they are school shoes, work boots or wedding shoes, new shoes often mark a point at which a new regime of bodily disciplines commences. If rites of passage are points at which the mechanisms through which the body is disciplined alter, then clothing is one of the ways changing disciplining practices are manifested. While the new shoe (with stiff leather, laces and straps) may psychically discipline the foot, putting on new shoes often also marks the commencement of larger institutional and social regimes of disciplining. The act of putting on new shoes (or the image or fantasy of that same act) is often linked with shifts in how the body, and thus the self, is produced and maintained. The body, its postures and gestures are produced not only by the performance of tasks and the organization of spaces but by the artefacts with which the body interacts. As Latour writes: 'The object does not reflect the social. It does more. It transcribes and displaces the contradictory interests of people and things' (Latour 2009: 152). Objects are afforded moral responsibilities and consequently play an active role in the disciplining of the body. However minorly, our shoes regulate our bodily behaviours, through their material form and in marking changes in how the body is disciplined. There is something about our capacity to see ourselves wearing shoes, to be able to look down and see the shod foot as a whole, that creates a particular experience for the wearer – a dual experience of seeing one's feet in shoes and of simultaneously feeling the shoe encasing the foot.[12] This process of looking at oneself, of simultaneously being the objectifying viewer and the subject of the gaze, can become both unsettling and scopophilic.[13] The subsequent dissonance and self-objectification might perhaps explain the compulsivity frequently said to accompany the purchase of footwear; shoes present an excellent site for narcissistic experience. The shod foot becomes an object of identification[14] for the wearer; the shod foot is both of the self and other to it.

Good shoes

If new shoes provide a locus for a narcissistic experience then they also provide a site for a moralizing one. There has long been a discourse of 'good' shoes, of shoes as a potential site of bodily, moral and ethical reform – from the Victorian Dress Reform Movement, as exemplified by Dr Gustav Jaeger (see Fig. 2.7),[15] whose adherents believed they could liberate and improve health via their clothes and shoes, to ways that masculinity and modernity are thought to intersect in men's footwear choices

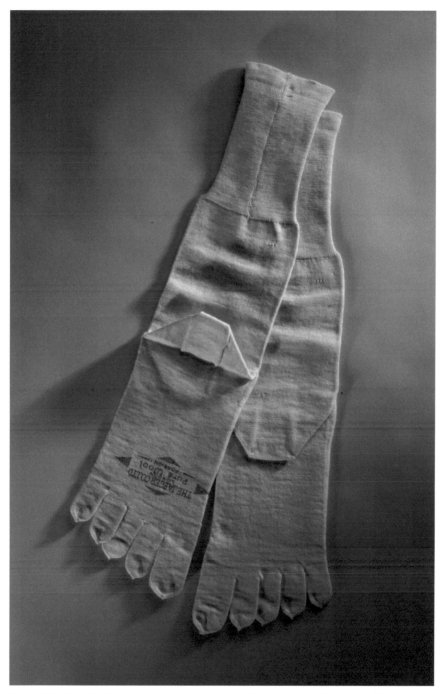

Figure 2.7 *Pair of ankle-length knitted wool socks with separate toes, Dr Jaeger's digital socks, late nineteenth century.*

(see Breward 2006). There is a pervasive idea that a 'well-chosen' shoe – frugal, of good quality and durable – is indicative of the wearer's morality. Conversely, 'poorly' chosen or ill-considered footwear, those shoes that are frivolous, poorly suited to the terrain or difficult to walk in, are interpreted as representing the frivolity or impracticality of the wearer.

The way the body is positioned in relation to the ground frequently demarcates social status (think of bowing or kneeling to pray). Similarly, a link is often made between physical balance and moral constitution; someone can be described as 'sure-footed', as 'off kilter' or as 'flighty'. Though the object of this research is the material shoe, these metaphors and the representation of the body through language offer insight into how the body in motion is interpreted. Different shoes are seen as representing different moralities and behaviours. Heel height, for example, is frequently interpreted as linked to power – the raising of oneself above others – and to pride. Extreme footwear has long held academic interest, both in relation to the high heel's incapacitating nature and to its capacity to raise the wearer up. For example Venetian courtesans, in wearing high wooden chopines, were both raising themselves off the street and making themselves more visible; this visibility was often interpreted as a lack of humility, or shamelessness. Vianello suggests that chopines produced a 'confusion about the moral and social identity' of the women who wore them (Vianello 2006: 77); stature was equated both with high status and low morality.

Shoelessness

Similarly, shoelessness has been interpreted as both liberation or subjugation; intentional or involuntary exclusions from the social contract. If the dressed body is the social body, the body without clothes is often excluded from the social contract. In choosing to be clothed, we are subscribing to a multiplicity of social demands and conventions. Often, to go without shoes is perceived as a strong marker of difference. We talk of the poor and disenfranchised in terms of their non-existent or shoddy footwear.[16] However, far from always being an impediment, deliberate shoelessness may be an act of power, a refusal. By going shoeless one marks oneself out as part of a counter-culture. For the hippies of the 1960s and 1970s, shoelessness was a form of liberation; DeMello (2009) suggests that their voluntary barefootedness referenced the perceived innocence and freedom of the bare foot, a foot without responsibility. The idea of the 'natural human', so dominant in Enlightenment discourse, presents the naked body and the bare foot as simpler, healthier and more moral. The bare foot is often perceived as more liberated than the shod foot. There is also a long relationship between barefootedness and ideas of humility, evident in the religious practice of barefoot pilgrimage and barefoot mourning, as well as discalced religious communities such as Franciscan monks and nuns. Eschewing the status afforded by footwear allows the pilgrim or mourner to materially manifest their modesty and submission to divine authority.

Opposite

Figure 2.8 *Black copper flip-flop – wear 1. Polaroid 2, 2015. Ellen Sampson.*

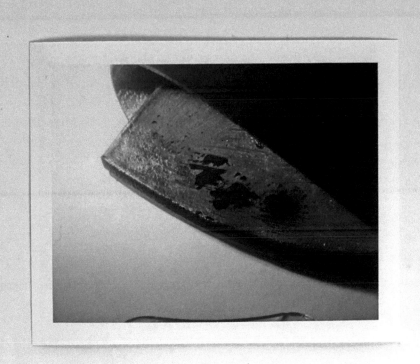

Shoe care

Similarly, acts of shoe care, of cleaning and mending one's shoes, are often presented as indicative of a disciplined and rigorous morality. Just as the body is disciplined through 'techniques of the body' (Mauss 1935), the objects with which we adorn it are also disciplined. The metaphor 'down at heel' connotes both the moral failure to maintain self-preservation and impoverishment. In no place is this more evident than in the ways that soldiers care for their shoes: bodily discipline through marching, drills and uniforms being extended to footwear. Boots are polished to a mirror-like sheen and their surfaces made impenetrable with dubbin and wax.[17]

The strengthening of the shoe's surface through care mirrors the fortifying of the body (and the army itself); boundaries sealed and leaks prevented, the impenetrability of the body and of the regiment is maintained. The maintenance of shoes is in itself interesting; beyond its practical benefit it is also an act of care. To care for one's clothes is to care for the self; it is the grooming of the 'bodily schema'. Repairing shoes may be due to necessity or economy but it is simultaneously an act of reparation: an attempt to negate the damage wearing does to one's clothes. Re-soling or re-heeling shoes is a form of erasure: the exterior records of steps one has taken, and the dirt one has stepped in, are erased through the replacement of a sole or heel tip. Kelley (2015)[18] writes of the ways that valued garments were repaired in order that they might be passed on. She examines the maintenance of clothing, not just as a domestic task necessary to 'keep up appearances', but as a way of negotiating personal and familial relations. To repair a garment is to acknowledge its value in one's life.

Empty shoes

Such a mountain I saw – of Jewish shoes in Majdanek. . . .
'We are the shoes, we are the last witnesses.
We are shoes from grandchildren and grandfathers.
From Prague, Paris and Amsterdam.
And because we are only made of stuff and leather
And not of blood and flesh, each one of us avoided the hellfire.'

(Moses Schulstein in Benstock & Ferriss 2001: 196)

Writing of the piles of shoes abandoned in Majdanek concentration camp, the poet Moses Schulstein poignantly captures the power of empty shoes, their capacity to function as both symbolic and material stand ins for absent bodies; the ways that, through use, they become records of the actions performed within them and the bodies they once held. The dirt and bodily imprints they contain are evidence of the wearer being in the world: traces of the interactions and experiences which altered

Opposite
Figure 2.9 *Black copper flip-flop – wear 1. Polaroid 5, 2015. Ellen Sampson.*

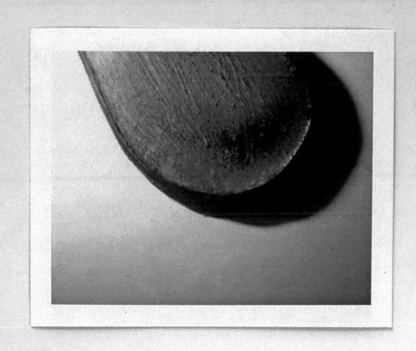

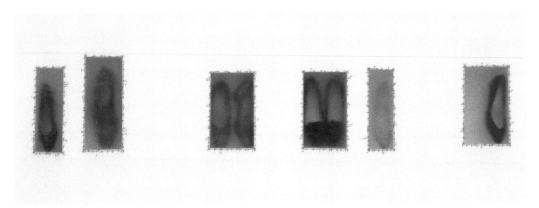

Figure 2.10 Atrabilious, *1992–3. Doris Sacedo.*

them. The insides of empty shoes often bear a footprint-like imprint of the absent wearer's foot, an index of the absent body. Even away from the body, empty shoes speak of the bodies which have inhabited them and the paths they have walked. They speak of these absent bodies in a way which is both symbolic and material – carrying physical traces of those bodies (footprints and sweat stains within the shoe) and simultaneously acting as referents to them. This poignancy, the empty shoe as a shoe empty of life, is often utilized to accentuate the horrors of loss. Artists such as Doris Salcedo and Elina Chauvet have drawn upon the signifying power of empty shoes to presence absence, disappearance and death, in works such as Salcedo's *Atrabilarios* (1992–7) (Fig. 2.10) and Chauvet's *Red Shoes* (2009–13).

In these works, shoes acts as a synecdoche, a part used to represent a missing whole: the shoe as metaphor, standing in for a body which cannot itself be present. Nowhere is the synecdochal power of the empty shoe more evident than in Holocaust memorials such as those at Auschwitz-Birkenau concentration camp, where multiple empty shoes stand in for multiple absent lives: for murdered people and bodies destroyed. Carol-Jones writes that the image of the empty shoe has become synonymous with the Shoah, so that one cannot help but connect these objects to the terrible events to which they were witness. Holocaust shoes are the 'abject survivors of the abjection suffered by men, women and children in the Shoah' (2001: 197) – witnesses to the horrors to which their wearers were subjected. Highlighting that these empty shoes recall the absent bodies of the murdered, Benstock states: 'The pile of 4000 shoes from death camps in Poland displayed in the United States Holocaust Memorial Museum recalls the piles of corpses in the streets of ghettos, in death carts in the camps, in mass graves' (Benstock & Ferriss 2001: 8). Beyond the shoes of those murdered in the Holocaust, the empty shoe has the capacity to make present other absent bodies (not least when those shoes bear an indexical trace of those who wore them). Benstock observes that 'At a 1994 protest in Washington, D.C., for example, 38000 pairs of shoes stood in for victims of gun violence. The same statement has been borrowed in Paris and other French cities to symbolize the 600,000 civilians killed by land mines' (Benstock & Ferriss 2001: 8). Similarly, the placing of 10,000 empty shoes at the Place de la République, Paris to stand in for the bodies of protesters who had intended to attend a march at the UN climate conference COP21, which was cancelled after the 13 November 2015 terrorist attacks (see Fig 2.11), drew widespread media coverage.

Worn

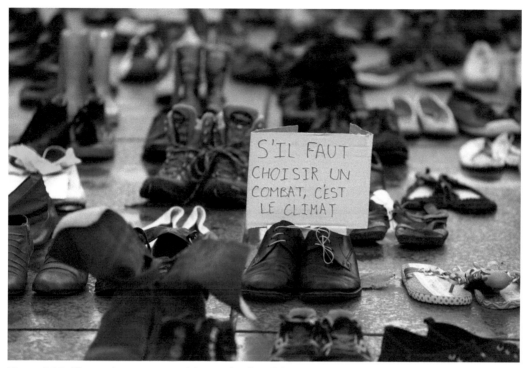

Figure 2.11 *Climate change protesters' shoes in the Place de la République, 2015.*

In these worn and empty shoes symbolic and material meanings converge, so that their affects multiply. The worn and empty shoe does not just symbolize the absent body, but with its scuffed soles and sweat-stained interior it is a material manifestation of that same absent body. The empty shoe is an absent-presence, a trace: a space where the body is both there and not there. Thus, the materiality of the shoe – its active role as a physical rather than symbolic agent – is brought to the fore. This book is concerned with the material agency of the things we wear, the ways that, through use, they act upon us. In addressing this material agency, this book does not deny the symbolic meanings ascribed to our shoes, or of clothing more generally. However, it suggests that in focusing on the symbolic meanings of garments other aspects of our relationship with them have at times been obscured – those aspects which are bodily and material. It suggests that beyond the multiple symbolic meanings ascribed to clothing, there is another side to our relationship with the things we wear: one that is bodily tactile and embodied, predicated on movement and touch. That a fuller understanding of our relationships with our clothes could be produced by attending to the intimacies of wear and of wearing – the way things feel rather than look. It positions footwear as an active agent in our networks of things, one that through its material presence, its physical form, impacts upon and becomes a record of our lived experience in multiple ways.

Overleaf

Figure 2.12 *Black copper flip-flop – wear 1. Polaroid 6, 2015. Ellen Sampson.*

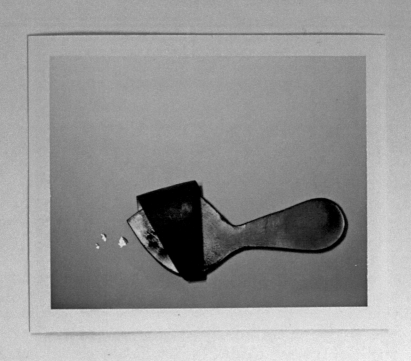

Wearing Diary 3

The shoes are biting me. The central strap pushing into the soft white flesh of my sole. Each step jars, a constant nagging reminder of what my feet are doing, of where I have to go. I move onwards slowly, conscious of my steps …

Bored and in pain, I pause on the street and break a conker under my shoe, the first of the year. I can feel the green needles of the shell through the sole of the shoe, a strange masochistic pleasure in rolling the fruit under my foot; as it cracks, the conker emerges, as white and under-cooked as dough, on the pavement. It is not what I want. I move on.

Later, on an escalator, I push the arch of my foot against the lip of the step; I want to feel the prickle of green needles again.

(Wearing Diary, September 2015)

Wearing and Being Worn

3

Beyond their symbolic function, shoes are tools that allow us to perform certain tasks: to walk further and for longer. Our relationship with shoes may be sartorial or fetishistic, but it is also practical and bodily. Whether we wear trainers, stilettos or wellington boots, our shoes facilitate bodily practices from which we might otherwise be excluded. Our bodily engagements with the materiality of footwear (rather than its symbolic signification) highlight our physical dependence upon it. We require particular shoes to negotiate the terrains and social spaces through which we move. To use Gibson's (1979) term, footwear 'affords' us certain behaviours – as a tool in identity construction allowing us to 'pass' in performing certain identities and selves, but also psychically and practically: shoes allow us to move through the world. Despite a cultural tendency to focus on footwear which is highly decorative and impractical,[1] most footwear retains its practical purpose; shoes 'work' for us. It is this 'tool-like' quality that this chapter explores, and how, in wearing, the shoe and our bodies interact. Frequently, shoes allow one to perform acts that the body alone would not be capable of. They aid movement and endurance, capacity to withstand heat and cold, to cross a rough terrain. If we think of shoes as tools both in the navigation of environments and the performance of identity, the significance of our bodily relationships with them is perhaps more apparent. It is the successful confluence of the body and a tool which permits certain actions to occur, so that the material form of the tool, alongside the skill, familiarity and agility of the body which uses it, dictates whether the task can be completed. Heidegger wrote of tools as often being 'ready-to-hand', objects which might be used without conscious regard for their form:

> The less we just stare at the hammer-thing, and the more we seize hold of it and use it, the more primordial does our relationship to it become, and the more unveiledly is it encountered as that which it is – as equipment. The hammering itself uncovers the specific 'manipulability' of the hammer. The kind of Being which equipment possesses – in which it manifests itself in its own right – we call 'readiness-to-hand'.
>
> (1962: 98)

Whilst Heidegger perhaps underestimated the tactile and tacit knowledges, the thought processes and muscle memory required to successfully use a hammer (to which anyone who has attempted to hang a picture can attest) it is true that there is a thoughtlessness in the use of everyday tools, which often extends to our relationships with clothing – we wear these things without being fully aware of them. Conversely, Heidegger also writes of things which are 'unready-to-hand' (a lamp with a broken cord, for example), objects which in their failure to work become present for us in a different way. The concept of 'unreadiness-to-hand' is useful when thinking about our relationship with clothing – our garments are frequently most present for us when they do not function. Like many tools, shoes may hinder us, either through intent[2] or by accident. Though these disabling qualities are sometimes interpreted as the work of an oppressive hegemony (high heels slowing our movements, old shoes making it painful to walk), they are also the physical work of the material shoe. At times, shoes are 'obstinate' objects, unwilling to bend to our wills. In their 'unreadiness-to-hand' they may hinder our movements or cause us pain; a pair of shoes with wrongly pitched heels will push the wearer off

Overleaf

Figure 3.1 *Cloth shoes – work in progress, 2015. Ellen Sampson.*

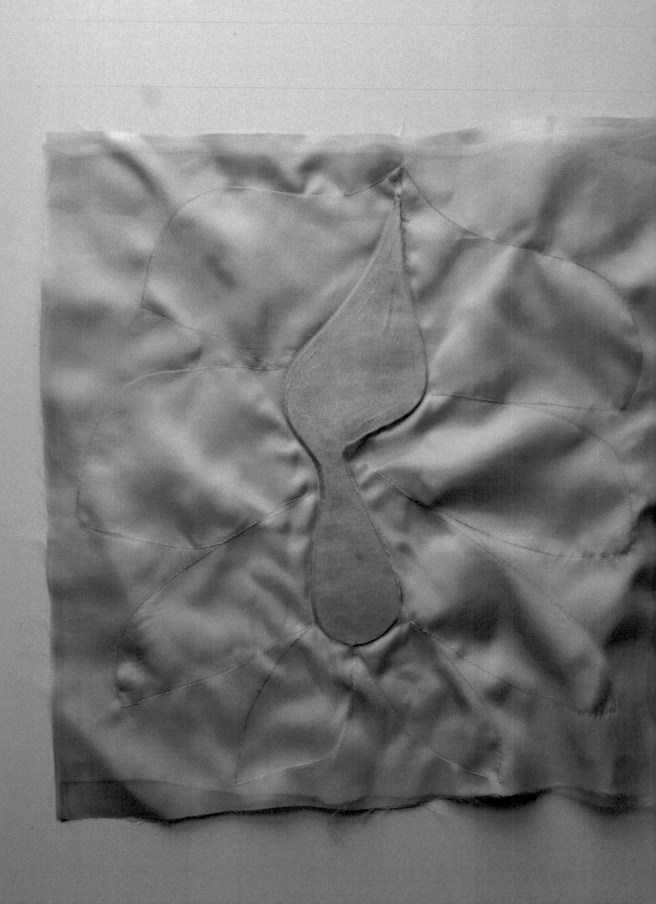

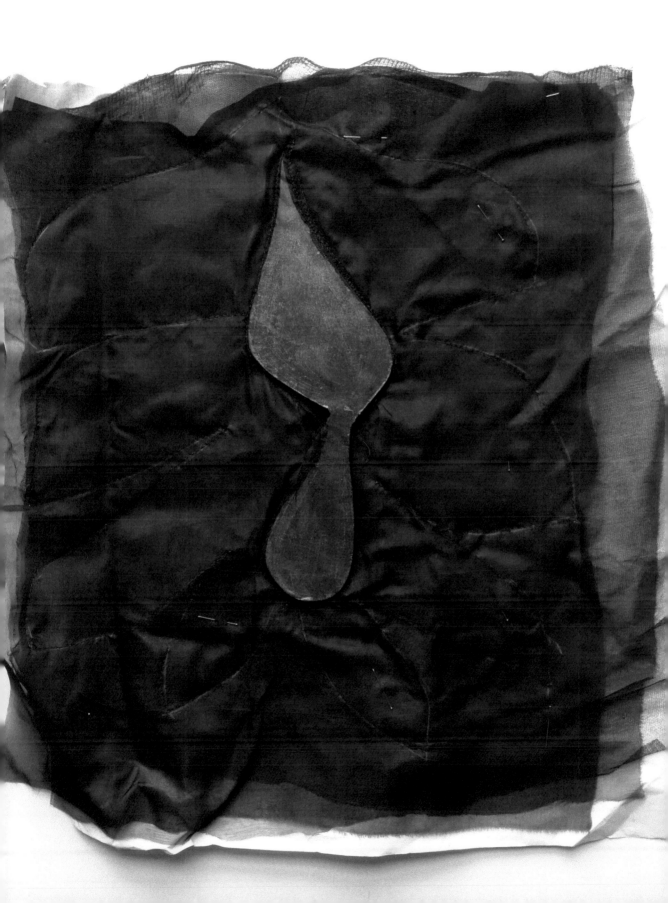

balance while a tight and unbending upper produces blisters and bloody heels. Such discomfort or hindrance may stem from our inability to manipulate them successfully; the more skill we have in utilizing an item (be it a hammer, a mobile phone or a shoe) the less aware of it we are; that when we have command of a tool, it recedes from view. The shoes we are most used to walking in and with are often those we are least aware of: shoe wearing is a learned practice. The shoe is an active material agent and the act of wearing is a continuous negotiation with its material form.

Armour

The shoe is a protective garment, armour for the foot. The sole of a shoe touches the ground in place of our feet, protecting us from the potential dangers of the street. Shoes allow us to walk; they are sacrificed to protect the foot. As with all garments, this skewed transactional relationship can be unsettling. Our clothes, simultaneously companions in our embodied experience, extensions of our bodily selves and visual communication tools, do not remain the same in perpetuity. With each wear, gesture and step, they are worn down and altered; though our shoes carry us, we are eventually too much to bear. Used shoes are frequently described as abject; sweaty interiors and dirty soles cause us to wrinkle our noses and turn our faces away.[3] Our footwear becomes polluted so that we are not. As we walk through the world, the substances which surround us adhere to our shoes; mud, rain, ash, urine: they carry traces of the places we have been. Although we may clean our shoes, the materials they are made from often prevent us from laundering them thoroughly – leather in particular cannot easily be washed without stiffening and cracking. As shoes absorb the dirt of the street, they become ambiguous objects, personal yet sullied by the public sphere. The shoe is often considered unacceptable when it is transformed through use and wear: the aged, creased and scuffed shoe is an uncomfortable, and intimate object. Used shoes are frequently linked with feelings of shame, whether as signifiers of poverty or as bearers of bodily trace.[4]

Used footwear is polarizing, viewed by some as the most abject of garments, dirtied both by the detritus of the street and by the excretions of the body. It is not surprising that in many cultures one must take off one's shoes before entering intimate and vulnerable spaces (the home, the temple). The purification of the extremities of the body, through the removal of shoes and washing of feet, is a common ritual in many cultures, emphasizing the tendency for the peripheries of the self to be most vulnerable to pollution.[5] Writing on purity and pollution in Japanese footwear, Chaiklin examines the literal and metaphorical pollution of shoes, highlighting their dual potential contaminants: 'footwear was unclean both from contact with the ground and the feet' (2006: 175). The shoe serves as a filter for these potential pollutions, sacrificed so that the self may remain clean. While external pollution may dirty the shoe, it is our bodily pollution that, for many, renders the shoe uncomfortable. The interior of the shoe, as a container for bodily materials, is an intimate space not usually visible to others. The used and empty shoe represents an absence, much as a fingerprint or still-smoking cigarette in an ashtray might represent an absent finger or mouth. The empty shoe always alludes to its missing binary: the foot.

Opposite
Figure 3.2 Cloth Triptych 1, *2015. Ellen Sampson.*

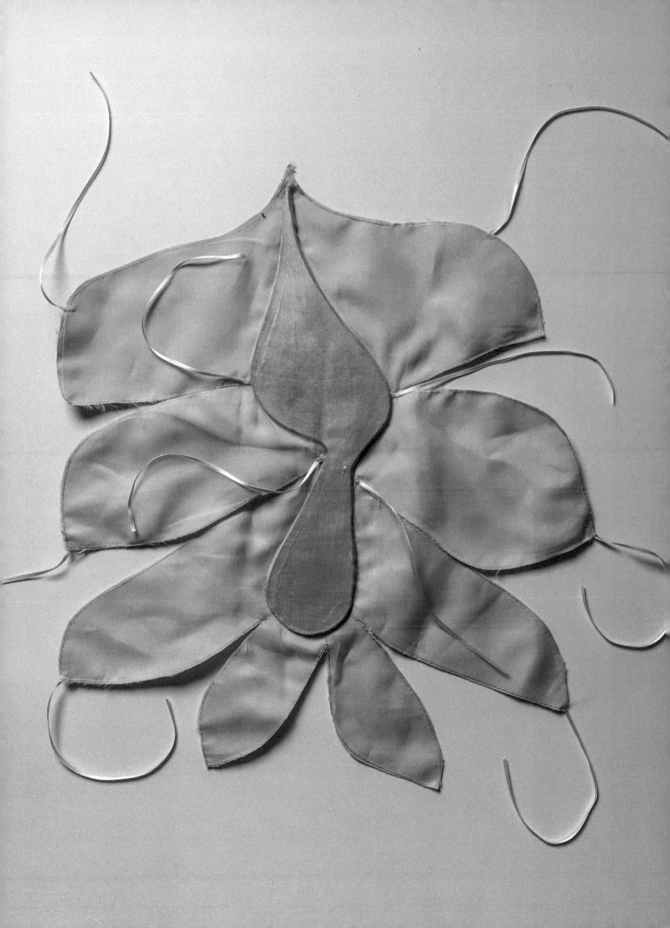

Used shoes have the potential to disrupt multiple binaries: those between the street and the home, the public and domestic, inside and outside, self and not self. The binaries of the clean/dirty and inside/outside are often vigilantly policed – so that footwear, standing ambiguously between them, must be managed with particular care. In the taxonomy of our garments, shoes are among the most peripheral, worn on top of other garments, at the edges of the body and touching the ground. Shoes sit at the edge of our bodily experience, and as a result are among the most potentially polluting of all our garments. As protective garments, shoes are boundaries of the body, objects which negotiate what may and may not be admitted. As artefacts that mediate our experience of walking, movement and the ground, shoes form a boundary between the self and the world. Shoes, like many garments, are simultaneously penetrable (one puts one's feet into them) and container-like (active spaces, capable of holding). As Douglas wrote: 'The body is a model that can stand for any bounded system. Its boundaries can represent any boundaries which are threatened or precarious' (1966 115). Conversely, shoes and other garments are artefacts which may stand in for the boundaries of the body.

Garments function as both literal and symbolic boundaries, protecting more than just our bodies. The pollution they filter is not only the dirt and detritus of the external world, but also pollutants that are potentially damaging to our sense of self. Just as shoes absorb the external pollutants from the street, so they also become receptacles for our own bodily excretions. As we wear our shoes, sweat and layers of discarded skin come to line their interiors, aspects of our body-selves absorbed into their material form. Although we may attempt to clean the dirt of the street from our shoes, it is difficult to remove these traces of our bodily selves; they are absorbed into the interior of the shoe so that the ambiguity and abjection of bodily excretion are present for us in dirty shoes. As our shoes absorb these aspects of the body, another binary is blurred: that between self and other, between object and subject. It is this breakdown in the symbolic order that Kristeva termed 'abjection' – a confusion between subject and object typified by substances which are at once bodily and separate from the body. Writing of the abjectness of bodily excretions, Kristeva writes: 'these body fluids, this defilement, this shit are what life withstands, hardly and with difficulty, on the part of death' (1982: 65). As the shoe absorbs our sweat and skin flakes, it is simultaneously a barrier between potential pollutants and ourselves, and a receptacle for those same substances. Rather than offering us the potential for transformation as a new shoe might, used shoes become vessels for our former selves; we remain incorporated into their material form. Worn shoes are material metonyms for the decay of the self; they are material links with our past selves, a literal vessel for the skins we have already shed. Instead of offering the release of transformation as new shoes might, they become a reminder of our pasts. The worn garment – and particularly the unclean and uncleanable shoe – is a repository, for both our public and bodily histories, where and who we have been.

Opposite
Figure 3.3 Cloth Triptych 2, *2015. Ellen Sampson.*

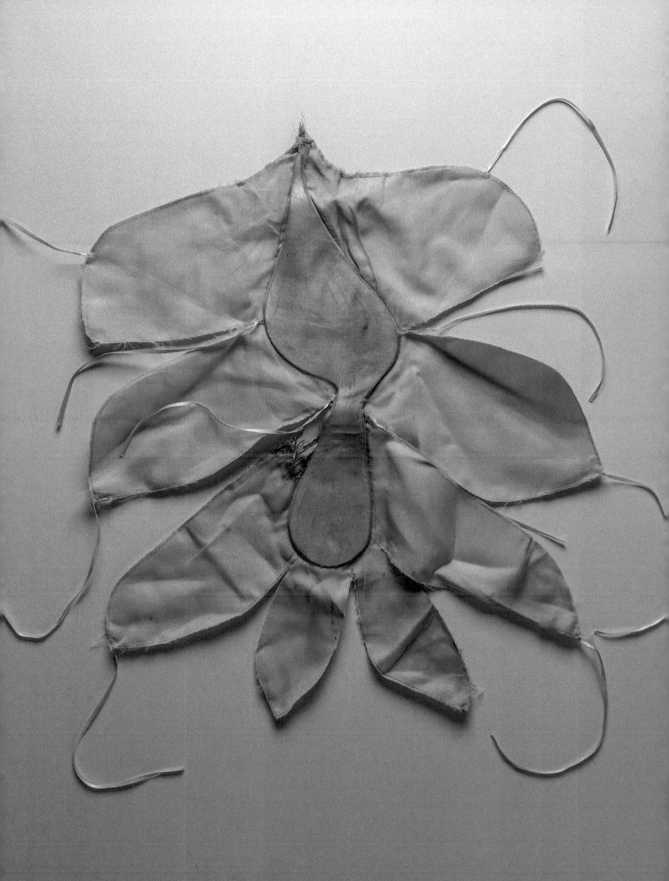

Interaction between the shoe and the foot

The shoe is an active agent and new shoes offer the potential for change; in being shod we are transformed. The idea of the shoe as an agent of change is seductive, but all too often new shoes are read as simply an illusory shift in the wearer's self-image. However, a new shoe causes us to alter our movements and thus our experience of our bodily selves. The way we walk and move is altered by our shoes, and simultaneously the material form of our bodies is altered with each new pair of shoes. Touching is fundamental to our experience of cloth and of clothing; though we experience our garments through other senses too, it is a relationship predicated on touch. It is through the tactile experience of our garments that we come to know them; to comprehend texture, fit and form. The experience of wearing is predominantly located in touch; in wearing, the dressed body is both touching the garment and being touched by it: wearing is both tactile and reciprocal. Shoes are intimate objects, worn close to the body for long periods. We often wear the same pair of shoes daily, for months or even years. In this sustained and habitual interaction, our relationship with our shoes often differs from our relationships with other garments; we come to know our shoes more intimately. This familiarity, a tacit and tactile form of knowledge, is often articulated as comfort – the well-worn item that has altered to accommodate our bodies. If wearing is a form of touching, and touch creates and maintains attachment (as psychoanalysts such as Esther Bick (1968) have suggested), then it follows that extended contact gives rise to a more enduring connection. Through extended use we become intimately attached to our clothes. In order for a garment to be worn for an extended period without discomfort, it must fit the form of our body, either through design or through alteration. Worn shoes have a close and continued relationship with, and correspondence to, the form of our bodies. If we were to categorize the significance of our relationships to artefacts by the duration of wear and proximity, shoes, along with spectacles[6] and jewellery, would rank highly. It is, in part, through this proximity and duration that we develop an enmeshed relationship with our clothes.

The shoe is not a static object; it alters through use. The shoe that we take off at the end of each day is different from the one we put on that morning. We are familiar with the idea of 'breaking-in' shoes and of the comfort and reassurance of a well-worn pair.

Through habitual wear a transactional relationship develops between shoe and foot. As the shoe moulds to the body it becomes a mirror, a cast of its form. As we wear our shoes they become casts of our body-selves; records of our form. The interior of a shoe that has been worn for an extended period resembles nothing so much as a footprint in leather and cloth. Footprints are records of gesture, the body progressing through space and time. The footprint is an index, a referent to a now absent body. Forster, in discussing the work of Peirce, states: 'My footprint represents my foot – as opposed to some other object of the same shape and size, because it is my foot that caused it. This causal connection is what qualifies the footprint as an index' (Forster 2011: 90). However, the footprint is not only a signifier of an absent body, it is also the trace of a gesture, of a body 'being' and moving in

Opposite

Figure 3.4 Cloth Triptych 3, *2015. Ellen Sampson.*

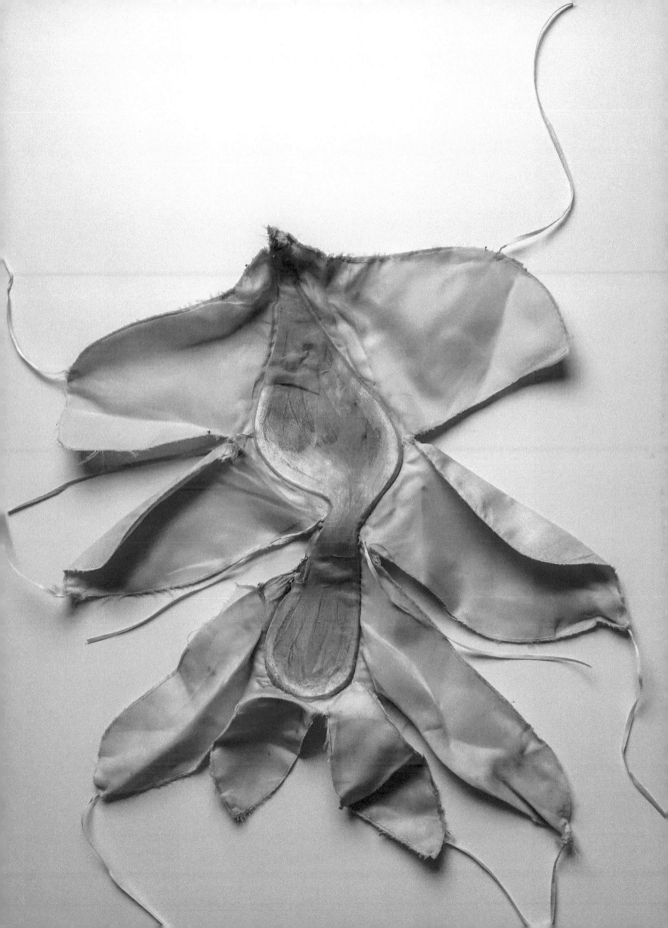

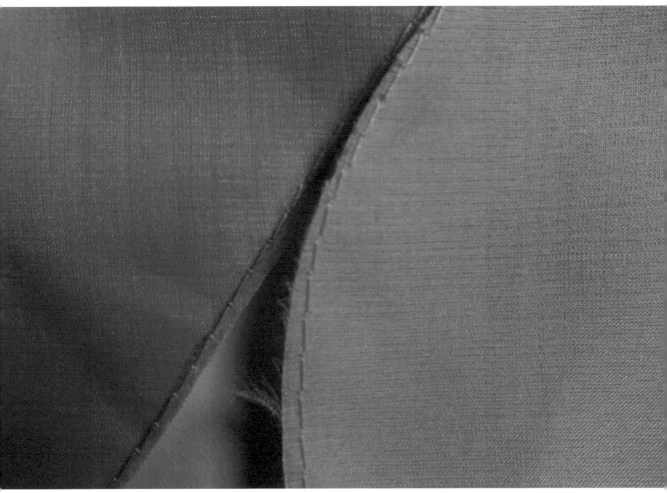

Figure 3.5 Cloth 2, *2015. Ellen Sampson.*

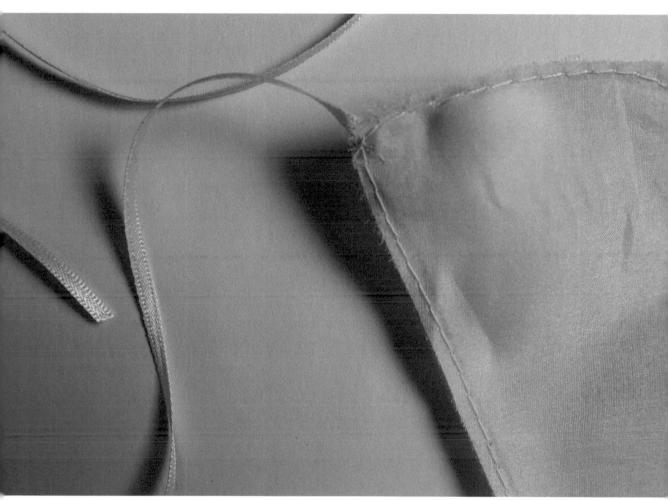

Figure 3.6 Cloth 3, *2015. Ellen Sampson.*

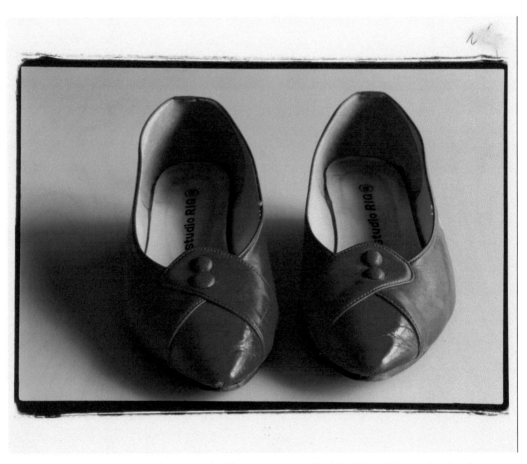

Figure 3.7 Mother's #57, *2004. Ishiuchi Miyako. Chromogenic print. The J. Paul Getty Museum, Los Angeles.*

the world; a footprint is a gesture materialized. The interior of the shoe becomes a reflection of the bodily self and this reflection is, in turn, projected back on to the foot with each wear. Wear alters its material form, so that the shoe is a continuously updated reflection of the wearer's body over time. The shoe is, thus, an ever-changing mirror of the self; it is a map of the spaces we have occupied and the gestures we have made.

If the foot shapes the shoe, then it is equally true that shoes shape the feet. The sole of the shoe suffers wear in place of the wearer's foot; in exchange, the shoe demands a distortion of the wearer's foot – the shoe asks the foot to perform. In placing their foot into the shoe, wearers are compelled to draw in their toes and heighten their arches; the foot dances for the shoe. Frequently this process is intensified, the shoe not simply asking the foot to contort itself, but permanently altering its shape. Shoes worn over a period of time change the shape and structure of the foot, altering the way that it can be used. Toes are pushed under one another, tendons become shortened, bones distort and arches collapse. Beyond these more extreme forms of footwear, our feet, formed of small flexible bones and cartilage, change frequently throughout our lifetimes and our footwear impacts upon them. The bones of the feet may tell a forensic archaeologist much about the activities they performed. The shoe changes the body – its shape, movements and behaviours – and though individually these alterations may be minor, they are cumulative and impactful. Feet and shoes correspond to one another increasingly over time. Through wear the fabric of the shoe is personalized, the shoe becoming a mirror of the foot: an unintentional portrait of the bodily self. As leather stretches and heels wear away, the shoe becomes a reflected image of the wearer, an indexical imprint. It could be said that the frequent aversion to wearing second-hand or borrowed shoes stems from this intermingling, the obvious imprint of another's body on one's shoes.

> In this instance, the notion of being in someone else's shoes becomes doubly powerful. You are placing your foot into a shoe shaped by a foot, which will in turn attempt to exert its shape onto you. In other words, in wearing another person's shoes, one's feet are, minute change by minute change, being turned into theirs.
>
> (Sampson 2003: 56)

Indebtedness

This process of reciprocal imprint – the touch and counter-touch of body and shoe – is central to the experience of wearing clothes. Feet and shoes rarely correspond to each other precisely[7] and must alter each other's form to produce a closer fit. The material outcomes of wear are the dual processes of imprint and wearing away. In wear, the shoe's form is altered through the simultaneous processes of addition and diminishment; matter is added and taken away. The exterior of the shoe is eroded through its contact with the environment: the pressure of our bodies wears down soles; rain dissolves dyes and discolours leathers; laces age and break; dirt builds up. As we move through the world, the surface of the shoe is changed. These marks – the hole on the sole of a shoe, the marks where oil dripped from a can, the grass stains on white running shoes, a heel snapped in a grate – are records of the garment's interactions, the ways that it and the body are together in the world.

The interaction between the foot and the interior of the shoe are equally complex. The body pushes the shoe away but simultaneously, minutely, adds to it in layers of sweat and discarded skin. The shoe becomes both a record of the bodily form and an archive for discarded aspects of the self. It is a container in multiple ways. As we wear our clothes, they break down; in use, the things we wear are slowly destroyed. If the shoe is sacrificed for the sake of the foot, then we, in turn, are indebted to it; it gives us something and asks that we reciprocate. It could be said that, in a manner akin to the obligatory reciprocity of gifting, we become entangled with the things we wear. The touch and counter-touch of the body create a reciprocity and entanglement which is resonant with anthropologist Marcel Mauss' writing on the gift. For Mauss the circular exchange practices such as the Kula, where debt moves not between two participants but in a forward-facing circle,[8] were particularly significant. In Kula exchange the object carries the agency of its owners, even when it is given away: 'What imposes obligation in the present received and exchanged is the fact that the thing received is not inactive. Even when it has been abandoned by the giver, it still possesses something of him' (Mauss 1928: 11–12). Through our relationships to artefacts, personhoods and agencies can be distributed further than the bounded surface of the body. In a similar way reciprocity, a process of touch and of counter-touch, of adding and taking away, underscores our relationships to clothing. While Mauss wrote of relationships between people negotiated through objects, here it is the relationship between a person and object itself which is of interest – the reciprocal relationships between persons and things: attachments produced in the interactions where the body and garment meet. Like the Kula, attachments and entanglements between person and artefact are cyclical and forward-facing, the agencies and attachments of previous users remaining present for each new user.

Skin, surfaces and boundaries

The surface of the shoe is in tactile interaction with the skin; walking is not merely the projection of the body forward but a process of touching and of being touched. The process of giving and taking, which typifies our relationships with clothing, echoes the reciprocal, touch-based, relationship between mother and infant. Attachment is, from the outset, located in touch. Although touch mediates internal desires, its manifestations occur not within the interior but at the peripheries of the body – the skin, the hands, the feet, the eyes. Visual and tactile mirroring is central to the development of mother/infant reciprocity (see Brazelton et al. 1974). The mirroring of touch becomes one of our first experiences and negotiations of the other. Benthien suggests: 'It is through the skin that a new-born learns where she begins and ends, where the boundaries of the self are. Here she learns her first feelings of pleasure and displeasure' (2002: 7). Touch is our initial and primary sensory experience, both in utero, enveloped by the mother's body, and post-natal, with the contact of the parent's skin. Similarly, in examining the psychic function of skin and touch, Anzieu proposed the 'skin ego', the 'psychic envelope' on which our sense of well-being and containment is founded. Anzieu's skin ego acts 'as a containing, unifying envelope for the self; as a protective barrier for the psyche; and as a filter of exchanges and a surface of inscription for first traces' (1989: 98).

Opposite

Figure 3.8 Cloth 20, *2015. Ellen Sampson.*

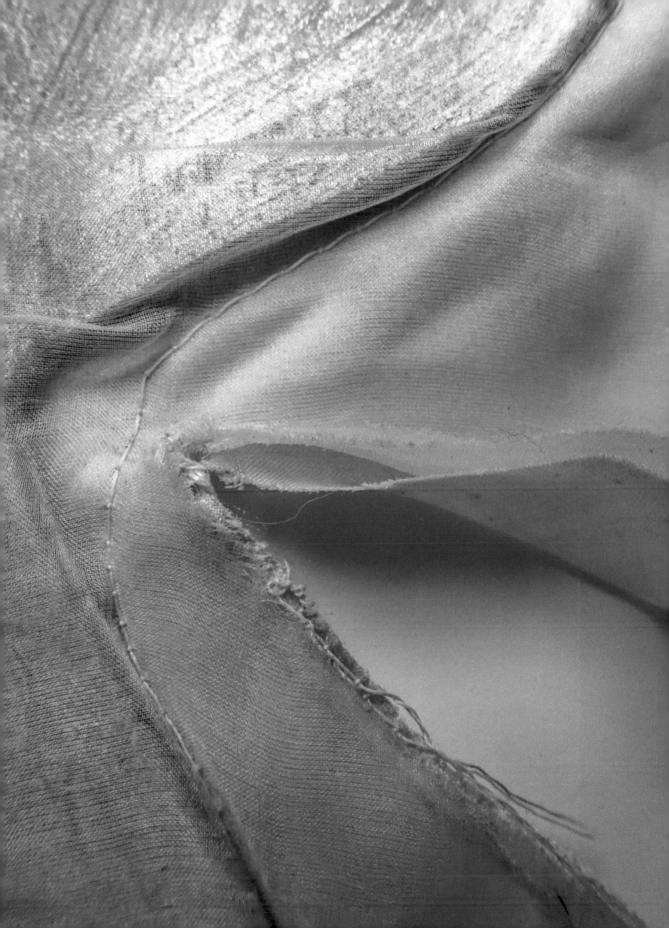

The surfaces of the self are ambiguous, simultaneously public (and accessible to the eye) and private (forbidden to touch). It is complex to define what constitutes the boundaries of the self, what are the edges of our personhood? – our skin, our clothes, our houses, our things? If we understand that we are constituted, in part, by our material culture, then where does a person stop and an object begin? Bachelard writes of surfaces which are interchangeable so that interior and exterior may be exchanged or transposed: 'Outside and inside are both intimate – they are always ready to be reversed, to exchange their hostility. If there exists a borderline surface between such an inside and outside, this surface is painful on both sides […] the centre of "being there" wavers and trembles' (1964: 217). In the embodied process of dressing, we add layers to the body-self. We laminate and build upon the edges of our being; colouring skin, dyeing hair, lacquering nails and lips: are these modifications parts of us or not? Next, we add fine layers and then thicker ones, stockings and bras, t-shirts, jeans and coats. At what point does the body-self stop and the world begin?

The skin is a semi-permeable but bounding surface of the body; the edge of the naked self at least. The skin is also a site where attachment and incorporation are negotiated. Reflecting on skin and containment, Benthien states: 'Notions about the psychic protection and integrity of the self, find enduring symbolic representation through the skin. It would appear that contemporary concepts of the self are necessarily linked to images of envelopment, of coherence, and at times, of something skin like' (2002: 9). Like skin, we use clothing to conceptualize a coherent and intact self: a self that manifests as complete and whole. The 'boundary' of a space is simultaneously the route of its coherence and its separation; its edges both define and separate. Skin is a boundary, but it is a permeable one; it absorbs and excretes, it stains and scars; the skin of the self is constantly changing. Like the skin, the surfaces of the shoe (often made of leather, a skin itself) are permeable and ambiguous; they absorb, they damage, they change. Insides of shoes are ambiguous; moulded by the body and hidden from view, they are a space that is felt rather than seen. It is a space of touch, where different surfaces meet. The skin is a boundary of both bodily and psychic experience. Thus, where the garment touches the skin, it touches the psyche as well. Our interior selves and the material world meet on the skin surface.

Incorporation and the bodily schema

As we dress our bodies the garment becomes an additional boundary to the self, a layer into which we are absorbed. In wearing a garment it is incorporated into the self, into the numerous layers that we use to produce ourselves in the world. In wearing, the boundaries between the self and the garment blur; the garment becomes incorporated into our selves, and we – materially and psychically – are incorporated into it. Phenomenologist Paul Schilder used this entanglement of the self and the world to formulate a conceptualization of the body that was not bounded by the skin. He termed this augmented body-self the 'bodily schema' – a body and its attendant, incorporated artefacts. Schilder's 'bodily schema' incorporates multiple proximate artefacts and technologies into the self: any object that is held or used has the potential to become part of the self. 'The bodily schema does not end with the human skin as a limiting boundary. It extends far beyond it and, from the point of view of motility, perception and emotions, includes all the objects we use and to which

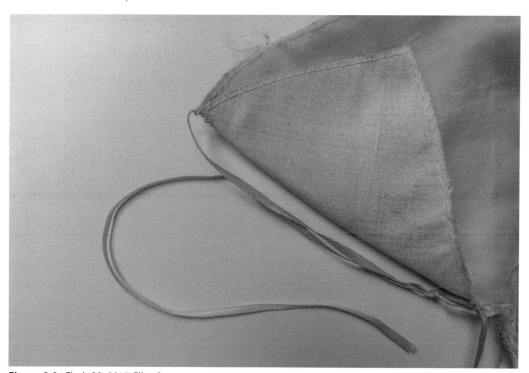

Figure 3.9 Cloth 22, *2015. Ellen Sampson.*

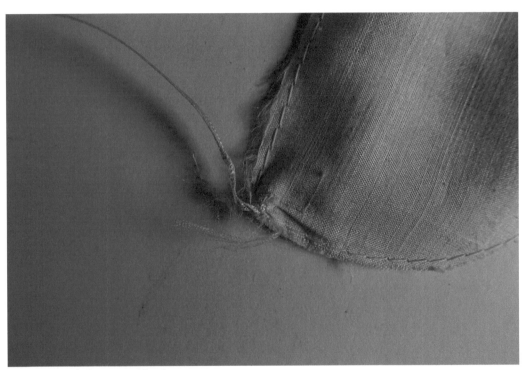

Figure 3.10 Cloth 14, *2015. Ellen Sampson.*

we are geared' (Schilder 1935: 56). Though not all objects are incorporated into our bodily schemas, for Schilder habitual bodily objects like clothing, shoes and prostheses are likely to be incorporated. This incorporation is not simply the accommodation of the artefacts into the psyche, but a reciprocal negotiation of the edges of the self – a negotiation of personhood. The garment is not subsumed but instead remains separate, a distinct but incorporated aspect of the self. Lucia Ruggerone (2016) terms these confluences of people and garments 'assemblages', borrowing not from Merleau-Ponty and Schilder but instead from Deleuze and Guattari (1987): 'The bodies/assemblages are clusters of connections between a variety of material and immaterial elements: molecules, neurons, cells but also ideas, signs, cultural symbols, etc.; all these elements and their constantly moving relations impact on the affective potential of the body' (Ruggerone 2016: 8).

In the context of these assemblages of person and thing, do habitual garments, those worn frequently or for extended periods of time, become incorporated into the bodily schema more readily than others? So that the more we use a garment, the more it becomes part of our selves? Does the reciprocal cycle of imprint, the continuous process of touch that is wearing, allow certain garments to become incorporated more readily? Through touch and counter-touch, the garment and the self become entangled. These processes of identification and incorporation are central to understanding our relationships with the things we wear, both shoes and garments more generally. In this context, the dialogue between the shoe and the foot is a process of giving and taking, the body and the shoe are in an ongoing process of mutual exchange. In the act of touching, we come not only to know the world but to produce and maintain the surfaces of the self.

Attachment

The attachment – and ambiguous sentiments – we experience towards our shoes is contingent upon mediated materiality and co-produced processes of incorporation. The material form of the shoe – its material rather than symbolic agency – is an active co-producer of this attachment. The materiality of a garment is a critical factor in our relationship to it – how it feels – but also how and where it touches the body. Not all garments enfold the body; a garment that is too tight, too loose or cut wrongly for the body upon which it is placed will constantly remind (and discipline) the wearer of this fact. Though traditionally undergarments have served as disciplining garments (bras, girdles, corsets and the like), other stiff materials like denim may have a similar effect. In the essay 'Lumbar Thought', Umberto Eco writes of the bodily experience of being gripped by his jeans:

> As a result, I lived in the knowledge that I had jeans on, whereas normally we live forgetting that we're wearing undershorts or trousers. [...] As a rule I am boisterous, I sprawl in a chair, I slump wherever I please, with no claim to elegance: my blue jeans checked these actions, made me more polite and mature. I discussed it at length, especially with consultants, of the opposite sex, from whom I learned what, for that matter, I had already suspected: that for women experiences of this kind are familiar because all their garments are conceived to impose a demeanour – high heels, girdles, brassieres, pantyhose, tight sweaters.

> (1986: 192)

The insistent nature of garments that Eco writes of is their material agency, their capacity to shape and discipline our bodily selves. Shoes are stiffer and more structured than many of the clothes we wear; they hold their shape away from the body, so that they look much the same whether on or off the foot. This structure makes them resistant objects; rather than enfolding the skin, as a woollen jumper or silk scarf might, they push back. They may damage our body by causing blisters and callouses, or compel us to walk in a different way. This resistance is the shoe's material agency at play, an agency in dialogue with the agency of our bodies. The shoe's capacity to push against our body creates a cycle of imprint and alteration. The shoe and the foot come to correspond more closely to each over time, through a series of small but cumulative alterations. A shoe may become so bodily over time, so imprinted and imbued with the agency of another owner, that there is a distinct discomfort in wearing the shoes of others. There is little market for second-hand shoes and we may view the shoes of the deceased as analogous with their bodily selves, and hesitate to dispose of them.

The incorporated shoe

The duration of wear and proximity of a garment to the body impacts upon its incorporation into the bodily schema. Extended tactile engagement with a garment creates imprints, both on the body and the garment itself. Each imprint is a record of our body-selves or the garment at a particular time and place: it is unique and unrepeatable. In the process of wearing, this image of the self (the imprint) is then reflected back on to the foot as the shoe exerts its force on the foot, in a perpetual cycle of tactile mirroring. Thus the worn shoe becomes a continuously updated mirror of our current and former selves: an external vessel for experience.

The shoe, as part of the bodily schema, holds a curious position: both incorporated into the self and materially separate from it. It is, to borrow Winnicott's (1971) term, an object which is both 'me and not me'. Winnicott formulated his theory of the transitional ('me and not me') object to explain the processes through which a child might separate itself from the mother. The function of a transitional object, a scrap of blanket or soft toy, is to allow the child to differentiate between what is 'me' and 'not me'; it is an intermediary object between internal and external worlds. The transitional object is neither a fully internal object (it exists in the infant's external reality and has material form) or an external object (it is part of the infant's interior world). Of this complex position, Winnicott writes that: 'The transitional object is not an internal object (which is a mental concept) – it is a possession. Yet it is not (for the infant) an external object either' (1971: 10). For Winnicott the transitional object is one that mediates psychic and external reality. It is the transitional object's capacity to remain me (of the self) and not me (external to the self) that gives it this function: a bridging object between internal and external worlds, which keeps inside and outside apart and yet interrelated. The infant uses an object (frequently a comforter or soft toy) to negotiate the separation of the self from the mother. Winnicott suggested that these objects and phenomena are 'neither subjective nor objective but instead partake of both'.

It is this idea of an intermediary space, one which mediates internal experience and external reality which, I suggest, the garment embodies: part of the self, yet materially other from it. They

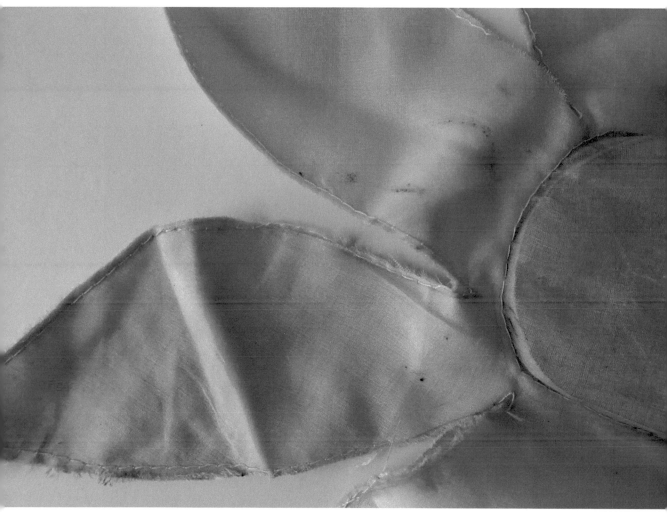

Figure 3.11 Cloth 15, *2015. Ellen Sampson.*

are akin to transitional objects, objects that mediate inside and outside worlds. Garments act as a boundary between bodily and external worlds, between us and not us. They allow us to mediate space, to 'be' in the world. Clothing with its literal and metaphorical capacity to mediate inside and outside is a bridge between the imaginary and the material. Clothes are a surface through which we are able to mediate our relations with the external world. It is the role of the transitional object to keep insides and outsides apart – separate yet interrelated. In this role – that of the intermediary – the garment is akin to a second skin: a two-sided surface, touching the body-self and the world. These incorporated objects function as both literal and metaphorical boundaries. The garment is, as a substitute or second skin, the site on which multiple tactile encounters occur.

In the same paper, Winnicott writes of the transitional object (the blanket, soft toy or other tactile fabric thing) that:

> Its fate is to be gradually allowed to be decathected, so that in the course of years it becomes not so much forgotten as relegated to limbo. By this I mean that in health the transitional object does not 'go inside' nor does the feeling about it necessarily undergo repression. It is not forgotten and it is not mourned. It loses meaning, and this is because the transitional phenomena have become diffused, have become spread out over the whole intermediate territory between 'inner psychic reality' and 'the external world as perceived by two persons in common', that is to say, over the whole cultural field.
>
> (1953: 27)

Decathexis (a process of disinvestment of emotional energy in an object) is the fate of many things we wear and in many ways this is a central function of the fashion object (the sought after, desired and loved garment). The garment must, in order to remain an important part of the wardrobe, withstand being worn much in the way that the transitional object must withstand being 'affectionately cuddled as well as excitedly loved and mutilated', 'never change' and 'survive instinctual loving, and also hating' (1979: 7), only later to lose its power, or agency, in the relationship and slowly fall out of favour. If garments (and, one might say, shoes as objects of desire, in particular) share qualities with Winnicott's transitional objects (intermediate objects between me and not me), is some part of the fashion system predicated on object relations? The idea of fashion as a transitional phenomenon leads us to Bollas's formulation of the transformational object. For Bollas the transformational object is one 'identified with the metamorphosis of the self' (1979: 27); it is identified as producing or facilitating the occurrence of internal change. The object as a process (transitory and shifting) rather than a thing: "The infant's first experience of the object is as a process, rather than a thing in itself […] For this reason I have termed the first object the transformational object, as I want to identify it with the object as process, thus linking our notion of the object with the infant's subjective knowing of it' (ibid.). Though for Bollas this identification is pathological, the transformation needing to occur within the patient rather than through the object, could the idea of the transformational object – an object which mediates fantasy and reality – be a tool in examining the object relations embodied in the things we wear?

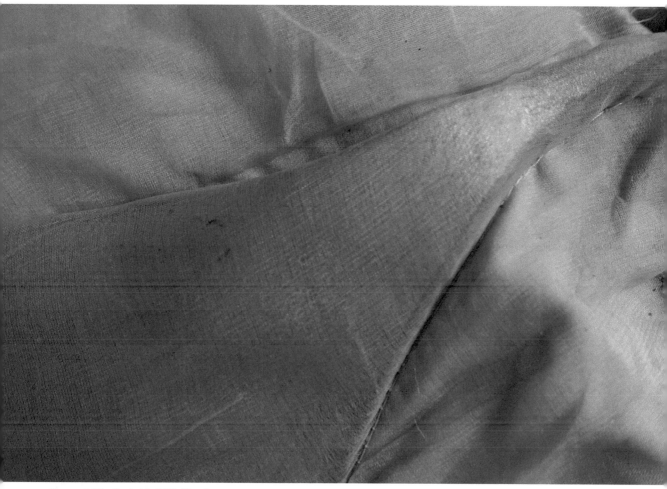

Figure 3.12 Cloth 16, *2015. Ellen Sampson.*

Wearing Diary 4

Today the noise of my shoes, the slap of flip-flops against my soles, is mirrored by the sounds of the street outside. Outside my window thousands of feet hit the floor in rhythmic time as they run the thirteen miles of a half-marathon. The paced rhythm of marathon running is so at odds with the usual patter of the street.

Their feet hit the ground: one foot, two feet in time with one another; the sound of the impact amplified as though their bodies are singing as one.

The sound of my shoes reminds me that I am walking, that they are there with me: companion and aid. They mirror my movements, each step followed by the fleshy slap. Slip slap slip slap I sound across the kitchen floor. A woman accompanied by her echo.

(Wearing Diary, May 2015)

The Dressed Body
in Motion

4

If wearing clothes is a relationship predicated on touch, then it is impossible to separate the experiences of wearing from those of movement, from the shifts of our bodies in time and space. The tactile relationship of wearing clothes should not be considered in isolation but only in the context of the activities that the dressed body undertakes; so that wearing as the subject of research might be better understood as a compound verb: as 'wearing-whilst-doing'. If most of us are clothed for the majority of our waking hours (and often when we are asleep too) then most of our time is spent wearing-whilst-doing x or y. Wearing clothes is rarely the sole reason for dressing but is instead a process which facilitates other actions and behaviours.

This is perhaps the point at which the study of everyday clothing diverges most clearly from the study of 'fashion' as represented in fashion media and on the catwalk. The bodies represented in fashion media and imagery are frequently predominantly engaged with the activity of performing fashionability. There is no 'wearing-whilst' – instead, their aim is the fashionable wearing of clothes: wearing as objective, activity and outcome. This skilled construction and performance of a professionalized fashionable body is quite other from the day-to-day acts of dressing, as Evans (2001), and Armstrong and McDowell (2018) have noted.

When one considers the everyday activities that our clothing facilitates and produces, walking makes an excellent example. The way we move is determined by many factors: clothing, terrain, temperature, culture and the composition of our own bodily selves. However, our footwear (and clothing more generally) also dictates many aspects of our movements: our speed, our cadence and our gait. As Dean (2011) suggests, the way the dressed body occupies and interacts with space is dictated in part by the materiality of our clothes, a cycle which in turn moulds and shapes us as social beings. She writes that:

> … what we wear affects the way we move and how we are perceived. If I wear high heels, for example, I walk in an entirely different way than if I wear boots.
>
> (Dean 2012: 168)

The previous chapter addressed footwear as both an incorporated aspect of the bodily schema and as a boundary: a surface that contains and separates the self. As boundaries, garments maintain the distinctions between multiple kinds of interior and exterior space. Shoes both separate us from the world, covering our feet so that we can no longer feel the ground, and simultaneously allow us to cross it. This chapter explores the dressed body in motion, the dressed self not as static but as gestural and mobile. It looks at footwear, and clothing, as agents in our experience of crossing space and in turn presents walking as a tool for interrogating our relationships to and with clothing: for examining the dressed self as a coalescence of body, garments and world.

Overleaf

Figure 4.1 *Tan pointed shoe – unworn. Polaroid 6, 2015. Ellen Sampson.*

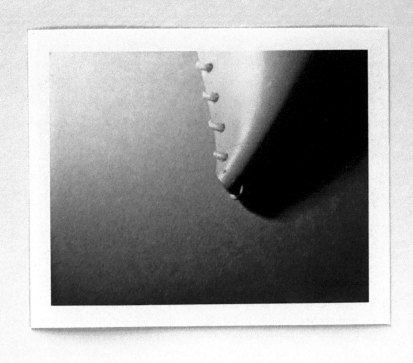

Movements

The dressed body is often understood as 'unnatural',[1] a space of artifice, where gesture and movement, learned over time, may conceal true experience[2] or feelings. However, for Mauss, all movements, not only those understood as fashionable or culturally specific, are learned, mediated and constructed:

> The habitus of the body being upright while walking, breathing, the rhythm of the walk, swinging the fists, the elbows, progression with the trunk in advance of the body or by advancing either side of the body alternately (we have got accustomed to moving all the body forward at once). Feet turned in or out. Extension of the leg.
>
> (1935: 114)

These gestures are the confluence of the body in space and time; a meeting of intentionality and unconscious or involuntary drives – bodily capacity and environmental agencies, creating a single and temporal line. Each gesture is unique; even if a movement may be repeated, it is never exactly the same. Though gesture is temporary and momentary, its affects may be lasting and profound and the traces of our movements often remain. These affects can be emotional, the experience of watching dance, protest (cf. Taussig 2011) or a violent act – the trance induced by certain religious practices, but they may also be material, the physical traces of our bodies moving through the world. Whilst these traces of movement are often understood in terms of the marks we leave in and on the environment – footprints and fingerprints, indents of seats and steamed-up windows – many of our gestures remain within our clothing; as wrinkles in elbows or holes in our socks. In 'A Garment in the Dock; or, How the FBI Illuminated the Prehistory of A Pair of Denim Jeans', Kitty Hauser writes of how the traces of wear on a pair of jeans were used convict a bank robber. In this case the traces of wear, which are unique to the garment's owner, emphasize the particular bond between garment and wearer. Hauser, writing of FBI photo expert Richard W. Vorder Bruegge's testimony, asserts:

> … [the findings] remind us of the indivisibility of clothing and the bodies that make and inhabit them; and not just in abstract terms, but understanding bodies as physical entities with their own habits, movements and suppurations. His work offers, then, an intimate engagement with the materiality of garment, wear and the body often called for in the study of fashion and material culture but rarely achieved.
>
> (2004: 309–10)

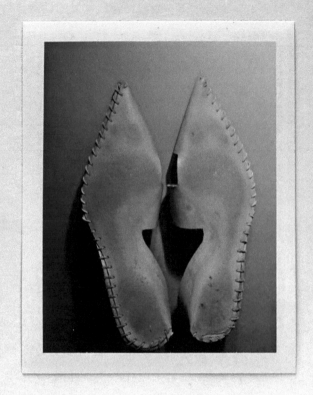

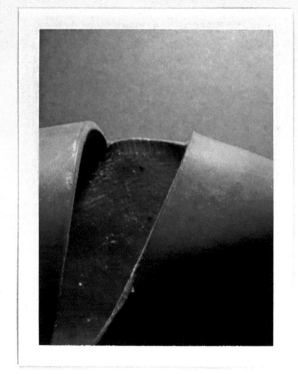

Walking as learned practice

Walking holds a particular place in our culture; not only are our movements learned, but they are socially and culturally specific: the way we walk is indicative of both who we are and who we would like to be. In 'Techniques of the Body', Mauss described his ability to identify people by their walks, not only in situations where walking is fundamentally performative, as in the case of a regiment marching, but in less explicitly performative settings such as walking down the street: 'for example I think I can recognize a girl who has been raised in a convent. In general, she will walk with her fists closed. And I can still remember my third form teacher shouting at me: "Idiot! Why do you walk around the whole time with your hands flapping wide open?" Thus there is an education to walking too' (1935: 458). Walking is an intersection of the social, the biological and the personal; it is learned, enacted and performed. Walking, more than almost any other activity, renders us social beings.[3] Walking is the act of being present in the world. It is a means of presencing the self, the conflation of intention and existence in the public sphere. In walking, the body, the self and the personal accoutrements that make up our material culture are placed on display. One is not simply being, but being in relation to the material world. Acts of self-display are often described in terms of walking, of strutting and striding, of sashays and streaks.[4] To walk is to make oneself into a social being, to take oneself outside. De Certeau famously commences *The Practice of Everyday Life* with a passage describing walking from the heights of the World Trade Center down into the streets of New York. The marks mapped out by our footsteps are, for De Certeau, cartographies of social structures; they are material and temporal manifestations of our social networks:

> Their intertwined paths give their shape to spaces. They weave places together. In that respect, pedestrian movements form one of these 'real systems whose existence in fact makes up the city.' They are not localized; it is rather they that spatialize.

> (1984: 97)

The pathways we take are our routes through the world, our negotiations with the multiple forces and agencies at play. The paths we take produce and confirm our identities in an iterative cycle of repetitions and performances. As Ahmed so beautifully describes of paths and the orientations of the body: 'Lines are both created by being followed and are followed by being created' (Ahmed 2006: xix–xx). These lines might be physical, such as those De Certeau writes of, or social, the ways we navigate familiar and unfamiliar cultural terrains. If we understand our identities as performative and iterative, then the paths we walk, the way we navigate and negotiate the material agencies which surround us, are one of the ways we are produced and presented as cultural beings. In walking we make ourselves social. In crossing space we become social beings in dialogue with multiple agencies beyond our own. These encounters, the meetings of both human and non-human affecting bodies, are individual, bodily and frequently public. They are also cumulative and iterative. In making our way

Opposite
Figure 4.2 *Tan pointed shoe – wear 1. Polaroids 6 and 10, 2015. Ellen Sampson.*

through our social and cultural terrains, we frequently meet the same bodies again and again: we are affected by both the familiar and the new. The spaces and objects we inhabit most frequently affect us in different ways to those we experience anew. The affect of the familiar is quite different from the affect of the new.[5] These meetings of agencies are the spatial, material and social networks that locate us within the world. We are produced by the spaces we inhabit and, in turn, negotiate those same socially and materially imposed identities by crossing and re-crossing space. To draw upon Bourdieu,[6] our networks of things, our habitus, provide the arena in which we both conform and rebel. In dressing the body is both affecting and being affected, complying with and rebelling against social and cultural norms. The clothed body and the environment are in a constant iterative cycle of affecting each other.

The material culture which surrounds us mediates and produces our lived experience, so that 'stuff' both locates us within the field and co-produces our body-selves. If people and things are entangled and inseparable, then clothing, as some of our most bodily and tactile of our possessions, has a direct and immediate impact on the ways we navigate of these networks and paths. We see this mediating capacity clearly in the way the things we wear impact upon and alter where and how we walk. The social and cultural structures we negotiate in walking are materialized in and mediated by our clothes. The practice of walking is fundamental to our relationships with footwear and clothing more generally. Clothes allow us to negotiate spaces and social situations from which we would otherwise be excluded both materially (keeping us dry or warm, protecting our bodies from damage) and symbolically (by being appropriately dressed). They may also allow us to cross borders or transgress boundaries. One need only think of the way that clothing is described in fairy tales (cloaks of invisibility and glass slippers[7]) to be made aware of the potentially transgressive and transformative nature of clothing. Habitual and mundane acts, such as walking and dressing a certain way, may in themselves be acts of resistance – points at which the body moves beyond the strictures of the hegemony. Though these hegemonic forces and affects are frequently discussed in the context of monumental buildings and sites of power, they may also apply to the material minutiae of our lives, our clothes, consumer electronics and everyday possessions. It is thus the case that the larger hegemonic structures which mediate our lived experiences and bodily practices (buildings, borders, transport networks and education systems, for example) are simultaneously working with and against the agencies of material minutiae which surround us, so that the habitual material culture both reinforces and rebels against the systems in which we reside.

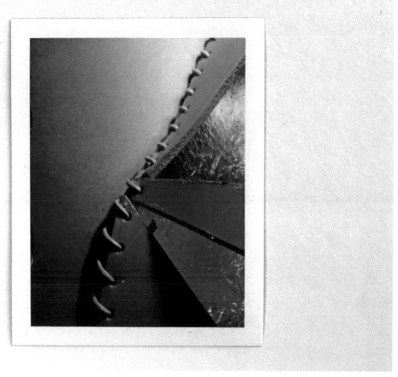

Figure 4.3 *Tan copper pointed shoe – unworn. Polaroid 3, 2015. Ellen Sampson.*

Meetings of bodies

Walking is a confluence of agencies: as we cross space we negotiate the social structures which contain us, veering off track or toeing the line. Though the forces we negotiate may be social or political, it is our material culture which enacts these structures upon us. The things we meet in the world affect us. The shapes of our environments afford us certain movements just as our garments do. In moving our dressed body through the world, we are wearing-whilst-walking-in-'environment-x', in an entangled and complex negotiation of the body amongst the agencies which surround it. Meyer's description of how landscape shapes and reframes human experience, so that the spaces we have built shape not only our movements but also our conceptualizations of space and time, illustrates this particularly well:

> The steps themselves represent a local time; the minutes required to climb up. In Venice, the steps of the stairway rhythmize the walk through the city. […] The city walker experiences the transition from the rhythm of the steps to another rhythm, clear, yet unknown, still to be discovered.
>
> (Meyer 2008: 158)

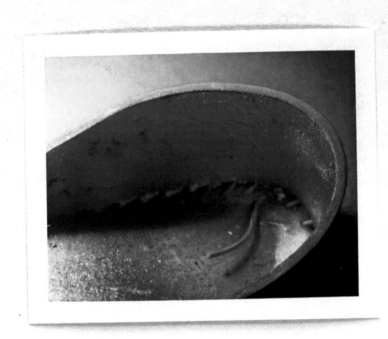

The dressed body in the world

Whilst the affects of our environments many be profound, it is equally true that we are affected by the small and mundane artefacts that surround us. These affects are not simply transpositions of hegemonic power (a way in which feminine items of clothing such as corsets and high heels are frequently described) but instead confluences of agencies so that the material agency of the artefact may affect us just as freely as the power dynamics it embodies. The body and the garment are in a constant reiterative cycle of affecting one another. This cycle of affects is the nature of our relationship with the material world. Our garments, the boundaries of the social self (and perhaps particularly our shoes which allow us to navigate the pathways we are presented with) mediate these external agencies. The mediating capacity of our clothing is central to the embodied experience of dress – we experience much of the world 'through' our clothing. Many of our sensory and particularly tactile engagements with the world are mediated through multiple layers of cloth – I do not, for example, feel the wood and leather surface of the chair I am seated in to type, but instead the sensation of leather and wood through the fabric of my dress. The same might well be said of the experience of the paths we walk on – we feel the texture of sand or the crunch of fallen leaves indirectly. We come to recognize these materials and textures despite their rarely meeting the surface of the skin. In turn, much of our sensory understanding of the world is mediated through dress (looking through the lenses of glasses, grasping something in a gloved hand) so that our perception is constructed through a composite bodily schema rather than through the body alone.

These groupings of bodies and things are the construction of the self in the world, so that 'bodily schema' (Schilder 1938) extends beyond the surfaces of the body into both the things which surround it and the environments (landscapes, bodies, screens) it inhabits. The spaces we move through act upon us just as do the agencies (material and other) in the things we wear, so that we are in a constant position of being affected, whilst at the same time affecting. Walking is an immersion in a cycle of affects: of meeting bodies that affect us. Walking is 'being in the world' – and in this 'being in' we are also becoming – changed and transformed by the meeting of agencies other than our own. The transformative nature of our encounters with the world is recorded both in the body-self – we are changed both physically and psychically in these meetings – and in our material culture. Ruggerone terms these transformations becomings:

> The living corporeality of our practices, the fleshy experience of life we sense but cannot fully describe, like the feeling of walking through the city (De Certeau 1984), or sinking into a warm bath or wearing our favorite dress, all these are examples of perpetual becomings, events in which our bodies transform as a result of encounters with other bodies (human and non-human).
>
> (2016: 8)

Opposite

Figure 4.4 *Tan copper pointed shoe – wear 1. Polaroid 3, 2015. Ellen Sampson.*

The affects we experience are unique to us, both because our body, material culture, environments and dispositions are unique, and because we are affected in the context of all the other affects we have experienced; our becomings are unique because of what we have already become.

The mediating capacity of clothing is particularly apparent in relation to footwear, which impacts on both our ability to walk and our capacity to negotiate complex social terrains – like all garments, shoes are both materially and symbolically useful. The material form of the shoe directly alters the way one moves: one's gestures and gait. In selecting footwear, task specificity often comes into play: we are aware of the necessity of selecting the correct tool for the job. Much is made of shoes which aid and facilitate our physical exertions – running and walking shoes, but also those for dancing, climbing, yoga and golf. This task specificity is, in part, a transference of responsibility akin to those that Bruno Latour (2009) describes in relation to the architecture and machinery, such as seat belts and door closers, which complete tasks we might otherwise avoid. In the performance of good health (so often perceived as entwined with morality, cf. Metzl & Kirkland 2009) our garments are made surrogates for our own obligations and needs. When highlighting the physical and moral responsibilities we assign to our clothing, I return to Gibson's (1979) idea of affordances, the ways that things permit us certain behaviours, movements and postures. Though Gibson wrote in terms of physical affordances, we are also afforded social and cultural behaviours by our clothes. The status that certain garments afford frequently relates to the ways they physically mediate our environments. Whilst this may correlate to physical facilitation (the popularity of fur coats in Moscow, for example) it is also often the case that the status afforded to garments correlates to the hindrances they produce (very high heels which make it difficult to walk, for example): impracticality affords status whilst hindering bodily freedom, in a complex cycle of empowerment through subjugation.

Opposite

Figure 4.5 *Tan copper pointed shoe – wear 2. Polaroid 1, 2015. Ellen Sampson.*

Shoes alter the way we walk and in doing so change our experience of the spaces we occupy. One needs only to walk the same path in different shoes (ill-fitting sandals and comfortable trainers, for example) to know that one's experience of the environment is profoundly changed by one's shoes. They are indicative of the ways in which we depend upon the material world – its agency in our interactions. If shoes aid our movements, then it is also true that they often hinder them. The tool-like nature of footwear – its functionality – presupposes that our shoes function as they should, that they are 'ready-to-hand'. The 'readiness-to-hand' of our clothing is not a certainty: our clothing may become physically or socially impractical, as environments and fashions change and equally because, as we wear them, our garments alter. The search for an ideal garment through shopping and dressing (cf. Clarke & Miller 2002; Woodward 2007), one which is 'the right tool for the job', is a complex negotiation between fantasy and material. Often garments cease to serve their desired function because they have altered through use. As we wear our shoes, they stretch and mould to better accommodate our bodies; eventually they break down and becoming 'unready-to-hand' – and in this unreadiness our awareness of them is heightened. It is often in this unreadiness that we are made conscious of our relationship with our clothes: of the way they mediate our lived experience, the things that they allow us to do. Malfunctioning garments make apparent the entangled nature of our relationships with the things we wear – our dependence on them and the extent to which they mediate our experience of the world. In the discomforting act of non-compliance, our garments make their material agency known.

Opposite
Figure 4.6 *Tan copper pointed shoe – wear 2. Polaroid 2, 2015. Ellen Sampson.*

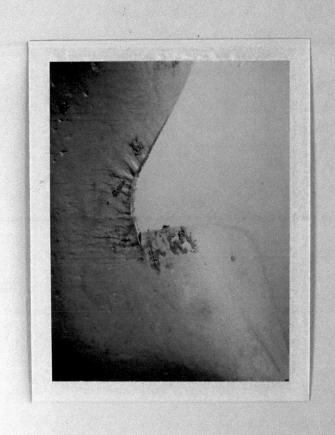

Wearing Diary 5

The dew has crazed tiny lines across the surface of my shoes. They have become a network of creases, the skin of my shoe aged from wear.

I am pleased my shoes have remembered my steps, that they have taken this task from me. They remember what I do not.

When the shoes dry, the tiny lines disappear.

(Wearing Diary, May 2015)

The Cleaved Garment: The maker, the wearer and the 'me and not me' of fashion practice

Clearly things make people, and people, who are made by those things, make other things. The central question, however, is not whether this does or doesn't happen, but in what kind of way it happens. What is the modality of this relationship?

(Pinney 2005: 256)

As makers and wearers of clothes, we implicitly understand that people and the garments they wear are entangled. The intimate nature of this relationship is highlighted in the way it is expressed through language: 'It's just not me,' somebody will say, or 'it fits like a second skin'.[1] We think ourselves into the garments we wear and through this projection they become integral parts of our selves. Our garments are simultaneously signifiers of identity, participants in and witnesses to our embodied experience. Though our skin bounds our physical bodies, it does not bound our psychic and emotional selves – our capacity to integrate with the objects that surround us.[2] This chapter explores the ways in which the self and the garment become entwined – how through making and wearing clothes, the garment and the self become cleaved, to and from one another. It presents the processes of making and of using garments as both a negotiation with the garment's materiality and the projection of the user's fantasy on to their material form – a process through which the maker's or user's agency becomes entangled with the material agency of the garment. Though the focus of my research was footwear, this chapter addresses our relationships with clothing more broadly, in order to explore both the generalities of our relationships with the things we wear and the embodied experience of making for the maker. I have chosen the word 'garment' specifically to include not only fabric clothing but footwear, accessories and other worn objects such as jewellery, watches and spectacles. The word garment is interesting, linked etymologically to the old French words 'garnir' and 'garnement': to decorate or garnish but also to protect (oneself) or armour up. The garment is one of the ways one equips oneself to be in the world.

The relationship between the self and the garment, simultaneously bodily and not of the body, may be encapsulated in the verb 'to cleave'. To cleave, one of Freud's (1910) antithetical words, means both to join together and to split apart. We may refer to things cleaving together and also cleaving apart. Freud considered antithetical words, or anti-autonyms, to be one of the multiple trickeries played out by the unconscious mind, particularly in dreams; in the unconscious, a thing may be represented as both itself and its opposite. In their ambiguity, these words represent, for Freud, a way into our unconscious desires and fears, a crack through which to peer. In 'On the antithetical meanings of primal words', Freud observed that:

The way in which dreams treat the category of contraries and contradictories is highly remarkable. It is simply disregarded. 'No' seems not to exist so far as dreams are concerned. They show a particular preference for combining contraries into a unity or for representing them as one and the same thing.

(1910: 353)

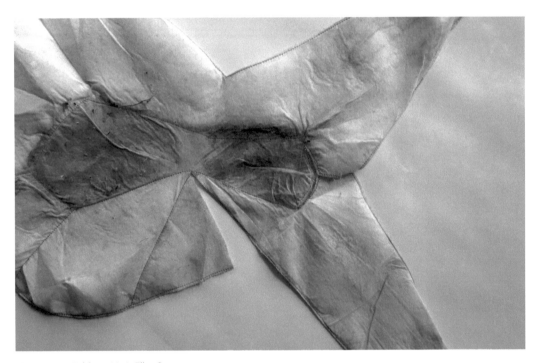

Figure 5.1 Fold 11, *2013. Ellen Sampson.*

This chapter examines the intermingling of selves that constitutes the practices of making and of wearing clothes. Though the relationships between the wearer and the garment and, to a lesser extent, between the garment and the maker, have been addressed,[3] these two sets of relationships are often viewed as bounded or mutually exclusive.[4] The distance between maker and user in contemporary commodity cultures often renders the maker inert in the experience of the wearer; the maker's agency is viewed as bounded within the transaction of making. This chapter suggests a rethinking of this dynamic, examining the ways in which the maker is present for the wearer in the latter's experience of the garment.

The 'me and not me' garment

Our relationships with clothing are often discussed in relation to labour, commerce and exchange – clothing as a commodity within a network of transactions, rather than a vessel of lived experience. Theories of commodity, gifting[5] and exchange underlie much of our thinking about clothes; the points of acquisition and of disposal are the loci of much research into fashion and dress. This research examines the tactile and psychic transactions that take place among artefact, maker and user, looking at the triangular nature of these relationships and exploring the capacity of garments to function as both mediator and transmitter of internal relations and relatedness. In his essay on the gift, Clive Dilnot writes of this relationship, of the gift or artefact as a relational device:

> But this means that to make and to design something is to create something whose end is not in itself but is rather 'in' the subject for whom the object is made (whether that subject is individualized, or is ourselves, collectively, as a whole). On this argument, then, the object is never autonomous, never just 'for itself'. It is, in fact – as Elaine Scarry puts it […] always 'only a fulcrum or lever across which the force of creation moves back onto the human site and remakes its makers (Scarry, 1985, 307).
>
> (Dilnot 1993: 57)

That is to say, the artefact and the maker are in a constant and reiterative dialogue, and in the act of making the maker themself is remade.

To return to the ideas of the previous chapter, Schilder suggests that 'the bodily schema does not end with the human skin as a limiting boundary. It extends far beyond it' (1935: 56). The bodily self extends beyond the skin surface of the body and into the artefacts that surround it, into the things that are habitually and intimately used. Artefacts that mediate our sensory experience, as garments do – keeping us warm and dry, helping us to run further or to see more clearly – are integrated into the bodily self. For Schilder, clothing is integrated into the wearer self, not simply as a form of expression, a mark of allegiance or a signifier of wealth, but as a central aspect of the self. If for Schilder the bodily self may extend beyond the boundary of the skin, for Winnicott (1971) it is the psyche that is not limited by our bodily form. For Winnicott, infants use artefacts in order to negotiate and separate internal and external realities: to separate the self from the other. Similarly, the garment, tactile and encompassing, mediates the relationship between the wearer's internal imagined self and the projected bodily reality presented to the world. The garment is transitional in the sense that it is the site on which a shift from internal desire to external performance is achieved and maintained.

Opposite
Figure 5.2 Fold 6, *2013. Ellen Sampson.*

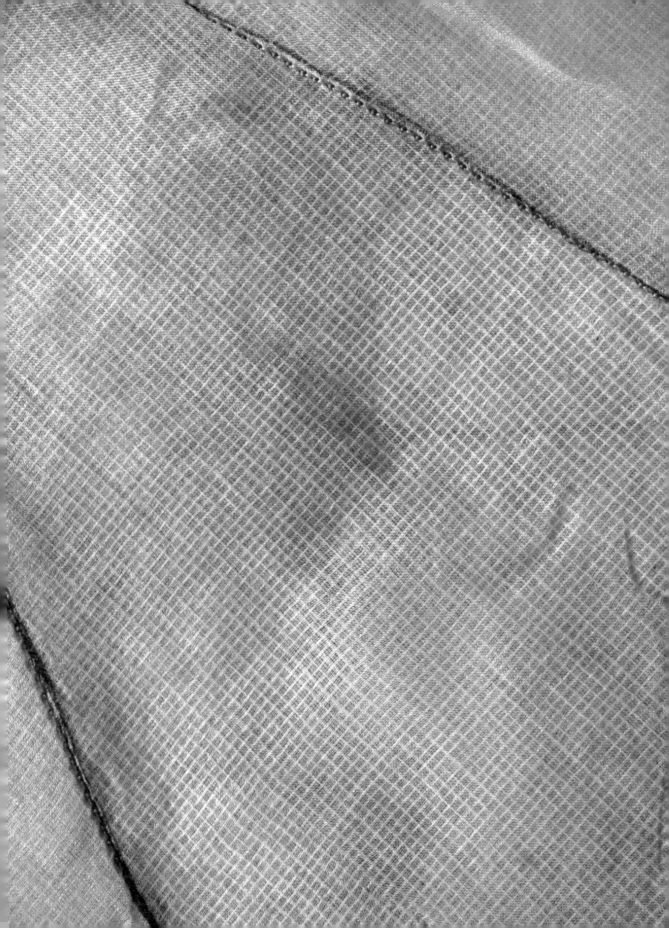

If the garment functions as an extended and externalized aspect of the self, then this relationship presents a paradox; for artefacts that are incorporated into the self may disintegrate, be discarded or lost. How is it that, despite their incorporation, the disintegration or loss of the incorporated garment occurs without compromising the integrity of the wearer's bodily or psychic self? – that the wearer's internal self is not destroyed or damaged with each laddered stocking or fraying hem? How is it that garments might act as internal objects for their user, without risking damage to the unity of that internal self, as the garment breaks down over time? Though we may keenly feel the loss of a beloved garment or comfortable shoe, that loss does not cause us permanent harm. These lost garments may present a sadness or melancholia for the wearer, who may never retrieve the sensory experience of wearing them again. This tension – the incorporation of the garment into the bodily schema versus the garment's material frailty – suggests that incorporation is not total or permanent, and that the garment is capable of straddling bodily and non-bodily divides. It is simultaneously part of the self and materially not of the self; it holds a place of partial incorporation, never wholly of us or not us. The material frailty of the garment presents a continual risk; garments, made of yielding fabric and leathers, do not last as long as we might psychically require. They are temporary repositories, parts of us for a short time only. Though with careful use and care a garment may last many years, it presents a risk, for the more it is worn the faster it will degrade. Just as we must care for the body in order that it might thrive, garments must be subject to grooming and ablutions. We tend to our clothes as an extension of our bodily selves.

In *The Art of Forgetting*, Adrian Forty presents monuments, edifices of stone, bronze and concrete, as sites of communal forgetting, the permanence of the material artefact freeing the viewers from the necessity of holding the event in their mind; monuments permit us to forget. Forty contrasts this idea with Riegl's conception of an 'Aristotelian tradition [in which] if objects are made to stand in for memory, their decay, or destruction (as in iconoclasm) is taken to stand in for forgetting' (Forty & Küchler 1999: 3). For Forty it is the very transience of a material thing – the fading of a Polaroid, the fraying of a hem, the crumbling of a wall – which forces us to remember. For the artist Christian Boltanski, this material impermanence could be utilized to maintain memory:

If you make a monument in stone, everyone will soon forget what you have commemorated. The city will pay for the monument in order to forget it. What I wanted to do was to make a monument that would have to be remade each month, using very fragile materials, like the little prayer houses that observant Jews construct for Sukkoth. Of course, the monument would fall down and have to be continually reconstructed. If at any time it disappeared, it would mean that times had changed, and the reasons for its existence were forgotten. The only possible monuments are those that must be continually re-made, that require a continuous engagement, so that people will remember.

(Boltanski, quoted in Solomon-Godeau 1998: 1)

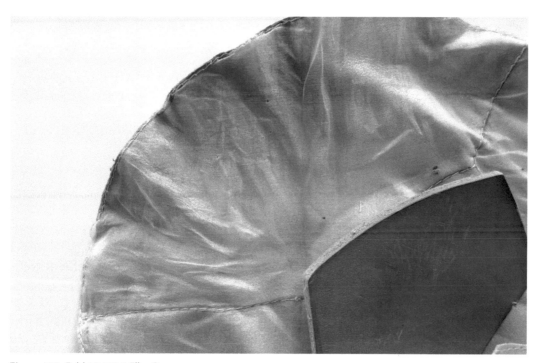

Figure 5.3 Fold 10, *2013. Ellen Sampson.*

In turn, it is the psychic 'work' of keeping a frail or decaying thing whole and complete within the mind that maintains it there; we cannot let the artefact go for fear it may disintegrate and crumble. The wearer or user must attend to, and be vigilant of, the fragile object, for fear it may disappear. Though one does not wear a garment in perpetuity – outfits are changed, styles come and go[6] – a bond between user and garment frequently remains.

The capacity of the self to remain whole in spite of the loss of a garment suggests that the nature of the relationship between the self and the garment is in a constant state of cleaving: intermingling both physically and through their incorporation into and separation from the psychic self. The ambiguity of the antithetical verb 'to cleave' is central to our relationship with garments; they are both incorporated and yet other to us. As an artefact pulls away from the self through decay, it is grasped by the mind and vice versa, a continuous backwards and forwards between selfhood and otherness. Central to this process is incorporation through touch. Our relationship with the things we wear is produced as much through touching as through looking. As Matthew Ratcliffe suggests:

> the ubiquity and indispensability of touch becomes even more apparent once it is acknowledged that what we perceive through one sense includes an appreciation of what could be perceived by means of other senses. A visually perceived cup looks graspable; a surface looks smooth to the touch. Tactual possibilities permeate all experience.
>
> (2018: 19)

If the garment's capacity to integrate and separate from the self allows it to become both 'me' and 'not me' of the wearer, then might the process of cleaving also extend to the relationship between the garment and its maker, through the touch and counter-touch of cutting, sewing and pressing?

An artefact that can simultaneously be part of the self and separate from it presents the potential for the self to be distributed beyond the confines of the body. If the garment becomes an aspect of the self, then may we also become an aspect of the garment? Do we inhabit the clothes we wear even when they are not on the body – even when we are gone from them? The idea of a self distributed into clothing recalls Peter Stallybrass's 'Worn Worlds' in which the author relates how his dead friend Allon is suddenly present for him when he wears his jacket. Allon is intermingled with his clothes and remains in them even after his death:

> I was inhabited by his presence taken over. If I wore the Jacket then Allon wore me. He was there in the wrinkles of the elbows, the wrinkles which in the technical jargon of sewing are called 'memory': He was there in the stains at the very bottom of the Jacket, he was there in the smell of the armpits.
>
> (1993: 2)

Stepping back from the hypothesis that garments and the body are cleaved, continuously integrating and separating from one another, in what ways do garments act upon their wearers? Clothes, like all artefacts, are an amalgamation of multiple processes, experiences, materials and agencies. They carry both symbolic (representational) and indexical (bearing trace of) meaning. A garment is a point, in space, in time, in culture, where a range of meanings converge and from which they will, in time, diverge again. Garments are an accumulation of agencies. In *Inalienable Possessions* (1992), Annette Weiner explores the ways in which, through the exchanges of artefacts, agencies and personhoods are distributed. She argues that the artefact and the self are not separated when the artefact is given away or gifted; that an artefact may retain the agency of its owner ('mana' or 'spirit' in Weiner's discussion) even when passed on to another. Weiner writes of artefacts that may not be exchanged or gifted but which remain within families or groups and eventually become inseparable from them, of how through years of ownership, the garment develops a cumulative identity. It is not simply representative of its current owner but of those who have owned and worn it before. Of the wearer of a Maori ceremonial cloak, she comments that, in wearing the precious garment, 'she is more than herself – […] she is her ancestors' (Weiner 1992: 6). The artefact thus becomes a synecdoche of the people who have owned it; it stands in for them and is invested with their agency: 'These possessions then are the most potent force in the effort to subvert change, while at the same time they stand as the corpus of change' (ibid.: 11).

Such artefacts accrue agencies just as they accrue the patina of use or wear. Similarly, Marilyn Strathern writes of the initial owner retaining an aspect of the gift after it has been distributed: 'when we give something maybe we don't keep it, but we don't lose it either' (1988: 198). Expanding upon Mauss's supposition that the gift is central to forming cohesive social relations in Melanesia, Strathern argues: 'objects are created not in contradistinction to persons but out of persons' (ibid.: 171). Objects and selves are merged in their creation and in the exchange of artefacts aspects of the self are distributed into the other:

> As an exchange, an unmediated relation works through the directness of the effect which partners have on one another and, in the case of the metaphoric gift, creates a mutual dependency between them each for their own definition. They 'exchange' identities as it were […] Here, however, it is the replication not of individuals as singular, same-sex persons, which is at issue, but the replication of substance. Thus we might imagine its effect as bodily growth or as the transmission of bodily tissue from one person to another.
>
> (Ibid.: 207)

The gift is not merely a representation of the person but a non-divisible part of them. The act of distribution separates neither the artefact from the person nor the person from the artefact; instead they are 'extracted from one and absorbed by another' (ibid.: 178).

These accrued agencies or incorporations do not have to sit comfortably with one another. An artefact may be the site of several conflicting discourses or experiences. In any contested artefact or space, one will see multiple agencies at play. Even a non-contested artefact may be the site of multiple agencies. As Janet Hoskins suggests, 'Even those objects which seem to be without a directly identifiable function – that is, objects which have previously been theorized as simple objects of aesthetic contemplation – are in fact made in order to act upon the world and to act upon other persons' (2006: 76). Material objects thus embody complex intentionalities and mediate social agency. When you sit on a chair, the maker or designer, the person who placed it by the desk and the other bodies who caused its seat to sag through use are all present and acting upon you through its material form. No artefact contains just one agency; they are always an accumulation and, in the layering of these agencies, new ones may be produced.

In his call for an anthropology of art, Alfred Gell examines the agent–patient relationships embodied within the art object. Gell understands viewing an artwork as a 'transmission of power'

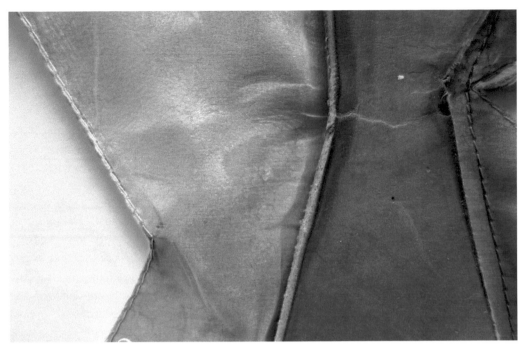

Figure 5.4 Fold 8, *2013. Ellen Sampson.*

in which recipients abduct information and experience from the artwork. According to Gell, art comprises 'social relations in the vicinity of objects mediating social agency' (1998: 7); that is to say, anything may be an art object if it is mediating agency. For Gell, these social relations are not only human-to-human but may also be between the person and the 'thing':

> The immediate 'other' in a social relationship does not have to be another 'human being', my whole argument depends on this not being the case. Social agency can be exercised relative to 'things' and social agency can be exercised by 'things' (and also animals). The concept of social agency has to be formulated in this very permissive manner for empirical as well as theoretical reasons. It just happens to be patently the case that persons form what are evidently social relations with 'things'.
>
> (ibid.: 17)

Gell maps the multiple agencies which come together in the production of the work of art and looks at how these may act upon the viewer as 'patient'.[7] Through the drawing up of an 'art nexus',[8] Gell presents numerous agents whose intentionality or agencies are at work within the art object (the index). The artist, the patron, the material, the viewers and the objects which inspired it, may all be agents in the production of the art object – their agency is bounded within its material form. These agents may be human, as in the case of a patron or gallerist, or non-human, as in the landscape that inspired Constable or the urinal co-opted by Duchamp. The art object is both the outcome and the 'index' of these agencies; it bears indexical trace of their agency. Thus, the viewing of a work of art becomes a transmission of power or agency. The interaction with any artefact is in fact similarly transactional; agency is exchanged, through looking, touch and use. The abduction[9] of this agency – in Gell's case, the art object's 'affect' – is not predetermined and will vary depending on the recipient and the physical, geographical and social relationship they have to the artefact. The intentionality of different agents may be at odds with one another, whilst simultaneously being bounded within the artefact's material form.

Artefacts are active agents within both human-to-human and human-to-artefact interactions. Tim Ingold (2013) writes of the convergences within or between artefacts and forces; the points at which materials and people meet. He terms the objects that facilitate such convergences 'transducers' – artefacts that act as links between materials, forces and intentions. It is interesting here to think about intention, for both the making and wearing of clothes are often typified as unconscious or unthinking acts. The conceptualization of wearing and making as not only tacit but also separate from thinking tends to negate the role of fantasy and imagination in the production of both the garment and the outfit. Craft has often been presented as a process outside of the imaginative, the maker as custodian of tradition and continuity rather than experimentation. However, the imaginative leap is vital to the process through which we 'think' garments in both making and dressing. If we apply the idea of the transducer to fashion, does the garment act as a facilitator or link between fashion 'thinking' or intention and fashion action or performance? The idea of the garment as a facilitator or point of transition is useful, the garment allowing internal experience to emerge in material form. These confluences between intention, agency and materiality are not fixed or permanent but are always in a state of flux or cleavage. Once fashion thinking has been transformed into fashion performance via the making or wearing of a garment, it will continue to alter, through both entropy and use. Artefacts are amalgamations of agencies brought together in material form, inseparable from their environments and users. Artefacts, environment and users are in a constant state of flux.

The maker and the garment

Taking the idea of a distributed personhood in a chain of affordances, and of the artefact as both mediator and facilitator of intentionality, we are presented with personhoods that may spread out from the body via artefacts and artefacts that can facilitate or hinder a user's intentions. How is this intention or 'thinking' incorporated into the garment and how is it distributed through use and wear? This question might be explored by looking at the points when a garment and a person cleave, where they either join or pull apart. The first instance of cleaving is between the garment and the maker. As referred to above, for Schilder (1935) and Merleau-Ponty (1962), an artefact that was in habitual tactile contact with its user was incorporated into their bodily self. Thus, makers as well as users mingle with the artefacts they produce. Handmakers, such as craftspersons, seamstresses or shoemakers, who have repetitive tactile engagement with the object's materiality through its production, incorporate some aspect of that artefact into themselves. Simultaneously, the maker is incorporated into the garment, the two becoming entangled or enmeshed.

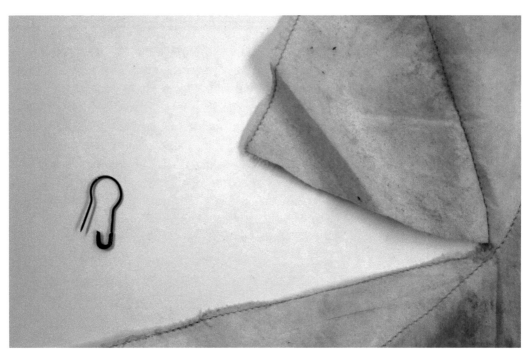

Figure 5.5 Fold 5, *2013. Ellen Sampson.*

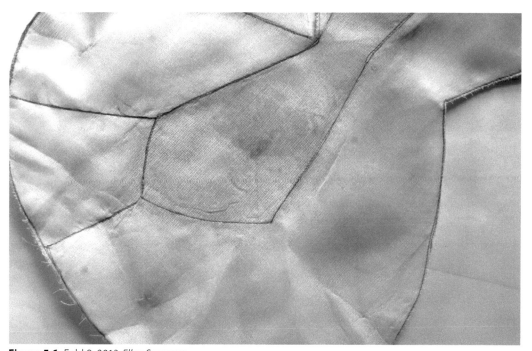

Figure 5.6 Fold 9, *2013. Ellen Sampson.*

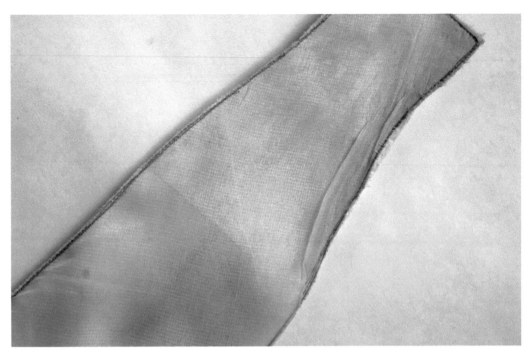

Figure 5.7 Fold 7, *2013. Ellen Sampson.*

Though the means through which a garment is produced may be complex, multi-faceted and frequently include many agents and processes, in this instance I wish to focus on the relationship between a handmaker and a garment. Without straying too far into the politics of garment production, it is worth acknowledging that even in the simplest acts of making there are multiple agents at play. Each material and its producers, as well as designers, inspirations and clients, are present for the maker in the making of an artefact. One could easily apply Gell's 'art nexus' (1998), in which he outlines the multiple agencies at play within the art object, to the agent–patient relations embodied in a garment.

Before the garment exists as a material form, it exists as an idea, image, intention or impulse. It is a fantasy or desire held in the mind of the maker. It is through the projection of this intention on to the material form, and through negotiation with agency of materials themselves, that the realization of the garment takes place. It is important to acknowledge the role of fantasy and the imaginary in the creative process, the ways that in order for intention to cross into action, a fantasy must be developed, tested and approved. Fantasy is the trying-out ground for experience, a space where an idea may be examined and amended before it becomes fixed. The object as fantasy is malleable, and at times ambiguous; it is made solid only through its examination and testing out within the mind. Just as one might grasp a new artefact and turn it in one's hand in order to comprehend its weight and form, so the maker must turn the imaginary artefact over in their mind until it becomes clear to them. However, unlike a material artefact, the imaginary artefact is never truly graspable and thus never truly complete. It is ephemeral and transitory; its essence eludes capture.

Frequently, it is the maker's or user's capacity to accurately translate this fantasy object into material form which is interpreted as the essence of makerly skill. This capacity to successfully transition inside to outside, internal desire to external product is viewed as the goal of the creative process. Though the notion of the craftsperson's skill as solely located in the accuracy of this transmission may be out-dated, the ability to manipulate and tame the agency of the materials one uses is central to the maker's work. The material of the garment may facilitate this realization or it may not, fighting back and resisting transformation. Thus, the process of materialization is always one of negotiation: a to-ing and fro-ing between the fantasy of the object and the means through which it can be produced. The garment becomes an actualization not just of the maker's desires[10] but also of the processes of materialization, and of the accidents and affordances that occur during its making.

The process of materialization is conflicted. Just as our outfits rarely look quite how we imagined them, the garment is not a direct transposition of the maker's ideal but a culmination of a series of divergent and at times conflicting agencies. The fabric may pucker, stitching come undone, pattern pieces not fit together.[11] Though the maker's skill and experience may mediate and lessen the material's agency and resistance to change, the process is rarely simple or without problems. All this time the maker is, through repeated tactile engagement, incorporating the garment into their self; the garment becomes an extension of the self. Other incorporated or cleaved objects may mediate these incorporations, such as the familiar tools a maker uses, the chair they sit on, the garments they themselves wear. Returning to Gibson's (1979) affordances, it is not merely the skill of the maker that affords the transition of the object from fantasy to material form. The objects that surround the maker – their tools, their landscape and the materials available to them – are all active agents in the actualization. The maker must negotiate with these agencies as well as with the agency of the materials used to make the object.

The negotiated material garment is not an ideal but an ambiguous object, embodying both the maker's fantasy and the maker's failure. The ideal or fantasy object may never be fully achieved. This is both because the ideal object is rarely unified and static (it is malleable and transitory in the mind) and because the process of materialization must be negotiated with the agencies of the materials with which the maker interacts. The garment cannot be fully and permanently incorporated into the self because it represents a chink in the armour of the ego. It is 'of the maker' but never fully part of them. Through extended tactile engagement, the maker and the garment become entangled, the maker internalizing the garment's failures or flaws, the garment existing as a material projection/extension of an internalized ideal. Despite the intimacy of the making relationship and the intermingling that occurs, garments rarely remain with their maker but are distributed onwards to wearers. The distributed garment retains elements of this ambiguity; it retains the 'me and not me' of the maker. To return to Dilnot, 'The basis of this re-description is a transformation of how things are thought: not as "dead" possessions or signs or markers but as "live gifts" working, at base, "for" us, and working in their "circulation" between and among us to establish a circle of making and self-making' (Dilnot 1993: 59).

The wearer and the garment

Just as a process of projection, negotiation and incorporation typifies the relationship between the maker and the garment, the relationship between garment and wearer is one in which material agency and the body are in constant dialogue. The process of dressing, like the experience of making, starts with a fantasy of confluence, the outfit and the body uniting to form an ideal. Unlike the maker's ideal, the garments that will constitute the wearer's fantasy already exist. Fashion is dependent upon the wearer's agency as a maker of meaning: mass-produced garments are made original and idiomatic through appropriation and use. Both the ideal and its material manifestation require the utilization of pre-constructed objects and imagery. The ideal or imaginary dressed body is constructed in reference to both external artefacts and imagery and the wearer's conceptualization of their own bodily self. Many different agencies collaborate to produce the fantasy of the dressed self: fashion, culture and politics. We are perpetually surrounded by imagery of the dressed body and cannot help but incorporate elements of this imagery into our ideal and imagined selves. Conversely, the manifestation of the ideal, in material form, requires negotiation not with imagery and symbolism but with the materials or garments available to the wearer. In order to create a 'look', the wearer must work with what is available to them. Location, trends, financial means, social rules and prohibitions and, in particular, the wearer's own pre-existing wardrobe impact on the wearer's ability to successfully manifest their ideal. Simultaneously, once a garment or garments have been selected, the wearer must negotiate with the agencies already embodied within the garment and those of the other garments worn with it. The maker and attendant agencies are present for the wearer in the act of dressing. The wearer must negotiate the actualization of their fantasy with pre-constructed material forms rather than with raw material, and their ability to realize their ideal is limited by this.

Fashion thinking is turned into fashion performance via the collation and modification of garments: their styling. This confluence retains the fractious and conversational nature of all our relationships with material things; the agency of the wearer is in a constant negotiation with the agency of the garment itself. Sophie Woodward's research highlights the material agency of the garment: its capacity through form, rather than signification, to impact on bodily and embodied experience. The realization of a fashion fantasy cannot help but be, to some extent, a failure, for fantasy cannot comfortably accommodate agency outside the ego. The garment is never truly separated from the previous bodies with which it has been entangled. It is not simply a confluence of agencies, but also a confluence of selves, and those selves compete with the material agency of the garment. The maker is present for the wearer in the garment. This presence, however, is not always consciously or unconsciously acknowledged: few of us think on a regular basis of the hands and bodies which made our clothes.

Just as the body modifies the worn garment, stretching, straining and creasing its surface, the garment imprints itself on the body, rubbing, marking and, in the case of structured and resistant garments, permanently altering the form of the body. Through this tactile engagement, the garment

Opposite

Figure 5.8 Fold 12, *2013. Ellen Sampson.*

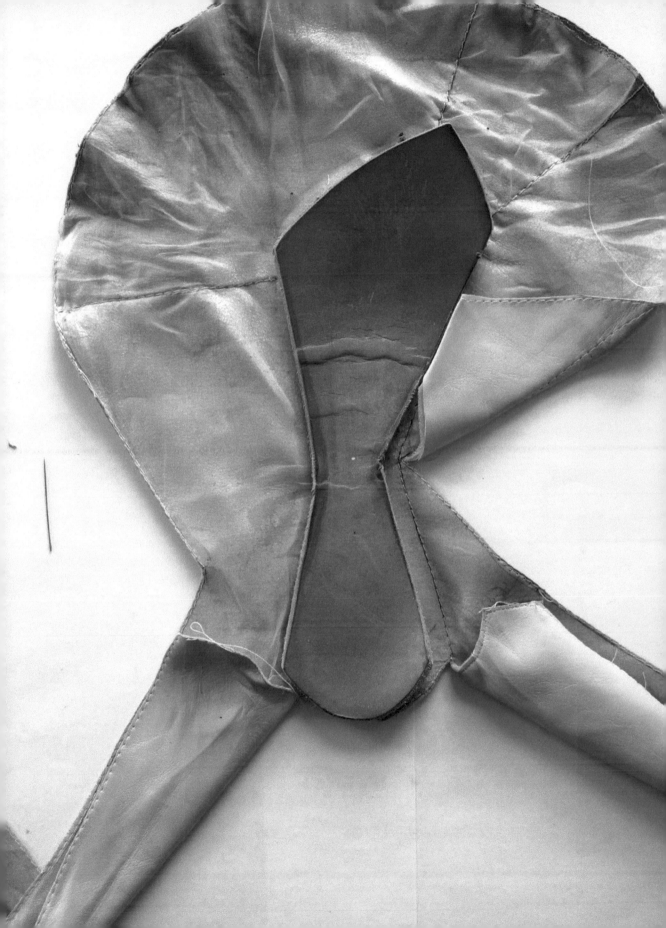

becomes part of the bodily self and can function as an additional psychic receptacle, carrying a history of our embodied relationships within it. Though wearing creates an attachment with the garment, it also hastens its disintegration. To return to the question posed earlier in the chapter, if this disintegration presents a risk, how may it be accommodated? Not only is the manifested artefact already a lost object, a poor rendition of the original ideal, but with each use and wear it moves farther from that ideal state. As the garment is worn, it becomes both more integrated and less ideal. Thus the paradox is present for us again: the more we use, the greater the incorporation and the greater the decay. In the negotiation between the body and the garment, it is the agency of the body that often wins. As attachment deepens, through reciprocal touch, garments start to fray, sag and tear. As the fashion is performed, the garment is sacrificed.

It is here that the transitional nature of garments becomes apparent: their capacity to be both of the self and other to it. It may also be useful to address the garment as a transformational object, as discussed by Bollas (1979). For Bollas the infant's first experiences of the mother are as processes rather than as an object. If not transitional, could the garment then be viewed as a 'transformational' object – one on to which transformational desire is projected and contained? Transformational objects are 'identified with the metamorphosis of the self' (ibid.: 27); much like Ingold's (2013) transducers, they are perceived as allowing change to occur. They are understood as facilitators of potential transformations, objects through which a new self may emerge. For Bollas this identification is pathological, the transformation needing to occur within the patient's psyche rather than via a material object or external experience. The garment is transformational in two senses: firstly, it allows for the transformation of the wearer/maker's fantasy into an enacted material reality, a shift from internal to external, which gives the maker/user the omnipotence the ego craves; and secondly, like all material artefacts, it is in a constant state of flux. The garment is not stable in its material form and it is this absence of fixity that prevents permanent and total incorporation. The garment pulls away from the wearer in this transformation, never fully allowing its agency to be subsumed by that of the wearer. For the maker this tactile entanglement results in the production of the garment, the drive forward resulting in a shift of form. Conversely, for the wearer the pressure of the body upon the garment leads to its destruction, its wearing away. The shift in form leads eventually to the degradation of the garment. The two processes of incorporation mirror one another, one a process of conscious construction and the other of unconscious destruction.

Cleaving and the failed garment

For both the maker and the wearer the garment is always, to some extent, a failure. It cannot appease the desire for an ideal object, and is condemned to fall short. Despite this inability to live up to the maker's and wearer's ideal, the garment is still incorporated through making and use into the maker's or user's self. However, on failing to live up to their fantasy or ideal, and simultaneously presenting the risk that it will disintegrate and be lost to them, the garment may be rejected. Despite this initial rejection, through continued use and tactile engagement re-incorporation of the garment occurs – only for it to risk rejection once more as it again fails to live up to the ideal. Thus, the relationship with the incorporated garment (the garment located within the wearer's bodily schema) is not continuous,

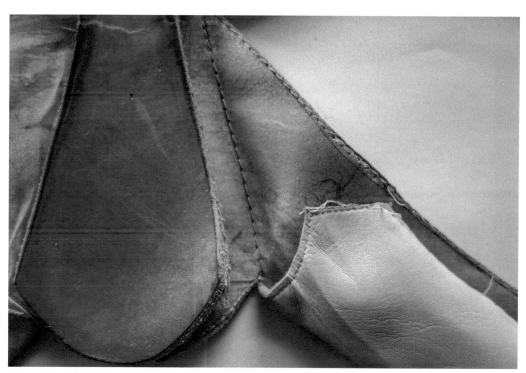

Figure 5.9 Fold 12 *(detail), 2013. Ellen Sampson.*

but one of repeated rejection and incorporation, a constant to-ing and fro-ing between fantasy, desire and loss. This cycle of re-incorporation and rejection is reminiscent of Freud's 'compulsion to repeat': the attempt, through an act of unconscious compulsive repetition, to master an earlier troubling experience. Freud wrote of this process of returning to the site of trauma or loss over and over again in the hope of overcoming the source of anxiety as 'like an un-laid ghost, it cannot rest until the mystery has been solved and the spell broken' (1909: 123). The repetitive incorporation and rejection of the garment into the psyche, the continuous cleaving, echoes the process that Freud describes.

There is always a dissonance between 'thinking', as the creation of an ideal object within the psyche, and 'being', as the materialization of that fantasy object through negotiation with the material world. The performance of fashion thinking can never be entirely successful because it requires the convergence of multiple external agencies. This inherent failure is at the heart of fashion: the compulsion to try and try again. In part, this imperfect realization of the fantasy occurs because the garment retains traces of the maker and previous users.[12] The garment is imbued with the agencies of others that threaten to over-ride the agency of the new user. Despite physical separation, others are still entangled with and acting through the garment. Just as Gell writes of the index as 'a detached part of the prototype' (1998: 103) or Weiner (1992) describes spirits transmitted via the Kula, the garment is a detached part of the maker and wearer. The word 'cleave', called upon earlier to encompass the me and not me qualities of the garment, its capacity to be both the self and other to it, can be called upon again to describe the garment as an object in flux, split between and incorporated into two or more bodies and selves.

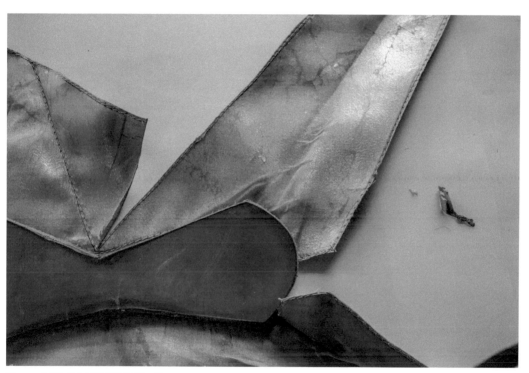

Figure 5.10 Fold 13, *2013. Ellen Sampson.*

Wearing Diary 6

There is, I think, a horror in scuffing one's shoe, inevitability, a loss. The shoe starts off perfect, a crisp clean surface, free from multiple layers of marks; the marks it does bear are intentional, they are meant to be. As soon as you put on a shoe for the first time you know that you will scuff it. Often to initially preserve the shoes, to acclimatize myself to their damage, I would wear them indoors for a few days, walking mindfully and gently around the house. However, at some point I would need to wear them outside. The tips of the toes, the point at which the body moves forwards, are the first place to mark. With each stride, as the foot leads the body forward, there is a new risk. The scratched hide is no longer smooth, its protective sheen abraded. Abrasions reveal the suede-like softness of the leather's interior, raw and vulnerable, insides laid bare.

(Wearing Diary, April 2015)

The Empty Shoe: Imprint, memory and the marks of experience

6

The previous chapters have addressed touch and counter-touch of the clothed body, the attachment that ensues from use: how, in holding an object, one comes to know it differently than through looking at it, and how, in the acts of making and of wearing one knows it differently again. They examine the intimacies of wearing and of making and the entanglements and incorporations that occur where the self and material meet: how wear increases attachment but also speeds up imprint and decay; how, through wearing, the incorporated garment is slowly lost to the wearer. Next, then, are the manifestations of wear: the scuffs, wrinkles and creases, which make apparent the embodied and material experience of wearing. These marks, the traces of our embodied relationship with our clothes, are prevalent and multiple: few garments survive use without being changed. Though we may launder our clothes and clean our shoes, our garments are progressively and cumulatively altered as body, environment and garment meet. Over time, garments become records of lived experience, covered with the marks of use. These marks are the records of the ways the garment mediates our passage through the world.

If these traces of use are manifestations of the passage of time, how then might they be viewed and read? As we wear ours shoe, our bodies imprint on their form: the shape of our feet and the weight of the body come together to alter the shoe, a repetitive and cumulative process, the shoe changing with each step and each wear. This layering of imprints is not linear or singular, one set of imprints masking the next; instead, the process of inscription is complex, imprints jostling together non-contemporaneously. These marks pile one on top of the other, becoming less intelligible and distinct with each movement and each step. Wear is materialized in objects in many ways, in stretching, tearing, abrading and creasing – marks made in a repetitive cycle, one mark begetting the next. These marks are not singular, or orderly; instead they overlap, each one impacting and producing another. As the shoe is worn, its surface becomes a map of the actions performed within it. The shoe becomes a record of the passage through time and space: of being in the world.

Time is present in all material things; they are both of 'a' time (when they were made, altered or used) and material manifestations of the passage of time itself. A Victorian button boot, for example, is not only a manifestation of when it was produced but also of the progression of time since that point. The passage of time is apparent and visible in the material world. This confluence of 'there–then' and 'here–now' is what Barthes (in reference to the photograph) refers to as 'spatial immediacy and temporal anteriority' (1977: 44): material culture always existing between two times. The marks of use and wear presence this dissonance, material records of the shift between there–then and here–now. Often we understand the passage of time by our distance from an event, object or location; time as a process of measuring. The incremental changes that mark its passage are too numerous and varied for our minds to comprehend or retain. Material things, however, do retain these incremental changes. The use of the material to record and mark the passage of time, to bear witness to what we cannot retain, is an important aspect of our relationships with the material world. We watch the tides, the sun and the seasons; we count rings on trees, measure shadows, watch clocks.

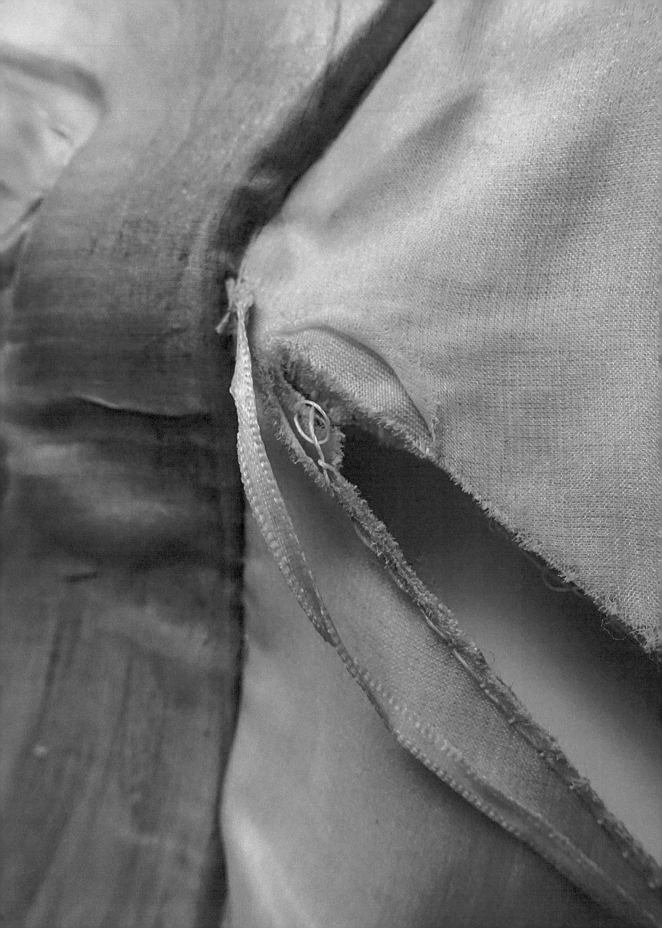

Gestures

Garments show the traces of use and wear in many ways; these marks are intersections between the imprints of the body, the resistance of the environment and the inevitable atrophy of all material things. Often the first signs of wear are creased or crumpled surfaces, wrinkling and folding to accommodate gesture. Gesture is the intersection of the personal (the bodily, involuntary and innate) with the cultural (both the learned and the unconsciously acquired): 'The ways in which from society to society men know how to use their bodies' (Mauss 1935: 70). Though a gesture – the cadence of our run, the length of stride – may be culturally proscribed, our performance of those gestures (its embodiment), dependent upon our environment, dress and physical form, is unique. Steven Matthews writes of the way that gestures and the material culture with and through which they are enacted are entwined – gestures as amalgams of body/space/thing:

> Like artefacts, situated within webs of meaning and signification, gestures too have widespread symbolic and material connotations within both specific and generalised contexts of social action. It is not enough to simply say 'here was a particular gesture' and this was what it did and this is what it meant. Gestures are both ambiguous and multifaceted and any particular gestural technique will almost invariably have a counterpart within another social, material or spatial context.
>
> (2005: 15)

If gestures and the object that they are performed with are entangled, then garments, the most bodily of our artefacts, are both agents in and the recipients of our gestures; producing and recording them as we move through the world.

Creases and folds

As my shoes creased, their surfaces became more appealing to me; they became bodily – more intermingled, more mine. Each crease felt poignant, an unintentional record; the surface of the shoe sacrificed unthinkingly in the process of my daily life. Creases are 'poignant' in a way that folds are not. There is, I think, a particular resonance to worn things, a particular sense of awe of their survival, of artefacts and of experiences. We do not feel that same awe for immaculate surfaces, the smooth surface has retained nothing; it has not experienced, learned or survived.

(Wearing Diary, November 2015)

Opposite
Figure 6.1 Cloth 26, *2015. Ellen Sampson.*
Overleaf
Figure 6.2 Cloth 8, *2015. Ellen Sampson.*

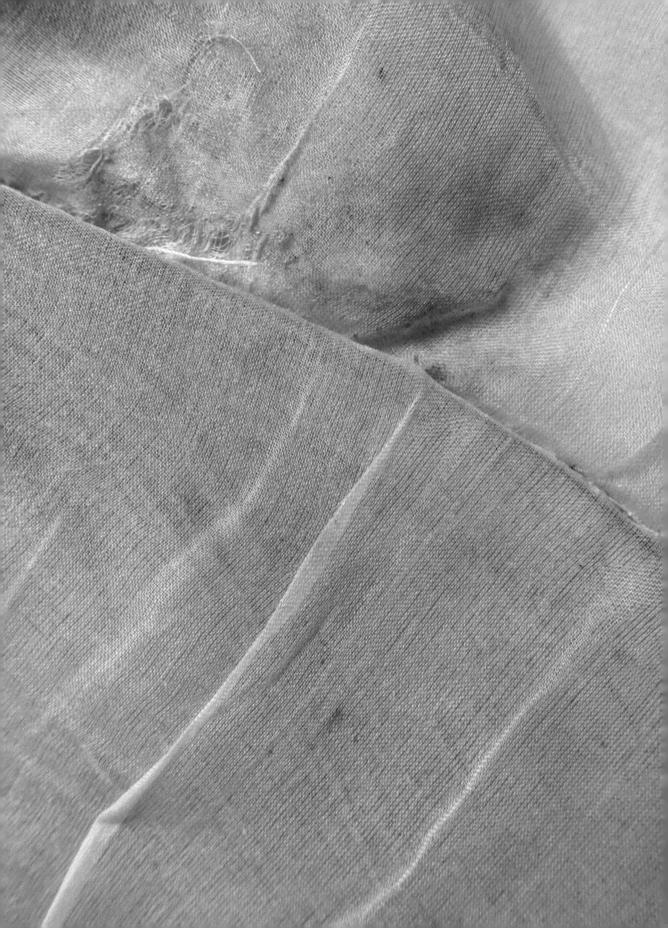

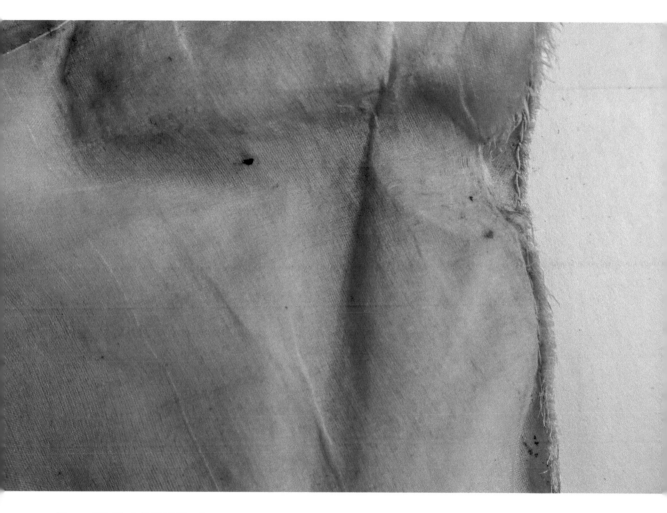

Figure 6.3 Cloth 7, *2015. Ellen Sampson.*

As we move, gesture is materialized on and across the garments so that creases, the lines our gestures draw, are their traces. Both our bodies and our clothes crease, as we inhabit them over time. To return to Stallybrass they are 'the wrinkles of the elbows, the wrinkles which in the technical jargon of sewing are called "memory"' (Stallybrass 1993: 2). Creases are lines drawn through movement, gestures retained in a physical form. Creases are both the outcomes of gesture and the commencement of subsequent deeper marks. The surface that has creased will, unless smoothed, continue to pivot along that line until eventually it ruptures. Ingold writes of the crease:

> The third major class of line [is] created not by adding material to surfaces, or by scratching it away, but by ruptures in the surfaces themselves. These are cuts, cracks and creases ... If the surface is pliant, then it may be folded without breaking, creating creases rather than cracks.
>
> (2007: 45)

Creases are not the wearing away of matter or a building up of residue, but an inversion, a contortion of the material's form. Creasing is the transformation of a surface through action; creases are gestures embodied in material. Most often creases occur where the joints of the body bend a solid but malleable piece of material, bringing together non-adjacent sections to create pockets, ridges and furrows. Creasing is a manifestation of the fabric's resistance to compliance: silicon cannot crease because it is infinitely pliant; rice paper cracks because it is incapable of pliancy; fabrics which crease must both accommodate folding and resist it. As Ingold writes, 'The lines on a letter that has been unfolded after having been removed from the envelope are creases, as are the lines of pleated fabric on curtains, upholstery or clothing. So, too, are the lines on the face and hands, caused by folds of the skin' (2007: 45). Creasing differs from folding, not in the end result – though a fold may imply something more precise than a crease – but in the intentionality of the action, the thinking behind the mark-making. Folding implies intentionality and a purposive agency; creases, on the other hand, are often unintentional, the resultant trace of an action rather than the aim of it. Creases are traces of experience, whereas folds are inflicted on matter.

Creasing a surface produces a network of lines, a map of our movements; each crease connects to another, just as each gesture flows into the next. These networks, alongside the other marks of use, create material cartographies of experience. The repeated movements of the body bring surfaces into contact and create reflexivity: a surface which turns in upon itself as the two surfaces on either side of the fold are brought into contact. The crease is both a record of a gesture and that same gesture continued: freed from the bounds of the body gesture continues as a line across the material's surface, a line of flight away from the body. This transposition of the movements of the body, into and across material things, is agency moving from one form to another – the transposition of bodily experience into the artefact: animating the inanimate. This transformation does more than simply alter the material's appearance; creases animate and articulate the surfaces of things. This animating quality, the capacity of the surface not only to withstand the force of our bodies but to be enlivened by it, gives worn surfaces a particular resonance and agency: a capacity to act upon us.

Scuffs and abrasions

Just as creases alter the surface of a garment by transforming it from smooth to wrinkled, so scuffing disrupts the surface of the object displacing mater in alternate ways. Scuffing is the displacement of matter from one space to another; as the surface is rubbed away, the garment's material form dispersed. During this research the first scuffs on my shoes, the first marks of my research process, often held a particular poignancy:

There is, I think, a horror in scuffing one's shoe, inevitability, a loss. The shoe starts off perfect, a crisp clean surface, free from multiple layers of marks; the marks it does bear are intentional, they are meant to be. As soon as you put on a shoe for the first time you know that you will scuff it. Often to initially preserve the shoes, to acclimatize myself to their damage, I would wear them indoors for a few days, walking mindfully and gently around the house. However, at some point I would need to wear them outside. The tips of the toes, the point at which the body moves forwards, are the first place to mark. With each stride, as the foot leads the body forward, there is a new risk. The scratched hide is no longer smooth, its protective sheen abraded. Abrasions reveal the suede-like softness of the leather's interior, raw and vulnerable, insides laid bare.

(Wearing Diary, April 2015)

Scuffs are records of the garment and body's relationship to their habitat, their interactions with spaces and objects which surround them. If, as Latour writes, 'an "actor" in the hyphenated expression actor-network is not the source of an action but the moving target of a vast array of entities swarming toward it' (2005: 46), then these marks, the scuffs and abrasions, are the traces of these entities, the technologies with which the garment and the wearer interact. Thus, the scuff is a map of affordances, the actions the garment allows us to perform. The scuff is created through the meeting of the environment and gesture; it is a record both of the body and of the networks of artefacts and technologies that it is part of. In analysing these abrasions, Bide writes of their ambiguous position as evidence:

The fabric at the back of the hems has frayed in an arc about the heel, indicative of the wearer's stride, and what remains of the hems is caked in dark traces of inorganic dirt, likely gathered from repeated contact with dusty London pavements. Although no record remains of where exactly these trousers were worn, their heavy marks of wear indicate that they probably traveled many miles on the city's bomb-damaged streets.

(2017: 17)

Beyond the scuff as a record of being in the world – of the bodies we meet and the affects we experience –scuffs are often indicative of the ways that the body has been protected by the shoe. A scuff records where our own skin might have been abraded, the way that our own bodies might have been marked by these interactions with the world. In scuffing, the skin of another species may be used by us as prosthesis for our own more fragile skins. The animal hide or cloth absorbs the impacts that would have wounded us.

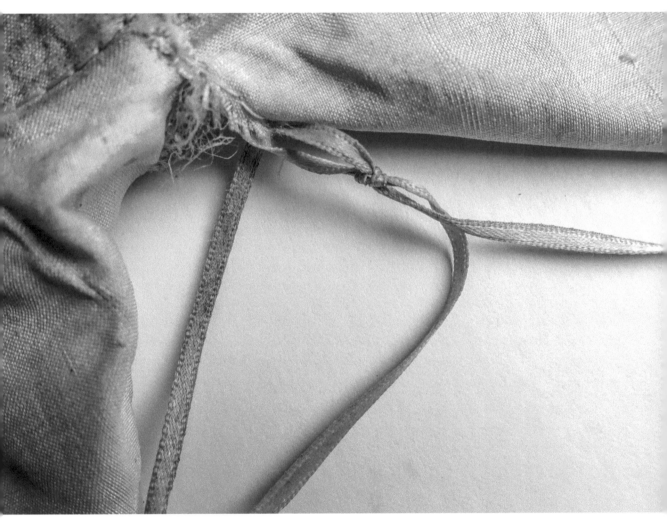

Figure 6.4 Cloth 25, 2015. Ellen Sampson.

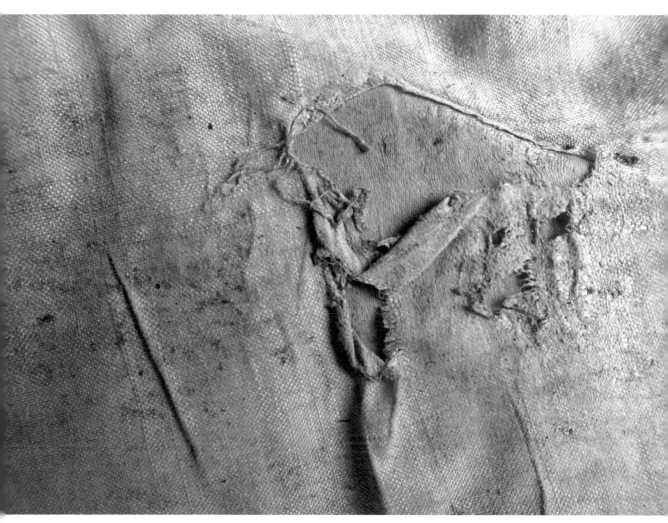

Figure 6.5 Cloth 6, *2015. Ellen Sampson.*

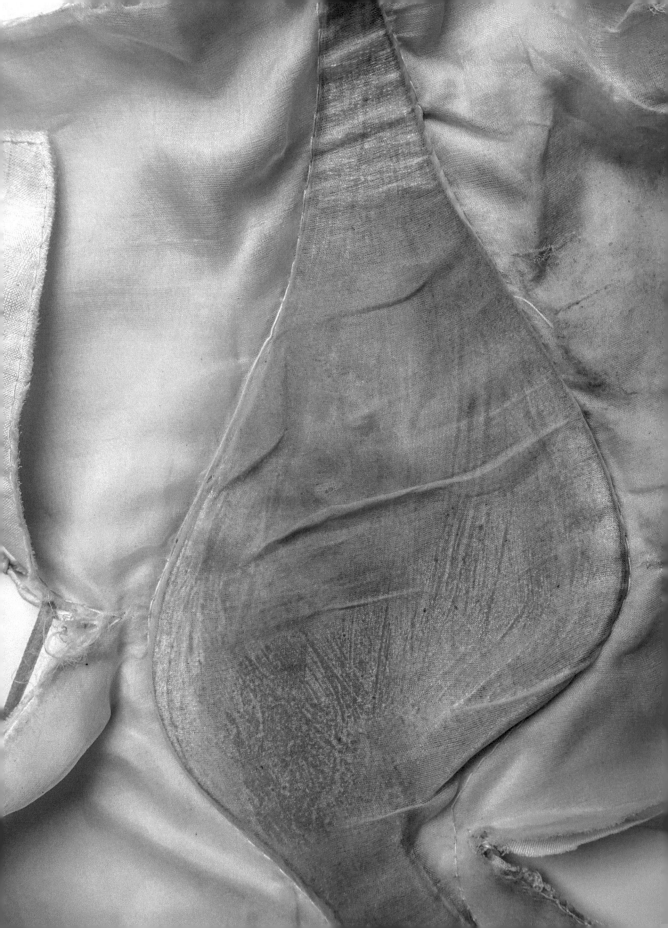

Stains

If creases are an inversion of the material's form and scuffs an abduction resulting from interactions with and in the world, then stains, the drips and seepages, which colour our clothes, are perhaps the most explicit manifestation of the intermingling of the self and the world. In staining, matter is displaced from one place to another: the matter of one agent is absorbed into the surface of another. Georges Didi-Huberman famously writes of the stain as an index: as a sign of an absent presence.[1] Didi-Huberman is a photographic theorist – he deals in negatives and positives, in image and reality, in the index and the sign. If for Didi-Huberman the stain is an index, then I would suggest that it is both that and more. For a stain is not simply an indent like a footprint or a thing left behind, such as the still-smoking cigarette butt, it is a transposition of the material of the original: a rearrangement of matter so that one becomes part of another. This intermingling blurs the edges of the object. This transposition is the exchange of material agencies. If one spills a drop of wine on a dress and it is absorbed, it is then unclear whether the stain is part of the dress (irreversibly absorbed by its form) or part of the wine one was pouring when the accident occurred, or both, an additional layering of agencies in an already complex object. Like Derrida's 'trace', the stain is an absent presence signifying not an absent object, but the residue of gesture performed (for the object, the liquid poured, the grass skidded on, remains, in part, both in and on the garment). Building on Didi-Huberman's work, Barbara Baert addresses the stain as a relic – clearly articulating its triangulated position in our networks of things – a mark that bridges time, recollection and location (both the location of the stain on the object and at the time it occurred). This triangulation recalls Barthes' writing on the temporal experience of viewing a photograph: the tension between the 'here–now' and the 'there–then' is materialized in the stain. Baert writes:

> The stain attaches itself to those same vectors within the triangle of time, memory, and place. The stain has a complex relationship with our body. First, many stains are made by body fluids. Intentionally or unintentionally, in various ways and places, we leave our own traces in the form of 'liquid relics.' A stain of this kind is an extension of our own physical boundaries and marks our dealings with the world (whether embarrassing, scabrous, or sexualized).

(2017: 285)

Stretching and imprints

The weight of my body and form of my feet are imbedded in the shoes that I have worn. Interestingly, on the thin-soled flat shoes these imprints are most visible, not on the inside, but on the outside, the soles of my shoes. The sole has curved to correspond to the undulating flesh of my feet, to the height of my arch and width of my toes. Thus, each time I remove my shoes and turn them over, I see myself reflected back.

Opposite
Figure 6.6 Cloth 19, *2015. Ellen Sampson.*

I am present in these shoes. Sometimes, if worn in the rain, or dried too quickly, the shoes lose their cast-like quality, their capacity to mirror my form. When I turn them over, the curves of my feet are gone from them – I have been erased.

(Wearing Diary, June 2015)

Stretching and imprints record the pressure exerted by the wearer's body on the garment. Stretching is not just a record of gesture but of continued force of the body against an object's material form. The garment's elasticity, which allows it to retain its original shape, decreases over time. Stretching, like abrasion, is a dispersal of the object's matter; however, unlike abrasions, the dispersed matter remains part of the object. These are processes of gradual rearrangement, of matter shifting in response to the body, its gestures and the environment in which it resides. Eventually, the impacts of the body and environment overcome the shoe and lead to its disintegration; wear hastens entropy. Although, in contemporary consumer culture, it is not common to wear a garment until it falls apart, using a garment will eventually destroy it. The time a garment takes to transform from pristine to rags is contingent on the wearer's body, movements and environment. The gradual process of material change is the manifestation of time in a material form.

Smoothness

The insides of my sandals have become smooth through wear, the pressure of my body impacting and burnishing the leather day after day. The shoes I wore after bathing are the smoothest, my warm damp flesh having made them pliable and slippery. The balms I rub into my feet have seeped into them, adding a sheen to their surface. They are luminously dirty, glossed not with polish but with oil and sweat. These shoes do not wrinkle and crease like the others do; their form is added to rather than depleted. These minute additions, of sweat and oil, swell the surface of the leather and fill in the abrasions of use.

(Wearing Diary, August 2015)

The smoothing of a garment's surface through use is interesting because the quality of smoothness is so frequently symbolically linked to ideas of newness. The near-fetishization of smoothness in contemporary culture is grounded in modernism; smoothness is interpreted as signifying newness, freshness, youth and, through these, progress. The late nineteenth and early twentieth centuries saw a particular engagement with and fixation upon the smooth and the sleek. In particular, transparent or impenetrable reflective surfaces such as glass, aluminium and Bakelite were presented as modern; as was the use of glass in both architecture and design – a material which often shows dirt and the traces of human interaction (fingerprints, smears on windows) so that considerable labour is required to maintain it. However, it is often the very reflective nature of glass that encourages its use within shopping culture: 'reflective surfaces in particular play an important part in the material culture of shopping; screens, glass and mirrors litter the spaces in which we shop (and in the context of online shopping are the spaces on/in which we shop)' (Sampson 2018b). This fixation on smoothness is apparent in relation both to product and industrial design, and also in the representation of female bodies. Smoothness has become increasingly linked to ideas around youth, cleanliness, progress, desire and the modern. Both the female body and the artefact (and indeed the female body is often treated as an artefact in commodity culture) have been corralled into a position where their attractiveness is dependent upon a sleek smoothness. Nooks, crannies, cracks, wrinkles, hair and patina have all been deemed old-fashioned, dirty, uncontrolled and undesirable. Ahmed and Stacey write that 'In consumer culture we are encouraged to read skin, especially feminine skin, as something that needs to be worked upon in order to be protected from the passage of time or the severity of the external world, or in order to retain its marker of gender difference in the softness of its feel' (2001: 1). This signifying quality of skin is emphasized by Connor: 'The skin figures. It is what we know of others and our selves. We show ourselves in and on our skins, and our skins figure out the things we are and mean: our health, youth, beauty, power, enjoyment, fear, fatigue, embarrassments or suffering' (2003: 50).

Smooth surfaces are often perceived as impenetrable, and thus immune to pollution or decay. A smooth surface as a protective layer, which cannot be easily unravelled or infiltrated. Smoothness, whether of a face or a garment uncreased by wear, may belie the wearer's internal experience: unreadable faces may be described as 'mask-like' (smooth, immobile and opaque). There is something seductive about this symbolic fusion of newness and impenetrability, and this seductiveness is writ large across twentieth-century design. Jonathan Chapman writes of our fixation on the new: 'Through a wide-eyed affection for all things new, mainstream industrial design has become technocentric, incorporating contemporary technologies within archaic product typologies – a skin deep discipline devoid of rich content that packages culture into slick consumable bytes, streamlined with synthetic polymers and metals' (2005: 10).

The newness implied by smoothness further suggests the potential for reinvention, whilst its impenetrability suggests a protection from pollution or harm. However, though surfaces may be smooth because an object is new, they may also have been worn away over time, smoothing through erosion. The soles of shoes, in particular, are often smoothed in this way. This smoothing is a form of erasure, of material forgetting; it wipes the slate clean. The ironing, for example, renders a garment amnesiac; it forgets the previous day's creases and gestures. The erosion of a surface to smoothness creates a paradox: the deletion of records through the process of their materialization. Smoothed objects may be appealing because they carry no record of the past on them; they are a blank slate, an absolution. Conversely, creases, whether on our clothing, skin or sheets, cannot conceal the actions that produced them. The creases on a shoe contain the records of the major events through which one might narrate a life (rites of passage, journeys or achievements), but also the habitual minutiae, the multiple repeated acts, of our everyday lives. A crease may start with a single gesture but is deepened by its repetition over time. Creases frequently relate our habitual gestures; at times one may even recognize a wearer through the creasing of their clothing (see Hauser 2004). This repetition does not require that each gesture be exactly like the one that preceded it. The exact repetition of a gesture is impossible, for it is performed in a different time. The repetition of gesture is one of the ways that tacit and somatic knowledge is produced and retained. Just as tacit knowledge is inscribed on the body through repetition, deep creases are incised into material, learning and responding to the practices of the body. A crease is a material memory, an archive of an act repeated over time.

As the material creases, its surface turns in upon itself, becoming a hinge that cleaves the surface, allowing discontinuous parts to meet. This inversion, through which non-adjacent parts of an object meet, brings to mind Michel Serres' description of time as akin to a crumpled handkerchief:

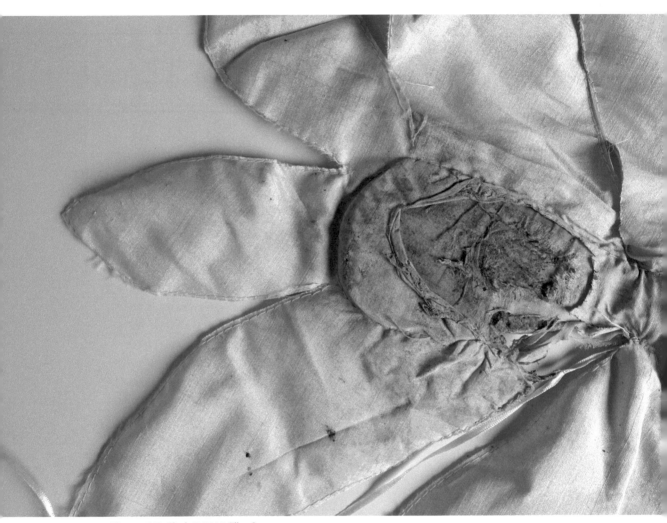

Figure 6.7 Cloth 5, *2015. Ellen Sampson.*

If you take a handkerchief and spread it out in order to iron it, you can see in it certain fixed distances and proximities. If you sketch a circle in one area, you can mark out nearby points and measure far-off distances. Then take the same handkerchief and crumple it, by putting it in your pocket. Two distant points suddenly are close, even superimposed. If, further, you tear it in certain places, two points that were close can become very distant. This science of nearness and rifts is called topology, while the science of stable and well-defined distances is called metrical geometry.

(Serres with Latour 1995: 60)

For Serres, the handkerchief serves as a metaphor for understanding time not as a metric system but as a topology. The surface of the cloth may be rearranged through crumpling or tearing, or be cast out and drawn back in like a net. While Serres uses the materiality of this habitual object as a metaphor for temporality, material things themselves function not as topologies but as topographies of time. The metaphor of maps is useful here: in stretching, scuffing and creasing, the surface of a garment becomes a complex map of experience rather than a linear chronological record.

Is attachment in part produced through the transmission of experience across surfaces – the cycle of imprint between body and the garment leaving traces on both bodies and things? These transmissions are transmissions of experience from immaterial into material and back again. They are the ways things and thoughts collide; a way that the solid and the ephemeral may relate to one another. As a surface creases, the geography of the object is disrupted; close becomes near, and near becomes far. As a garment wears down through use, the body is enveloped more closely in its folds, and simultaneously the creasing of the surface creates pockets or containers. The ridges and valleys of a worn surface capture both matter shed from the body and matter distributed from the outside world; the surface of a used garment becomes a container in this way. These pocked surfaces become imbued with a particular kind of resonance. The garment is both a mediating surface through which perception is filtered and a vessel for minute traces of the journeys and gestures the body undertakes. The creased surface becomes an archive. The dirt that creases gather is uncomfortable because it emphasizes our inability to move through the environment unsullied. Dirt threatens us because it disrupts the binaries we use to order our lives – inside/outside, me/not-me, safe/dangerous. The creased surface is risky because it sits at the edges of these boundaries, its insides and outsides touching and undefined.

The mystic writing pad

The marks upon our shoes are traces of the gestures performed within them, records of being in the world. The relationship between body, footwear and memory is one in which three agents are in continuous dialogue. The body imprints its form on the shoe, leather stretching and soles wearing away; in turn, the shoe alters the body, distorting bones and hardening skin: movement inscribing memory. Through the process of wear and bodily imprint, the shoe becomes a container for experience. Garments, in touching the skin, mediate our perceptive consciousness and become a site where internal and external experience meet. When addressing the transmission of experience through and across surfaces, Freud presents us with a useful metaphor in the form of the mystic writing pad. Material metaphors were crucial to Freud's explanation of the workings of the unconscious, from archaeology and ruins through to children's toys, the material rendering the immaterial more intelligible.

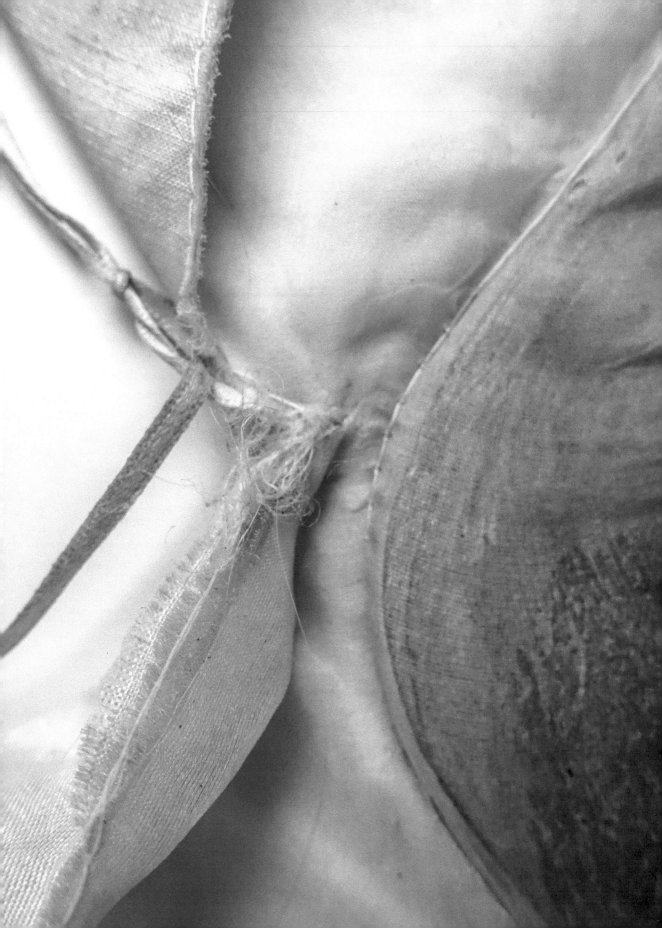

In 'A Note upon the "Mystic Writing Pad"' (1925), Freud takes the metaphor of a mystic writing pad to illustrate the way that perception, memory and the unconscious function in relation to one another. In searching for an adequate metaphor for the ways in which experiences are processed and retained, Freud examined different forms of writing and inscription. First, he rejects the metaphor of writing on a sheet of paper; though a sheet of paper can be permanently marked by ink, it is quickly filled up with information and once full cannot be used again. Similarly, he rejects the metaphor of a slate and chalk, upon which limitless information can be recorded, but only if the previous inscriptions are erased. For Freud, the most successful metaphor for the relationship between perception, memory and the unconscious is that of the 'mystic writing pad': a child's toy made up of a tablet of wax covered with a sheet of waxed paper and one of cellophane, on to which words are inscribed with a stylus.

The 'mystic writing pad' allows one to make unlimited notes which leave permanent (if not always legible) traces. By writing on the cellophane sheet, the waxed paper is pressed against the wax tablet and the written marks show. To clear the pad of writing, all one is required to do is to lift away the sheets of paper from the wax slab and the words will disappear. However, traces and impressions of the writing are still present as indentations, unseen on the wax slab below. Freud saw this device as analogous to the processes of experience and recollection: the cellophane as the shield of the perceptual apparatus, the waxed paper as the conscious perception of the event and the wax slab as unconscious record. For Freud this process of imprint and erasure was akin to the process through which experience enters the unconscious. The unconscious with its 'unlimited receptive capacity' (Freud 1925: 227) stores what the perceptive consciousness takes in but cannot tolerate or retain. The imprints of experience are produced on the surface (at the level of conscious perception) but retained in the core (within the unconscious). What is distinct about this process of transmission or transcription is that the marks made by experience, the records of perception, do not remain locked within the unconscious but instead have the potential to re-emerge. Within the mind, memories in the unconscious are also able to re-emerge both voluntarily and involuntarily. Freud considered 'the appearance and disappearance of the writing' as akin to 'the flickering-up and passing away of consciousness in the process of perception' (ibid.: 230).

These junctures are sites where conscious experience and the unconscious transfer across and between surfaces. Here, again, I wish to invert the trope of the material as a metaphor for the immaterial and ask if Freud's formulation of the layered relationship between perceptive apparatus, conscious perception and the unconscious might in turn be a useful tool in understanding how experience marks and is retained by the things we wear. Could this analogy be used to examine how experience is manifested in garments – the points where gesture and material meet? There are layers of experience and of retention, both in the mind and in material things and experiences embedded in the psyche, and the object may move between these layers, disappearing only to later re-emerge. As the garment and the body cleave, traces of the wearer's experiences move into their clothes, into layers of the bodily schema which are not materially of the body. While much of our memory is processed via the brain, the perceptive apparatus which allows us to recollect are located throughout the body, both on the surface and in its core. The skin, an organ of perceptive

Opposite

Figure 6.8 Cloth 22, *2015. Ellen Sampson.*

consciousness, is also a site of the unconscious, a juncture at which memories emerge and recede. The items we wear closest to the skin are in tactile contact with an organ of the unconscious: a site where immaterial and material meet. Garments pressed close to the skin become, at times, more bodily than object-like; as Stallybrass writes, they 'materialize the power of people to be condensed and absorbed into things and of things to become persons' (Stallybrass & Jones 2001b: 116). A well-worn garment that has rested long upon the skin's receptive surface comes to embody experience, rather than signify it.

Palimpsests

These traces of experience, the marks upon our clothes, often underlie the ambivalent relationship we have with the worn and used, artefacts which function as external rather than internal vessels of experience. Objects which are both intimate and revealing, precious and shameful; objects which are both us and not us: which bridge the gap between person and thing. The traces of experience that reside within and upon our own shoes make apparent the ambiguous attachment we have to them. However, this personal attachment created through the intimate experience of wearing does not in itself fully explain why viewing the worn shoes (and garments) of others has such poignancy: the particular affects of the worn and used. In exploring these affects of wornness, I draw upon another writing metaphor – not the magic slate but instead the palimpsest. Palimpsests are vellum scrolls which are inscribed and then, when the text is no longer required, scraped clean and used again, so that traces of inscription layer one above another. The production of the palimpsest has three stages: the initial writing, the erasure and the rewriting of text on to the cleared surface. The layering of texts in the production of the palimpsest is often used as a metaphor for intertextuality. However, here it is the materiality of the palimpsest I wish to explore; the ways in which the reading of one object might aid us in the reading of another. If we apply the metaphor of the palimpsest to a shoe or other worn item, we might interpret 'writing' as bodily imprint, and 'erasure' as the wearing away of the shoe's surface through use. Writing and wearing are both forms of inscription and erasure, of marking the surface and of scraping it away; both leave behind a trace. The scraped palimpsest is wiped clean but, like the wax tablet of the mystic writing pad, retains some traces of the previous inscription. The shoe carries traces of the wearer; bodily experience is written across its surface. Each movement we make is minutely recorded in the shoe's changing material form, only for those records to be partially erased as new records are imprinted on top.[2] In this ongoing cycle of erasure and inscription the shoe becomes like a palimpsest, experience inscribed over experience until its form finally breaks down.

Opposite

Figure 6.9 Cloth 13, *2015. Ellen Sampson.*

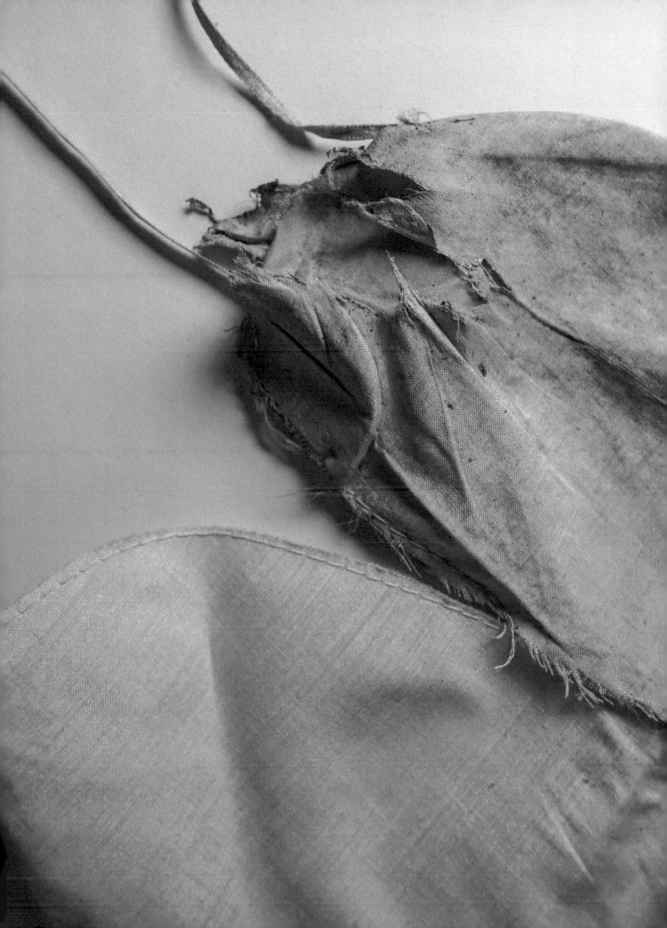

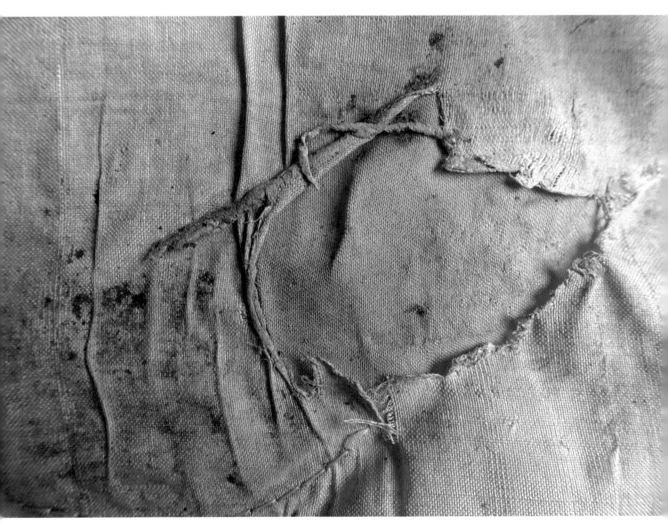

Figure 6.10 Cloth 14, *2015. Ellen Sampson.*

Erasure

This inscription of experience is not a single instance but is repeated each time a garment is worn. The worn shoe does not bear the marks of a single performance but, rather, the traces of many: our clothing contains multiple imprints of our lives. Frequently, garments become more resonant, more affective, the more they are worn:[3] the more entangled they become with the wearer and the world. However, the layering of the marks is cumulative but not linear. Marks are simultaneously partially erased and further embedded by the over-writing of the next. Erasure takes place through the performance of the next experience. The new partially obliterates the old and further embeds into the material of the shoe. As the shoe becomes a record there is always a partial forgetting: the wiping clean of a slate or even the scraping of the palimpsest. The empty shoe is a container of trace.

The worn shoe is a site of multiple non-contemporaneous records. Each new bodily imprint partially obscures the previous imprint, creating a mesh of overlapping and incomplete traces. So that when we look at a used shoe, we are not viewing the record of a single motion (as we do when we view a footprint), but instead the partial records of many different and disparate movements. Thus the worn shoe does not present a linear narrative but one in which multiple records sit side by side. The shoe is a site of non-contemporaneity. This overlapping of multiple narratives gives worn shoes their particular resonance. They do not represent a single trace but a complex record of many gestures performed and lost. These multiple overlapping narratives produce an experience for the viewer that is akin to looking at a well-used palimpsest. Previous acts of inscription are visible, despite their partial erasure, and compete with the most recent inscription to hold the eye. Thus the shoe becomes more resonant but less intelligible the more it is worn. The worn garment is difficult to read; the more worn it is, the less easily may one abduct an individual gesture: an individual trace. In *Art and Agency*, Gell (1998) presents the idea that an artefact may be 'cognitively sticky': this 'cognitive "stickiness"' of patterns is attributed by Gell to a blockage in the 'cognitive process of reconstructing the intentionality embodied in artefacts' (Gell 1998: 86). That is to say, our inability to comprehend the process through which an art object is manufactured gives it power over us; incomprehension leads to enchantment. Its affect stems from an inability to fully comprehend the experiences and gestures manifest within it; one cannot untangle the multiple imprints of events and experiences that the object contains. Is it the obfuscating nature of these bodily imprints that create such affect? The worn shoe's resonances stem not simply from its capacity to retain the marks of experience but from the fact that we can never fully untangle the web of interrelated experiences that produce a life.

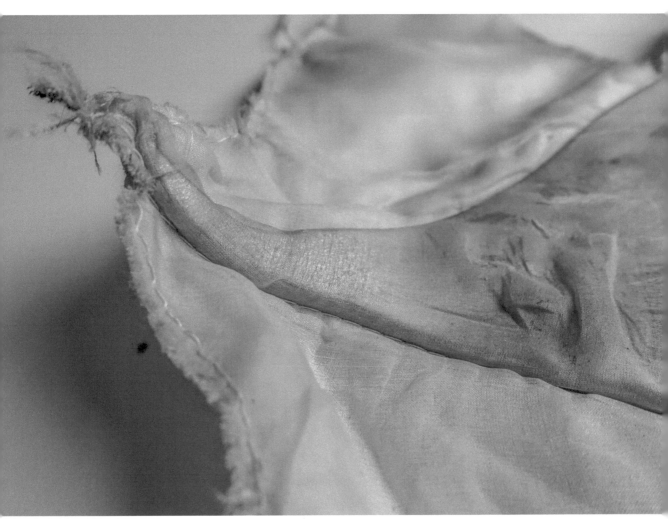

Figure 6.11 Cloth 33, *2015. Ellen Sampson.*

Wearing Diary 7

Today I find a new route. A different pathway to somewhere familiar; so that, though the start and end points are the same, the path is other to me. There is something magical in this tiny triumph. When you have lived somewhere for many years these moments are rare and precious, a secret of the city revealed to you once more. It is raining as I walk home, softly and still unseasonably warm. I walk across the grass in the park, enjoying the soft yielding of the damp earth. When I look down at my feet they are damp and striped with moisture. The skin-tone leather of the shoe (so much darker than my own skin anyway) has absorbed the rain and darkened from toe to waist. Darkened leather and the blue white of my own skin cross-cross over my feet. I am cold.

(Wearing Diary, October 2015)

Encounters and Affects: Garments and the memory nexus

7

A red wine stain on a wedding dress, a shiny pair of school shoes, the buttons on your father's favourite suit: even away from the body, clothing resonates with the aspirations and experiences of its wearers, of the lives lived within it. More than almost any other artefact, clothing demands that we recollect: from our own clothes, treasured or discarded, through the wardrobes of loved ones and lost friends, to anonymous dresses hanging in shops and museums, garments permit us to access pasts otherwise lost to us. There is something in the bodily nature of the garment, perhaps its skin-like quality or its ability to envelop our bodily selves that allows it to serve as a gateway, vessel or locus for recollection. As de la Haye writes, 'more than any other medium, worn clothing offers tangible evidence of lives lived, partly because it's very materiality is altered by, and bears imprints of, its original owner' (2006: 135–6).

The bodily material nature of clothing is a recurrent theme in fashion, textile and dress scholarship: from Stallybrass's (1993) haunting encounter with his friend Allon's jacket, to de la Haye's (2005) and Evans' (2014) explorations of the creases, scuffs and abrasions left through use, storage and wear. Davidson (2013), Bide (2017) and Ponsonby (2014) have examined the utilization of these affects in curatorial and research practice; the ways that a tear or imprint of the body on a garment may impact upon the viewer. In examining the entanglement between textile and the memory, Goett writes that 'laundry itself […] is a textile multiverse: every garment on the washing line of memories imbued with missed belongings; every textile process with its traditions, myths, histories and practices attached' (2015: 125).

It is perhaps a paradox that scholars of fashion and dress, a medium that is so fundamentally lived, enacted and performed, should focus on clothes no longer worn. What is the lure of the dress without the body, the shoe without the foot? Is it that we, in museums and archives, away from the bustle of the everyday, are surrounded by these bodiless garments – these absences of lives? Garments in museums and archives are quite other to the garment as a habitual and lived object – they are objects in stasis – preserved in order to retain a meaning or status. This tension between the disembodiment of the archival object and the need to preserve it is articulated by de la Haye who writes: 'When worn clothes enter a museum they embark upon a new "life" and serve new functions. In the process, what was once intimate can become impersonal – although often the very reason worn clothes are presented to a museum is to prevent them becoming part of the anonymous detritus of our material culture, and thus to retain their meaning' (2006: 135–6).

Overleaf

Figure 7.1 *Tan pointed shoe – unworn. Polaroid 1, 2015. Ellen Sampson.*
Figure 7.2 *Tan pointed shoe – unworn. Polaroid 2, 2015. Ellen Sampson.*

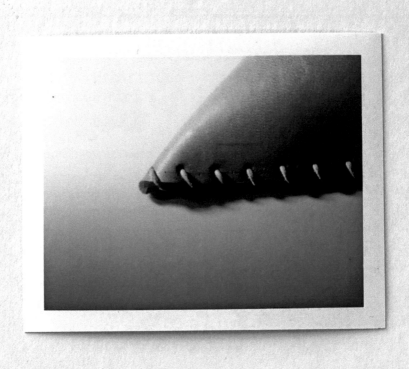

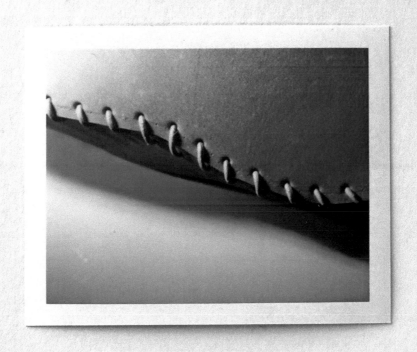

This book has explored the tactile and emotional encounters between the wearer and the worn; the ways in which, in the meeting of bodies and things, agencies and experiences are transcribed. This chapter shifts to focus upon the encounter with the worn and used garment away from the body; exploring the different ways these bodiless things affect us. The meanings of garments away from the body, which we seek to retain through collecting and archiving clothes, are as various and mutable as garments themselves. Each viewer encounters used garments through our own framework of knowledge and experience: we know garments only in the context of those we have known and seen before. Thus our encounter with the worn garment is always filtered through a matrix of knowing and not knowing, of what is sensed and what is seen. This chapter examines our encounters with used garments away from the body: unpacking the multiple mnemonic functions of used clothes.

It seeks to examine the idea of the garment as a memory object. Current writing about clothing and memory addresses many kinds of mnemonic and recollective processes and experiences, from those that relate to our own clothing to those that involve the clothing of others. Different kinds of 'memory object'[1] act upon us in different ways, and in order to understand how a garment may embody a memory or trigger recollection we must understand the viewer's position in relation to it. The position of a garment within networks of social and object relations is fundamental to how it is read. The garment exists only within this web of contexts and affordances and is inseparable from them. In framing the interaction with used garments as a meeting of bodies, I draw upon Ruggerone's statement that 'These embodied encounters are the stuff that makes up the material texture of our daily practices, actually rendering these practices possible; and because these practices are continuously flowing events (becomings), their meaning can only be partially captured by interpretative/linguistic discourses' (Ruggerone 2016: 8). Equally this chapter suggests that anthropologist Alfred Gell's (1998) formulation of the 'art nexus' is useful in exploring the role of the garment as memory object. Used garments like art objects are a locus of 'affect', a site of abductive experience for the viewer. To borrow from Gell, 'they fascinate, compel, and entrap as well as delight the spectator' (1998: 23). For Gell, art objects constitute a confluence of multiple agencies: the material agencies of the artefact, those of the artists and those of the patrons and viewers who receive it. By making these power relations explicit, Gell sought to examine how these groupings of agencies intersect. This book draws upon the work of Gell in suggesting that mapping the multiple relationships embodied in and made present through a used garment may help us to understand the manner in which it acts upon us. So that by creating a 'memory nexus' rather than an 'art nexus', we might understand some of the ways that clothing, experience and affect intersect.

This 'memory nexus' (see Figure 7.5) defines four broad categories of mnemonic encounter with the garment, and their intersections. The garments are divided by both materiality and their relationship to a recollected event: as indexical, symbolic, narrative and non-narrative, though in many cases a garment may be understood in more than one way.

The indexical and the symbolic

When thinking about the relationship of garments to memory, one must first define the nature of the garment itself: a distinction between indexical and symbolic artefacts. The indexical garment is one which was present at (and possibly altered by) the recollected event; it is a 'having-been-there' object, an object which bears indexical trace. The indexical garment's power as a locus of affect, its punctum, stems from a direct causal relationship to the event, experience or person recollected. Often these are garments that have been worn by a particular person or at a certain time or place. Their significance might range from the personal to the socio-cultural; from the dress you wore to your own wedding, to the shoes of Holocaust victims stored in the Auschwitz museum.

The indexical garment's affect quality stems from a causal relationship to the event, person or experience recalled: the fact that it was there. In Stallybrass's description of wearing his friend's jacket and in his larger study (with Jones) of memory and clothing, he examines how the material traces of wear or physical remnants of a body can evoke memory. In their resonance these artefacts challenge subject–object distinctions. Frequently, this blurring is due to the garment's capacity to conform to the contours of the body. Gloves, garments that, like shoes, are highly reminiscent of the part of the body they protect, 'trouble the conceptual opposition between person and thing' (Stallybrass & Jones 2001b: 118). This challenge to the opposition between subject and object (which I have termed 'entanglement' or 'cleaving') is also as apparent in artefacts which were once bodily but are now classified as things (artefacts containing hair, bones and skin) conceptually or culturally. The particular affect of these subject/objects, these cleaved items, has informed the debate on the display of body parts in museums. Writing of hair as a memento mori, Kate Hill addresses the ways in which these indexical objects act upon the viewer:

> The hair could produce an emotional or sensory point of contact between the viewer and the person it came from, thus was both subject and object, person and thing. Because hair meant memory and mourning, this meaning persisted even when the individual was historical or even unknown and therefore came to mean the collapsing of distance between now and any past, along with a sense of wanting to restore or access the past that can be captured by mourning objects.
>
> (2012: 164)

Similarly, Stallybrass and Jones (2001b) highlight the memento mori as both an indexical/narrative memory object and also a metonymic one: a part (the deceased person's hair) comes to stand in for the whole (their absence). These tiny mementos present a containment of trace within the artefact, a bounding of loss. Grief is contained within the object.

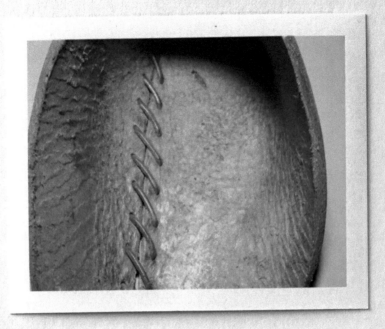

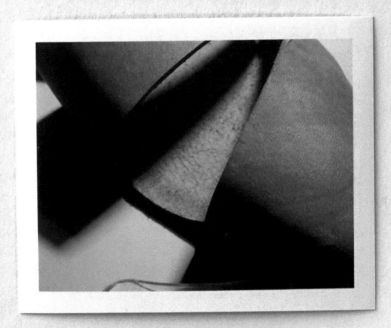

While an indexical garment may allude to a lost person, it may also allude more specifically to an absent behaviour or gesture. Writing about her mother's rolling pin, Susan Pollak (2007) addresses how the object as a record of gesture may compel us to recall, repeat and re-live movement. Again Stallybrass, in his writing on Allon White's jacket, stresses the capacity of the artefact to recall the immaterial, the movements of the body in time and space, so that the artefact is gesture retained. Indexical garments are often what Feldman (2006) terms 'contact points'. Contact points are, to use the terminology of this research, cleaved objects, objects which were once in contact with the body and remain entangled with it, so that they allow the viewer on meeting them to engage with them in an embodied and bodily manner. Feldman writes that they are a 'general category of object that results from physical contact with the body, and then subsequent removal or destruction of the body' (2006: 246). Though Feldman's category of contact points is perhaps broader than my own (including diaries and other ephemera) and are used in particular reference to the experience of artefacts in museums, the idea of an artefact as a contact point is helpful. If one understands the contact point as an index of a now absent body, then it is apparent how garments (and particularly those such as shoes and gloves which retain the shape of the body even when they have been removed from it and which become entangled with the body through wearing) might be particularly affective.

Opposite
Figure 7.3 *Tan pointed shoe – wear 1. Polaroids 8 and 9, 2015. Ellen Sampson.*
Overleaf
Figure 7.4 *Tan pointed shoe – wear 2. Polaroid 3, 2015. Ellen Sampson.*

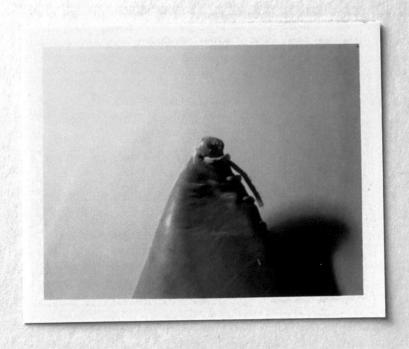

Symbolic garments

Conversely, when a garment acts as a symbolic memory object it stimulates recollection because it 'is like' another; it stands in for an absent original. These symbolic garments represent an experience, object or encounter to which they bear no causal relation – they are non-indexical. They may be similar in form or meaning to the original, or they may act as symbols representing it. Thus the symbolic garment may either be a visual or sensory stand-in for an original or it may be a mnemonic (a memento mori, a knot in a handkerchief, a pebble in a shoe). These objects induce recollection through their ability to remind us of something else. Perhaps the most famous of symbolic memory objects is the madeleine[2] in Proust's *A La Recherche du Temps Perdu* (1913). For the narrator it is not that particular madeleine or that particular cup of linden tea that causes his sudden and involuntary recollection, but the confluence of their properties at a particular place and time. That is to say, there is not an indexical link between the trigger (tea and cake) and the recollected act, but instead a likeness or similarity between the two sensory experiences; one is a 'material metaphor' for the other. Here, the object functions as proxy: a material thing reminds you of another, stimulating recollection. The artefact operates as a simile. In the context of the dressed body, such garments are those that recall another, whether intentionally or not. Thus this category might include garments which are intentionally 'retro' alongside others which trigger recollection. This likeness does not have to be visual; indeed, when the garment acts as simile it is often through the engagement of other senses. Chong-Kwan beautifully articulates these sensory simulacra, the way that the sensory affects of one garment might recall another:

> I have strong sensory memories of dress and can recall vividly the texture of a favourite childhood swimsuit and the silky feel of the pages of my mother's Vogue magazines permeated with the heady, grown-up scent of their perfumed inserts. I recall the smell of my father's polyester and cotton mix dental lab coats being ironed whenever I iron a similar fabric.

> (2017: 12)

Narrative and non-narrative garments

If the first categories (the symbolic and the indexical) define the way a garment relates to the original event or experience, then the next (narrative or non-narrative) attempt to define the ways a viewer might engage with and interpret that same garment; whether the encounter with the garment is located in and mediated through a verbal narrative. Those encounters which I have labelled as 'narrative' are those mediated through linguistic structure: the garment has narrative attached to it – a defined or definable story that may be articulated and understood. These narratives may be complex (these are the shoes in which Pavlova first danced Swan Lake, this is Princess Diana's wedding dress, or this is the dress I wore the day I got this job) or short (this is my dress, that is your hat). Equally these narratives might be personal or have broader cultural meanings. As Carole Hunt writes, ' … well-used fabric has a capacity – if not unique then unusually powerful – to embody both a communal, historical moment and a local individual, specific story: this is what a late nineteenth-century sofa looked like; this is what my mother wore in the 1930s' (2014: 226). Often the artefact itself may be less important than the narrative it enables the viewer to access, the recollection it triggers: its affect located within the narrative rather than the materiality of the garment. When one talks about the relationship between dress and memory, these narrative objects are often those which first come to mind. FIT's exhibition 'Fashion Unravelled' (2018), which explored incomplete and imperfect garments, included a digital section 'wearing memories' where members of the public were asked to discuss a particular garment and the memories they attached to it. Similarly, journalist Emily Spivak's (2014) website and book *Worn Stories* asks writers, designers and artists to describe the significance of particular a garment in their lives. Often the garments selected are those with a particularly high emotional affect – deceased loved ones' garments, or those associated with rites of passage such as weddings, new jobs and teenage misdemeanours.

Equally, Bide's description of her grandmother's fur coat highlights the fact that a narrative attached to a particular item of dress does not have to be one's own – it might be familial, social or cultural, so that we understand it not through something we ourselves have experienced but something we have learnt or been told about instead:

> Sitting with the coat on her lap, one hand carelessly petting a dangling sleeve, she narrated a chronology of memories evoked by this strange object: the smell of her mother's perfume when her parents went dancing before the war; the sensation of burying her face in its fur while the air raid siren sounded unexpectedly on an afternoon bus journey; watching her mother replace the worn lining with its current pink silk, repurposed from an old evening dress she no longer had occasion to wear since they didn't go dancing anymore. I had never heard these stories before, and it seemed as if the coat provided a new connection through which I could explore Grandma's memories and the complexity of her lived experiences.
>
> (2017: 2)

Many garments are ascribed certain symbolic and cultural narratives (from the Turin Shroud to Monica Lewinsky's blue dress) so that personal memory and the cultural meanings often become entwined. However, encounters with used garments are not always mediated by narratives; many are instead sensory and bodily, so that their affect stems from an encounter with the garment's material qualities. Callard and Papoulias wirite that 'an "affective event" is not consciously apprehended but is, rather, what happens to the body directly on the level of its endocrinology, skin conduction, and viscera' (Callard & Papoulias 2010: 47): affect as a bodily experience is felt rather than thought. Affect is not mediated through words but by the sensory experience of the garment itself, so that our encounters with used garments may be verbal and narrative or non-verbal and sensorially affective or a complex entanglement of the two: a complex web of different forms and experiences of recollection and evocation.

If we take these four categories, of the 'non-narrative', the 'narrative', the 'indexical' and the 'symbolic', and juxtapose them we are presented with four modes of encounter: the symbolic/ narrative, symbolic/non-narrative, narrative/indexical and indexical/non-narrative, each of which highlights one of the multiple ways a used garment may affect us; the ways worn clothes may act upon the viewer as agents of recollection, affect or aura.

	Narrative	Non-Narrative
Symbolic	Monuments Intentional keepsakes e.g. lockets, charm bracelets, friendship bracelets	Perfumes and textures Deja-vu and sensations unmediated by words. The texture of a garment held at a pre-verbal phase. Touching something in the hope of being transported back.
Indexical	Relics e.g. Princess Diana's wedding dress, baby shoes, memento mori	Other people's artefacts, abject objects e.g. Grave textiles (Davidson, 2013), Auschwitz shoes, Hiroshima dresses

Figure 7.5 *Memory nexus diagram.*

Voluntary and involuntary

It is perhaps important to note that there is a profound difference between the experience of voluntary and involuntary recollection in our encounters with things. There are things we make in order to remember and things we cannot forget; voluntary recollection is quite different from the sudden assault of an unwanted memory. The particular functions and mechanisms of memory and recollection are complex and varied. Increasingly, however, psychologists make a distinction between memories which are retained as narratives and can be recollected at will and memories that have no narrative attached to them and are experienced as involuntary or intrusive.[3] These recollections, unbounded by narrative, are considered more likely to re-emerge in response to sensory stimuli similar to the original event. Processes of recollection function in a number of ways. Often one recalls events without the intervening periods – recollection as a staccato series of exceptional events that stand out through the blur of the habitual. Alternatively, one may recall a whole period, each detail, event or action preceding the next. The difficulty with continuous remembering is that there is too much to take in or to later relay. In Borges' story 'Funes the Memorious' (1962), Ireneo Funes is able, after an accident, to recall an entire day's events precisely and accurately. However, the process of recollection takes an entire day, so that he can only recall one day if he sacrifices another. A similar paradox is discussed in Alexander Luria's *The Mind of a Mnemonist* (1987) where Shereshevskii, haunted by his inability to forget, attempts unsuccessfully to write down and burn his memories. The mind cannot retain infinite detail and also function successfully. Objects, however, have an almost infinite capacity to retain the markings of experience; to record and retain what we may not.

Symbolic/narrative encounter

The 'symbolic/narrative' encounter is a meeting with a garment that bears no causal relationship to what is recollected, but retains a narrative. Many artefacts used in memory and recollective practices fall into this category. Monuments are an example, as are intentional keepsakes such as lockets, charms and friendship bracelets. Objects intended to trigger recollection of a narrative that is familiar to you. Similarly, souvenirs (non-indexical but purchased at the site of a pilgrimage or holiday) may be understood as symbolic and narrative.

Garments which function as representations or substitutes for a past experience or lost object, event or person, and to which a narrative is ascribed, might be referred to as symbolic/narrative. Symbolic/narrative memory objects constitute a great number of public memory artefacts: memorials, objects in museums, portraits, etc. Their affect lies in their capacity to trigger recollection

Opposite

Figure 7.6 *Tan pointed shoe – wear 2. Polaroid 1, 2015. Ellen Sampson.*

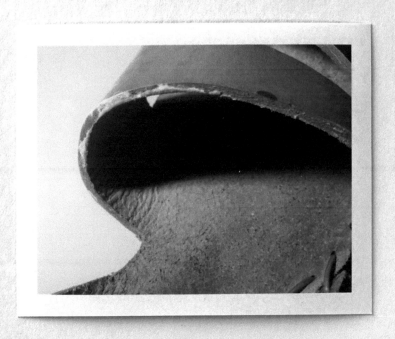

of something one has previously experienced or learnt. Frequently, these artefacts act as the cultural equivalents of a knotted handkerchief; they are a constructed reminder of something else. Though Forty (in Forty & Küchler 1999) would suggest that memorials are a tool for forgetting, it is apparent that the overt intention, if not the result, of the memorial is remembrance. To expand upon Forty's analysis of memorials, is it possible that the absence of an indexical link between artefact and event is what 'allows' us to forget? That there is none of that nagging urgency of the indexical garment, its commanding capacity to draw in and capture the viewer? The symbolic/narrative garment, however, does not have to be purpose-built – it may simply be that it resembles some other earlier artefact; an artefact may simply have enough commonalities with an original.

Symbolic/non-narrative

Just as one may be compelled by the symbolic/narrative encounter with a garment to recall a particular event or experience, the symbolic/non-narrative encounter also triggers affect because the garment resembles or stands in for an original. However, in contrast, these objects do not have an articulable narrative attached to them so that the affect they produce is not accompanied by recollection. The experience of these objects is not a verbal recollection but a sensory or bodily one: 'not consciously apprehended but is, rather, what happens to the body directly on the level of its endocrinology, skin conduction, and viscera' (Callard & Papoulias 2010: 47). Symbolic/non-narrative encounters are often with garments that are familiar yet unplaceable, stirring within us longing, desire or fear.

Scents are particularly liable to induce the affect of the symbolic/non-narrative encounter. Cut off from the grounding of vision, they discombobulate. As Benjamin wrote: 'If the recognition of a scent is more privileged to provide consolation than any other recognition, it may be because it deeply drugs the sense of time. A scent may drown the years in the odour it recalls. This gives a sense of measurelessness …' (1936: 184). However, these encounters are not the experience of the loved one's odour on a now empty garment, which Stallybrass so poignantly describes ('I cannot recall Allon White as an idea, but only as the habits through which I inhabit him, […] I know Allon through the smell of his jacket' (1993: 39–42)) but instead a smell which is like another: the catching of a long-lost lover's perfume on the subway, or the smell of talcum powder as one enters a changing room.

Textures, like smells, may stir within us experience that we cannot describe. Juliet Ash highlights the importance of the imagination in our encounters with the garments of others: 'the associative memory of an absent person, stimulated through the viewing or sensing of an item of clothing, requires us to be imaginative about the past, about the object or person when they did exist'

Opposite
Figure 7.7 *Tan pointed shoe – wear 2. Polaroids 6 and 7, 2015. Ellen Sampson.*

Overleaf
Figure 7.8 *Tan pointed shoe – wear 1. Polaroid 1, 2015. Ellen Sampson.*
Figure 7.9 *Tan pointed shoe – wear 1. Polaroid 2, 2015. Ellen Sampson.*

Worn

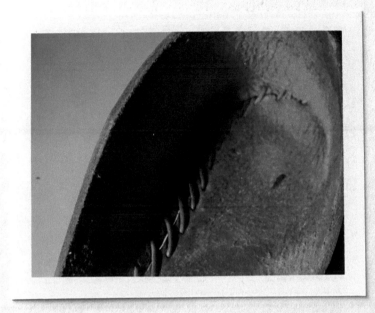

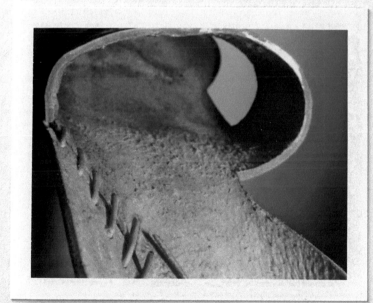

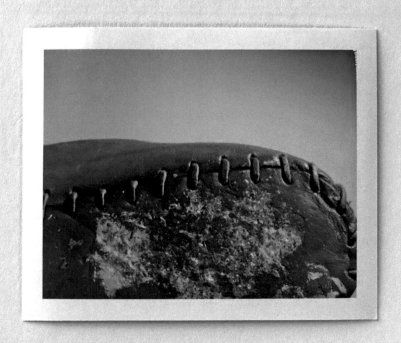

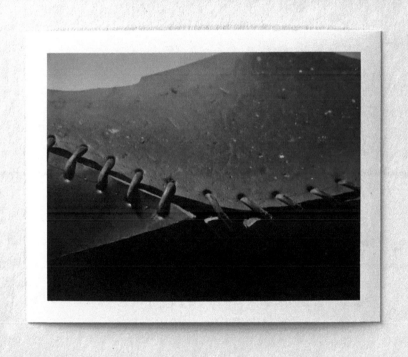

(1996: 20–2). Often the texture of a garment held in early childhood phase triggers particular affect: sensations unmediated by words. Goett writes of the frequency of these pre-verbal textile experiences in a BBC memory survey:

> … participants tell first memories of the safe smell of the pram's plastic lining, the soggy ear of a rabbit, the prickliness of the father's khaki uniform, the soft silky texture of the mother's petticoat, still vividly sensed in their minds.
>
> (2015: 121)

Similarly, the act of putting on an old garment may stir in us recollection without narrative, the memory of sensation rather than words. This capacity for one thing to stand in for another creates a world of affective echoes; one thing is resonant of another, again and again in a network of referents that come to bound our world. In many ways, the phrase 'is like' is the most profoundly informing aspect of abstract thought; that we come to know the world not just through 'me' and 'not me', but through our capacity to differentiate and compare.

Indexical/narrative encounters

> It wasn't merely the comfort of the silky softness of the wool next to my skin as I swaddled myself in it daily, nor was it the fact that it had belonged to her. It was the smell. Secreted away in the microscopic pockets of the warp and weft were traces of her perfume, her cooking, her garden, her books – smells from her life. But above all what lingered was her unique scent, a familiar milky sweet fragrance.
>
> (Campbell 2015: 4)

Victoria Campbell writes poetically of the comfort of her deceased mother's cardigan, the way the intermingling of wearing allowed her to recall her mother and in doing so be comforted. Encounters with used clothing are often both indexical and narrative: a worn garment about which you can tell a story. Items with a particular significance (those associated with rites of passage or periods of change) may be particularly resonant, but many of our own clothes fall into this category. The narratives attached to them do not need be of one's own (or true, for that matter[4]) but they must be connected to that particular object. These narratives may be passed on to you directly, or be part of a larger cultural narrative. We learn, for example, the story of Princess Diana's wedding[5] so that we recall it when we view the dress, whether we saw the wedding or not. An indexical/narrative encounter requires that we comprehend an artefact on viewing it; we see it, and can place it within our network of things. The indexical nature of a worn garment, its capacity to not signify but embody experience, lends these narratives an authenticity which can be deployed to great effect in museums and memorials. As Elizabeth Crooke writes of the ways in which this indexical/narrative memory can be used to highlight both personal narratives and larger cultural histories:

Opposite

Figure 7.10 *Tan pointed shoe – wear 1. Polaroid 4, 2015. Ellen Sampson.*

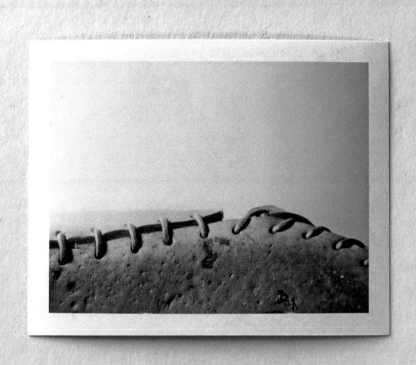

As we dig deeper the simplest object becomes evidence for our life stories [...] A faded cup may be favoured for its longevity, another for the memory of the day when it was bought or the connection between you and the person who gave it to you as a gift. On each occasion the value accorded to the practical nature of the object is surpassed by what the object might represent.

(2012: 26)

Indexical/non-narrative encounters

In a sense, these histories are secret; they are usually not recorded and often become lost forever. In the case of fashion, it could be said that these secret histories are stored in the creases, marks and scents of clothes left behind.

(Buick 2010: 136)

The final category is of those encounters with which my work is most often concerned. Indexical/non-narrative encounters are with garments which bear indexical trace of the original event, person or experience but which (unlike the indexical narrative) the viewer apprehends as a bodily rather than verbal affect. These encounters are often with the used clothing and possessions of others: objects that are simultaneously familiar and alien to us. Hilary Davidson writes of the experience of unpacking and cataloguing a baby's bonnet from a grave excavation:

They are a gap in the garment narrative I didn't know was there nor intuit the existence of, and startlingly close to our world. To see decayed what we are used to seeing whole is indeed uncanny, the familiar rendered strange. I felt the first influences of affect, 'as potential: a body's capacity to affect and be affected', where an 'outer skin envelope or other surface boundary' is a 'body': mine, the textiles', and those of the dead.

(2013: 8)

The affect of these encounters stems from their ability to bypass the verbal, the narrative and the symbolic, and affect us as material agents. Often their affect stems from their unintelligibility, like the palimpsest one cannot read, the tracks we are unable to decipher. These are garments to which we cannot attach a narrative, either because we do not know it or because it cannot be recalled. Unable to locate them within our web of meanings and words, we experience them in a bodily and non-verbal manner: interaction that often cannot be articulated, organized and contained. These affects are multiple: from Kristeva's (1982) horror at viewing empty clothes at Auschwitz, to the nagging uncertainty of a memory on the tip of your tongue, elusive and inaccessible. These affects, the horror of the abject, the loss induced by an object one recognizes but cannot locate, the electric thrill of the unknown, is the impact of the worn and used. Unbounded by narrative these are artefacts that circumvent our capacity to reason with them, to contain and control what they do, artefacts freed from signifier and signified. Unable to 'read' an object, we experience it psychically and physically; we cannot silence its insistent murmuring. We are unable to look away.

Opposite

Figure 7.11 *Tan pointed shoe – wear 2. Polaroid 2, 2015. Ellen Sampson.*

Overleaf

Figure 7.12 *Tan pointed shoe – wear 1. Polaroids 7 and 11, 2015. Ellen Sampson.*

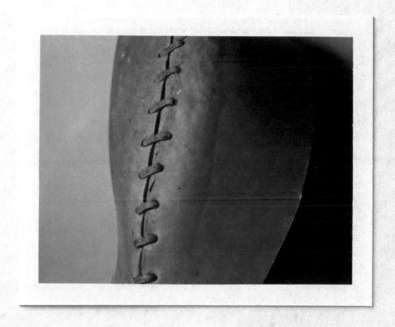

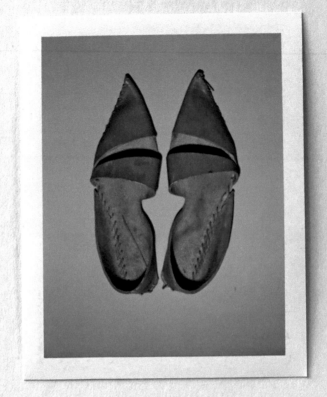
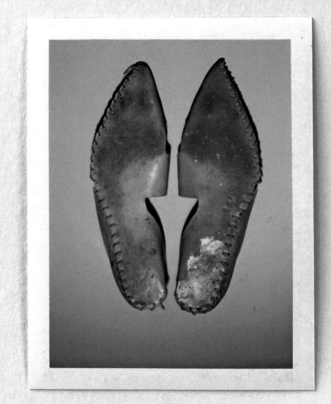

Wearing Diary 8

New shoes, this last pair have never been worn. Their form is deflated after months in a box in my studio, but as my feet fill them they swell. I bring them back to life; the waxy surface cool and smooth against my feet. I sit typing and scratch my toes across the insole – marking my territory. The shoes creak like floorboards, stiff and unfamiliar.

(Wearing Diary, November 2015)

Worn: Imprint, attachment and affect

8

This concluding chapter draws together these threads of thinking and attempts to bind them, to make them whole. It was the aim of this research to unravel some of the tactile and tacit connections and affordances that produce our relationships to our own clothing and that of others; to uncover the ways in which the worn garment may act upon us; to explore how garments and people may become entwined. This chapter explores the particular affect of viewing the used and worn shoe; to examine how the traces of our entanglements with the world impact upon us. How are the marks of an absent body understood? What is the affective power of this absence of presence, this trace?[1]

Garments are accumulations of agencies, agencies incorporated through production and use. The manifestation of these agencies is apparent in the ways in which a garment wears: the creases, folds and scuffs, which are the inevitable outcomes of use. Gesture is preserved within the garment – even when our bodies are gone from it, traces of motion remain. These marks form map of experiences: the worn garment is a repository of experience, a container of trace. Our relationships with worn or used garments run the gamut from comfortable and familiar, to abject and unknown. The distinction between garments we ourselves knew and wore, and those worn by others, is made more complex by a further difference between those with which we engage through narrative recollection, and those which induce a non-verbal affect. The inability to reconstruct the gestures which altered a garment lend to it a particular affect – a dissonance. Whatever our relationship to them, worn and used garments often produce a profound affect. They are uncomfortable, ambiguous objects, material traces of our own, or another's, past and present selves. They may disgust us, uncomfortable and abject, or trigger in us nostalgic longing, the desire to step back in time.

The knowing and unknowing

There is incomprehensibility to the marks of wear which create a dissonance for the viewer – an inability to retrace steps and gestures once performed within them. In order to fully comprehend an artefact we must already know of it, be able to place it within our network of things: both those that surround us and those which exist as internal objects. From a fragmentary knowledge produced through sensory engagement, we must use memory to contextualize the object in order to make it whole. Thus we understand objects not as discrete entities but as contingent parts of a much larger network, one which consists of both of our material culture and our internal world. In our encounters with the material culture which surrounds us, we rely on memory work as a form of reconstruction: rebuilding things which are no longer there. Jean Laplanche (1998) asserts that, in using the metaphors of archaeology and reconstruction, Freud presents a world in which no experience may be permanently lost. For Freud analysis and 'memory-work' … resembles to a great extent an archaeologist's excavation of some dwelling place that has been destroyed and buried or of some ancient edifice …' (1937: 259).

Overleaf

Figure 8.1 Cloth 25, *2015. Ellen Sampson.*

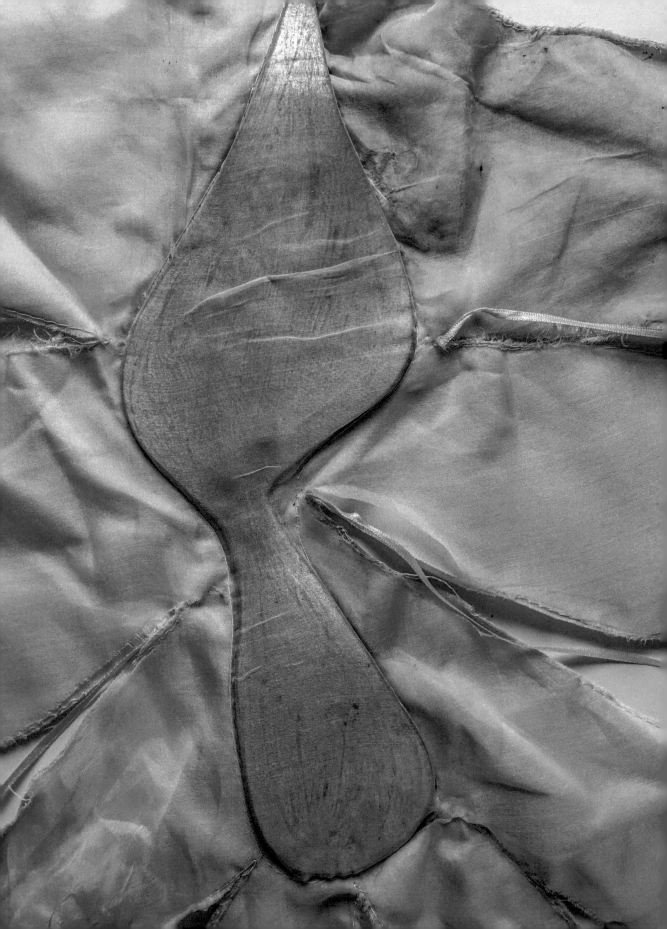

To understand an artefact one must be able to abduct from it (a sensory experience through sight, touch, taste or sound) and simultaneously contextualize it (memory-work). Thus, objects are always situated between these two realms: the perceptual and the subconscious. Memory is called upon to locate things within our internal and external worlds. Artefacts that cannot be contextualized through this meeting of perception and recollection often create a particular affect for the viewer, so that affect, in this context, is the experience of the artefact out of place. The artefact that cannot be contextualized takes on an ambiguous quality. Unable to be placed within our network of things, it may become miasmic or mesmerizing; by sitting outside the framework of the everyday, they may shock or enchant us; draw us in.

The affective encounter

For Freud, affect was positioned in opposition to *vorstellung* (1915): an idea, a memory or an image: a representational thing. This distinction between affect and representational memory is important; often affect does not depend upon recalling image or word. In discussing the affective turn,[2] Callard and Papoulias define it as 'concerned with non-representational and extra-linguistic aspects of subjective experience, aspects that its advocates associate with the very fact of embodiment and the particularities of our physiological responses to the world' (2010: 247).[3] Thus this affective turn reframes our relationships with the world as bodily and sensate: affect as the outcome of interactions, of engagement with and in the world. In his introduction to *Mille Plateaux*, Massumi writes:

> L'affect (Spinoza's affectus) is an ability to affect and be affected. It is a pre-personal intensity corresponding to the passage from one experiential state of the body to another and implying an augmentation or diminution in that body's capacity to act. L'affection (Spinoza's affectio) is each such state considered as an encounter between the affected body and a second, affecting, body (with body taken in its broadest possible sense to include 'mental' or ideal bodies).
>
> (Deleuze & Guattari 1987: 16)

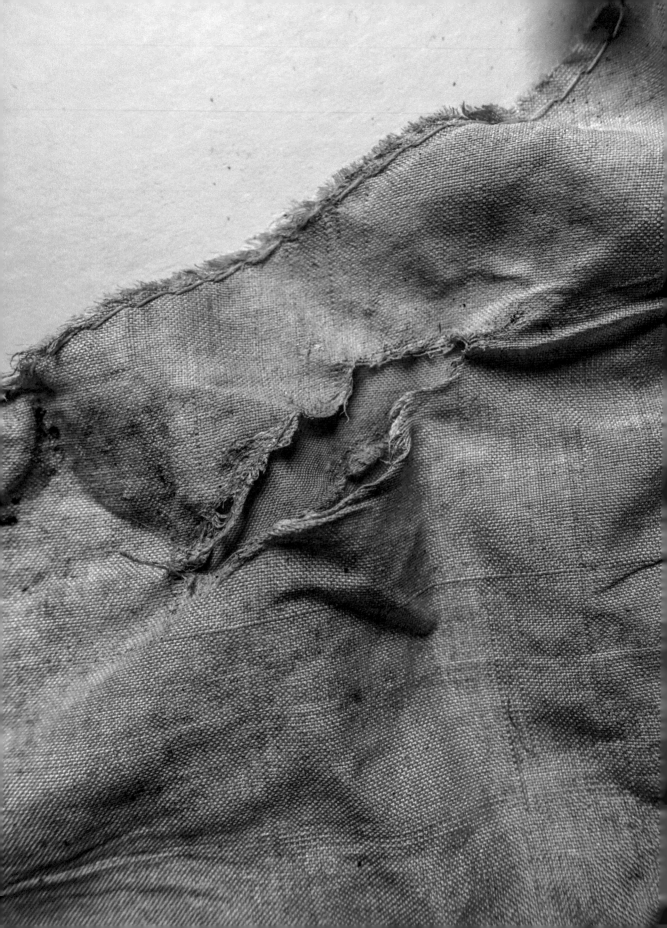

Deleuze and Guattari write of the encounter as the locus of affect, of the relationship of one 'body' to another – affect as a form of object relations. The experience of affect is one of encounter: affect is relational, it is the outcome of our intermingling in the world. Affect is bodily; it is experienced, processed and produced in the bodily self.[4] Thus affect is a meeting with the material world; an instance of a collision from which experience occurs.

In sensory engagement with the world, we experience multiple affects. The bodiliness of affect is pertinent in this context; often the encounter with an artefact bearing bodily trace induces an affect. These affects (both negative and positive) occur at points of dissonance or disjuncture, at moments of unknowing. Old and used shoes are frequently associated with the experience of negative affect – of discomfort, horror or disgust. Worn garments frequently induce in the viewer a discomfort that is difficult to articulate or define. We recoil from stains on dresses and from dirty shoes, unable to explain quite why this might be. Often the rationalization is that they are unclean, and yet the dirt they carry is rarely any more in quantity than we experience in other encounters with the material world. Though it is true that 'dirt is matter out of place' (Douglas 1966), the affective quality of the worn and used goes beyond displeasure at a disturbed binary. This negative affect recalls Kristeva's (1982) writing on the abject. For Kristeva, the 'abject' is a breakdown of the relationship between the subject and object, a blurring of the lines between self and other. She writes of the abject in the context of membranous or peripheral aspects of the body, those most liable to contamination – of things that have been excreted from the body and are thus simultaneously of the self and other to it. The horror of the abject may be understood as a fear of losing the self, boundaries blurred, insides spilled outside the body. For Kristeva, the affect of the abject stems from a disruption of the symbolic order: 'Abjection is above all ambiguity. Because, while releasing a hold, it does not radically cut off the subject from what threatens it – on the contrary, abjection acknowledges it to be in perpetual danger' (Kristeva 1982: 9). Worn garments present us with a different kind of intermingling: the intermingling of an 'other' (another person's body or our own anterior selves) and the garment. This intermingling, this breakdown of boundaries, is not potential but instead is something that has already occurred. While Kristeva's abject is located in a threat, a potential confusion of subject and object, in the case of the worn garment, artefact and user have already mingled – subject and object are already cleaved. Thus the affect of the worn and used stems not from the threat of intermingling but from a boundary already collapsed or obscured. This affect stems from the bodiliness of the garment, its imprint, creases and wear. The worn garment is affective, because it both represents an absent body and also remains a distrusted aspect of that same body itself.

Opposite

Figure 8.2 Cloth 27, *2015. Ellen Sampson.*

Overleaf

Figure 8.3 Cloth 28, *2015. Ellen Sampson.*

Figure 8.4 Cloth 29, *2015. Ellen Sampson.*

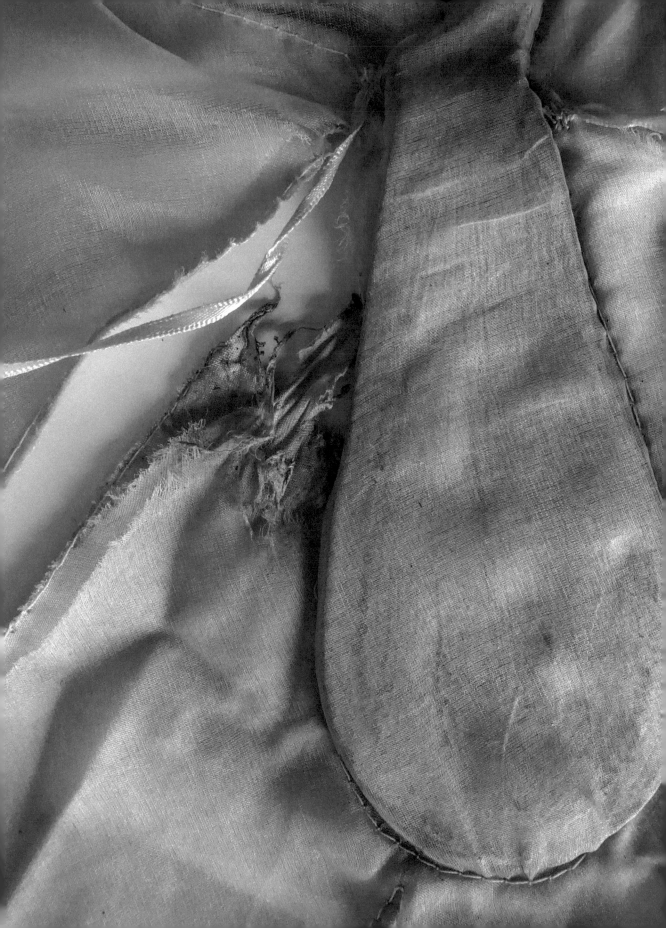

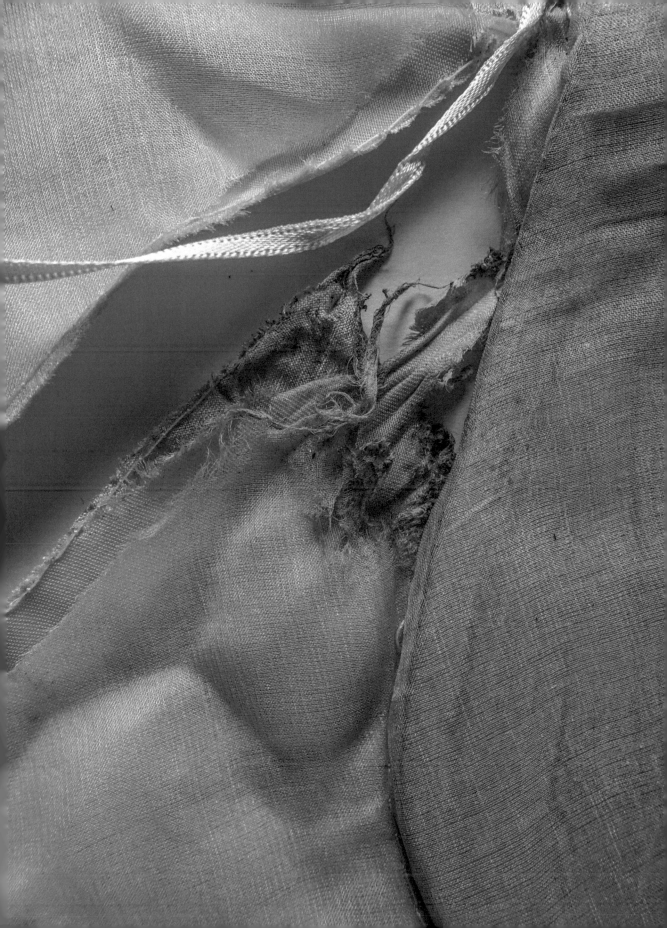

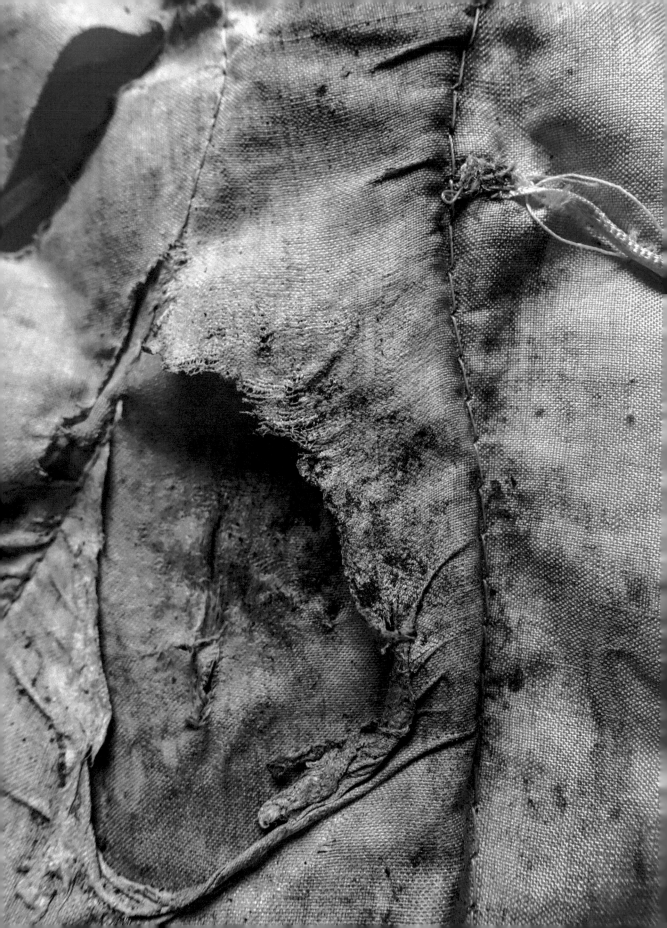

Aura and trace

The worn shoe is at once part of the absent body and separate from it; a shed skin, a discarded aspect of the self. It is neither entirely bodily nor fully clean. Inscribed upon it are the marks of previous actions and past selves. Even away from the body worn garments remain a locus of the agencies of those who have laid hands upon it: its users, its makers and its wearers. This intermingling has an obfuscating effect, as agencies build up, traces come to compete and overlap. These multiple records, the palimpsest-like quality of the worn shoe (or other garments), create dissonances and disjunctures for the viewer. Viewing these gesture traces, one is unsure which trails to follow, where one ends and the next begins. If the negative affects of viewing a worn garment are rooted in the garment's capacity to become a 'distributed' part of the self, then the positive affects are also rooted in this 'distribution' – an absent wearer made present for the viewer. Worn garments retain gestures, the immaterial and temporary made material, and also those parts of our body that we shed each day. This trace is an absent body, a body absent but still present for the viewer. These traces disrupt the binaries of there and not there, of animate and inanimate, of person and object. Discussing the affect arising from traces upon burial clothes, Davidson states:

> I like the ways what I found in the pieces eludes the documentary; slips into a silence that is eloquent if you can read its messages. I like the presence of absence, the holes left by stitches, the impressions and the corrosions and the challenge of unpacking incomplete, incoherent remains.
>
> (2013: 24)

If the cause of this gesture-trace is a now absent body, a meeting of self and world, then do these marks produce particular puncta or an 'aura'? Is the punctum of the worn garment, its piercing quality, a form of aura? Though aura is most commonly associated with 'The Work of Art in the Age of Mechanical Reproduction' (Benjamin 1936), the idea of aura and the auratic is woven into many of Benjamin's texts. Aura is an ambiguous term that links magical, religious and perceptual experience. For Benjamin, aura was linked to the irreducible quality of material and spatio-temporal originality.

Perhaps the most useful definition of aura in this context is Bratu-Hansen's description of aura as a form of perception that 'invests' or endows a phenomenon with the 'ability to look back at us' (2008: 4), to hold the viewer in its gaze and captivate us. Though aura is often associated with the artwork, Benjamin writes that 'genuine aura appears in all things, not just in certain kinds of things, as people imagine' (Benjamin quoted in Bratu-Hansen 2008: 1). So that mundane or habitual artefacts, worn garments, for example, might possess a certain kind of aura – a quality which allows them to captivate the viewer.

Opposite
Figure 8.5 Cloth 30, *2015. Ellen Sampson.*

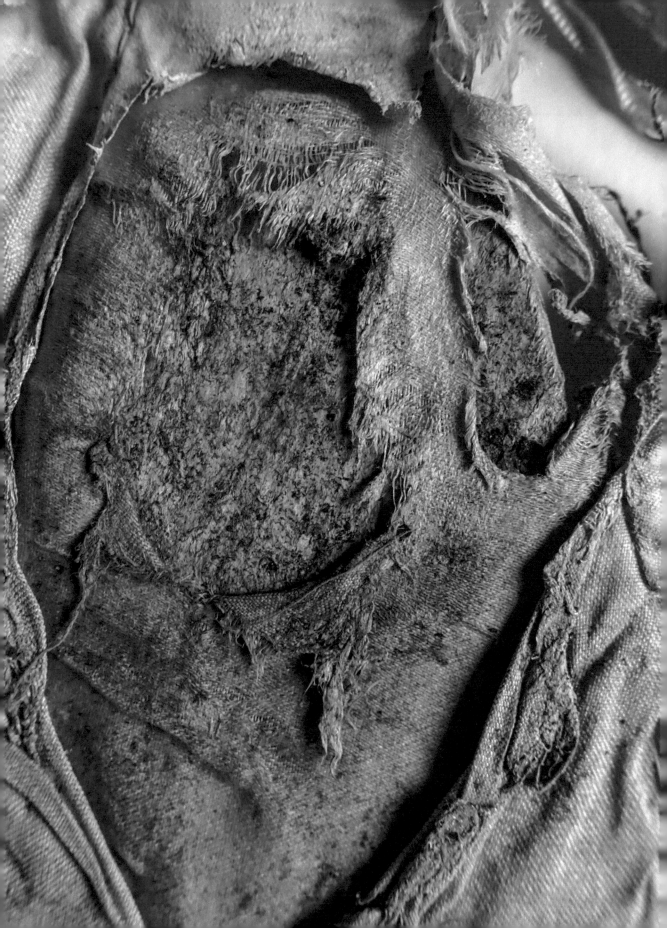

Relics

Thinking about the aura of habitual things leads us to the encounter with religious relics. Relics are presented as powerful indexical memory objects: artefacts that were part of a miraculous body, and are still invested with those same miraculous qualities. It could be said that the relic is believed to be invested with similar qualities to those that Benjamin afforded to the artwork, so that when one looks at the relic (an object invested with God's agency), God's agency looks back at you or, when one touches a relic, one is in turn touched by God – a tactile encounter with the divine. Though everyday artefacts, such as clothing, may seem at odds with the status afforded to relics, there are points where encounters with the habitual and the holy may overlap. Relics are loci of trace: (alleged) indexical records. Relics are not representations; they are the thing rather than the image of it. It is this indexical quality to which Didi-Huberman writing of the Turin Shroud, refers: 'The non-iconic, non-mimetic nature of this stain guarantees its indexical value. I might add that the word authenticity is common to the vocabulary used by Peirce to describe the index and to the cultural discourse of theologians concerning relics' (ibid.: 67–8). The stains on the shroud are for Didi-Huberman (alleged)[5] indexes of the absent body and this is what lends them their power. Perhaps the defining quality of a relic is that it produces an affect for the viewer, that it calls forth an absent body. Didi-Huberman writes: 'If all physical contact calls to mind the act that establishes it (in an indexical relationship), every act calls forth as well, and imperatively, the proper name of the actor: he who left some of his blood on this linen sheet' (ibid.: 68). Though they are very different forms of material culture, valued and interpreted in different ways, one might compare the affect of the worn and used garment to that of the relic, a similarly indexical artefact. Both share a particular kind of haptic visuality – an ability to 'touch' you through looking. The indexical artefact succeeds in calling forth its previous users: those who have intermingled with it. In looking at the artefact one must engage with the traces of use, and in engaging with these traces one is touched by them.

Opposite
Figure 8.6 Cloth 32, *2015. Ellen Sampson.*

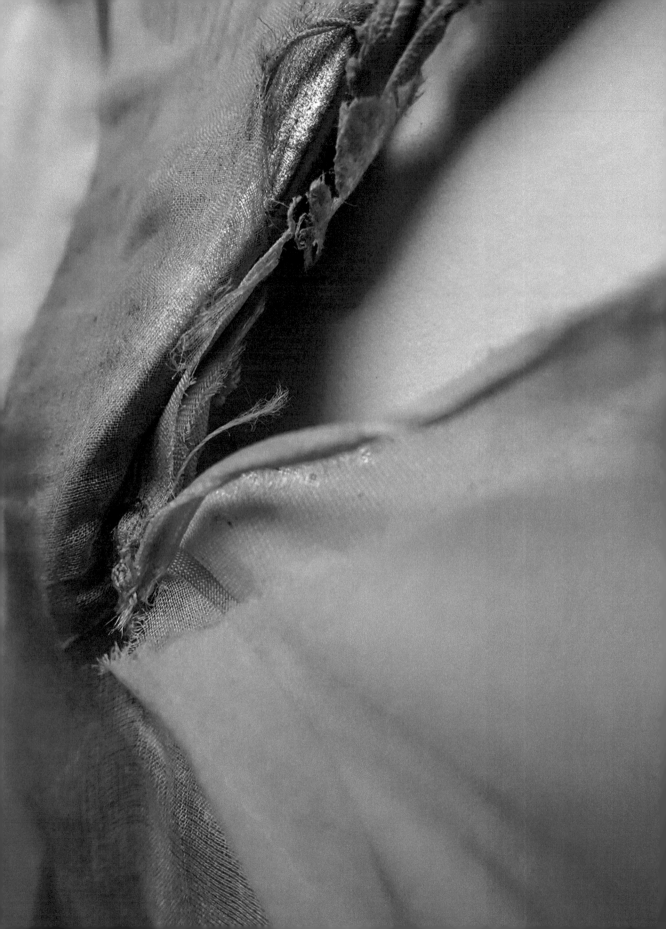

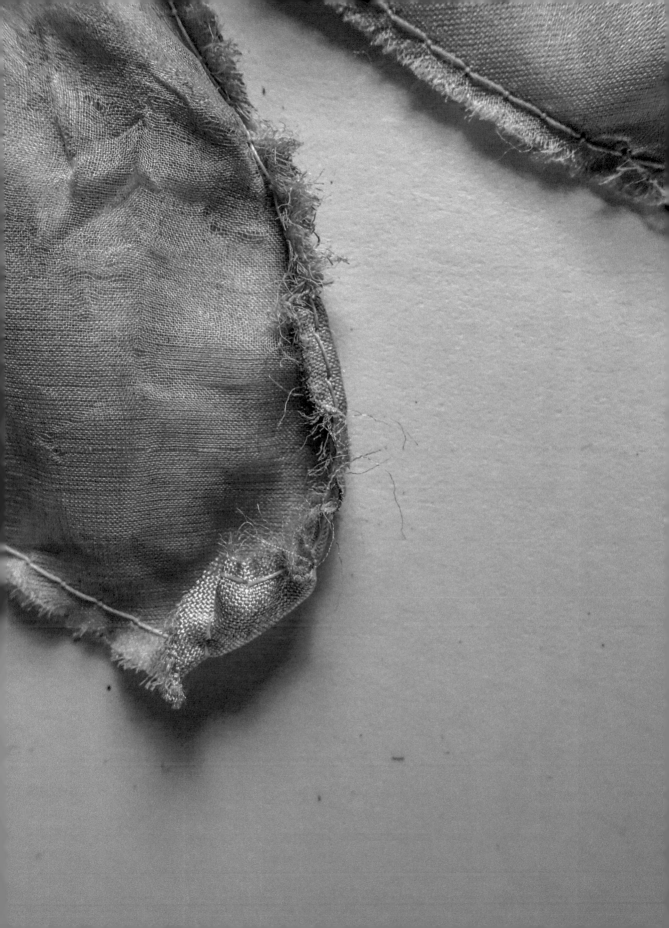

Originals and copies

If the power of the relic lies in its indexicality, then often the power of artworks is located in singularity and authorship – a spatio-temporal originality. Benjamin (1936) interrogates the relationship between the original and the reproduction: the power of the singular and multiple. For Benjamin, aura is present in the encounter with the original artwork; 'even the most perfect reproduction of a work of art is lacking in one element: its presence in time and space, its unique existence at the place where it happens to be' (Benjamin 1936: 50). Aura is the 'inalienable possession' of the original, a thing that cannot be taken from it. However, as Glenn Adamson writes, Benjamin acknowledged both the powerful democratizing nature of the mass-produced and the fact that the mass-produced may, over time, become unique:

> he (Benjamin) argued that because mass-produced copies lacked the 'aura' of handmade originals, they actually might be preferable, as they would afford audiences and users greater cultural determination. But if a copy is to be saturated with the same cultural value as, say, a traditional pot and weaving, we must have the same sense of ownership and intimacy with mass-produced objects that people of earlier times had with their own material culture.
>
> (2009: 337)

Though mass-produced items (newspapers, shoes, cars) may start out as near-identical, they are individuated through use and wear. That is to say, 'things can be said to have "biographies" as they go through a series of transformations from gift to commodity to inalienable possessions, and persons can also be said to invest aspects of their own biographies in things' (Hoskins 2006: 73). A newspaper, for example, may be read, folded, crumpled and used to wrap food or broken glass, over the course of a day; it is made original through its entanglements with agencies other than its own. Similarly, most mass-produced garments start out as near-identical but are quickly individualized by the unique qualities of the wearer's body, gait and environment. In her comparison of the works of Gell and Benjamin, Hoskins raises Morin's (1969) distinction between biographical object and commodity: 'Though both sorts of objects may be produced for mass consumption, the relation that a person establishes with a biographical object gives it an identity that is localized, particular and individual, while those established with an object generated by an outside protocol are globalized, generalized and mechanically reproduced' (ibid.). The distinction between biographical object and commodity is, I think, unnecessary; commodities become biographical through use and biographical objects may (as is apparent in the case of relics and museum acquisitions) become commodities. Habitual artefacts become unique over time. As the garment becomes bodily and entangled with its wearer, it becomes unique; wearing is a form of individualization. The 'aura' of used clothing lies in part in the customization of the habitual through wear. Just as aura is linked to the temporal and geographical specificity of the artwork, the worn object is inseparable from the movements that have produced it; gesture-trace makes the garment original.

Overleaf
Figure 8.7 Cloth 31, *2015. Ellen Sampson.*
Figure 8.8 Cloth 35, *2015. Ellen Sampson.*

Powerful objects

The worn garment is a record, a materialization of the actions performed within it. Each crease and scuff relates to a gesture, a body, a time and place. This record, original, non-representational and unrepeatable, shares the auratic quality of an artwork, both in its specificity and in its capacity to induce affect. The act of wearing transforms a mass-made garment from a copy to an original. The wearer is to the maker of clothes much as the reader is to the author. The 'interpretation' of the garment through dressing, styling and use renders it a different artefact. In the transformation of wearing, the garment and user become cleaved – neither fully integrated nor fully apart. The entanglement of wearer and worn allows for a distribution of the user beyond the bounds of their body; wearers are present in their empty and discarded clothes. This distribution of the self into things brings to mind the magical and talismanic artefacts. Old clothes are frequently presented as having a talismanic quality, as if the accrued markings of use make them powerful. We are familiar with the ways that a leather jacket or the ripped jeans of a musician may take on an almost relic-like quality, as though to touch them is to be transported back to the events they witnessed and participated in.

Talismans, relics and fetishes serve a particular purpose in the world of magical things; we afford them tasks of which we ourselves are not capable or dare not undertake: relics may heal, talismans protect, fetishes settle disputes. This is not to say that the worn and used garment is magical, only that the ways that magic has been used to explain the distribution of person into thing and thing into person might be helpful in interpreting the transpositions of wearers into their garments. It is to acknowledge that in a commodity culture we struggle with the transposition of persons and things through use, with the capacity of a thing to act in a person's place and of another person to be affected by that artefact's agency. Stallybrass writes of Congolese fetishes (*nkisi nkondo*) a source of both fascination and fear for colonial traders: 'what was demonized in the concept of the fetish was the possibility that history, memory and desire might be materialized in objects that are touched, loved and worn' (1998: 186). For Stallybrass, magical objects allow for agency abducted from one body to impact upon another; they serve as intermediaries and facilitators between wish and desire. In 'Function of the Fetish', Pietz (1985) writes of the 'irreducible materiality' of the fetish object: the fetish's power is dependent upon its material form. It does not stand in for another thing or idea (as a crucifix or icon might) but itself acts as direct agent within the encounter. The fetish's power is not as a symbol; the fetish's power resides within its form. Thus the fetish epitomizes the material agency of artefacts and in particular power brought about through touch. The tactile intermingling of the self and the artefact is what gives the object its power. When a person hammers a nail into a *nkisi nkondi*, they are in effect leaving a part of themselves in the artefact and through this transposition they are protected.

We often talk of clothing in a similarly talismanic manner; from ritual and rites of passage[6] to everyday practice, this intermingling of person and thing may be used to our advantage. We may use another's garment to conjure up their qualities, to wrap ourselves in the aspects of another person's personality and take on their traits.

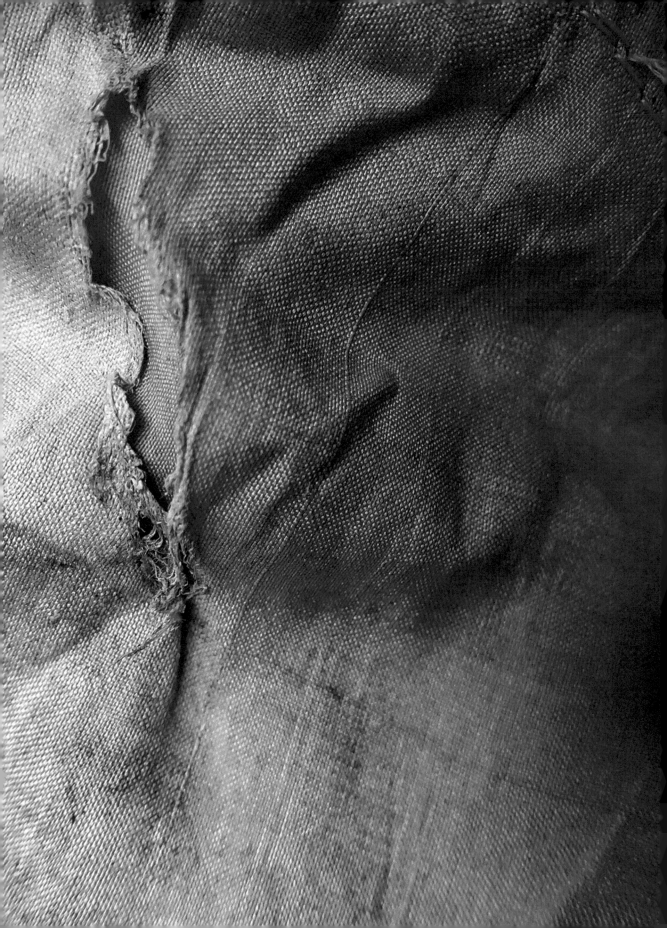

The talismanic qualities of well-worn garments, the protective nature of a well-worn sweater or the capacity of a loved one's garment to summon their memory is reminiscent of Gell's writing on art and magical objects. In *Art and Agency*, Gell describes the artist as a 'skilled technician', asserting that art is a technical system in which we, the viewer, recognize skill and are captivated by it: 'the power of art objects stems from technical processes they objectively embody: the technology of enchantment is founded on the enchantment of technology' (Gell 1998: 44). The capacity of the art object to actively engage the viewer is located, for Gell, in technology or technique. In particular Gell writes of a 'halo effect of technical difficulty' (ibid.: 68): that an object may affect the viewer because they themselves would not be able to make it. Though one may understand the way an art object was made, the viewer cannot fully comprehend the processes of its construction: 'It is the way an object is construed as coming into the world which is the source of the power of such objects – their becoming rather than their being' (ibid.: 46). For Gell, technical expertise can obfuscate, and this obfuscation is a root of enchantment.

For Gell, the affective power of the artwork lay in its ability to enchant the viewer through its technical prowess, 'the enchantment of technology' and the 'technology of enchantment' becoming one and the same (Gell 1992). I suggest that we might use the idea of the obfuscating power of unknown and unknowable, to think about the affects of the things we wear. That the marks of use upon a shoe produce an affect through their simultaneous familiarity and incomprehensibility: the disjuncture that the knowing and not knowing creates. This resonance, this affective quality, is all around us. We are assailed by it habitually. In our daily life used and worn garments may demand that we recollect or confront the unknown. This is not to suggest that art objects and dirty shoes are analogous (the intentionality of an artwork either through its creation or their positioning, is, after all, central while the shoe is made unique in the unthinking practice of everyday life) but instead that the affects of patterns and process might be helpful in reading the affects of things we wear.

Skilled bodies

Though Gell writes of art objects, he acknowledges that 'enchantment is immanent in all kinds of technical activity' (ibid.: 44), and thus this enchantment is present in the technologies and techniques of the body (one need only think of the affects of viewing dance to know this is true). The practice of everyday life is the mastery of these 'techniques of the body': learning to walk, move and interact in a socialized manner. Though techniques are acquired in the transmission of tradition, they become individuated; our movements are both cultural and personal, our gestures only ever our own. Thus, our movements are a form of skilled work, a bringing together of social and bodily knowledge in the performance of the everyday. The worn garment is made unique through the techniques of the body, the individual's assimilation and interpretation of bodily cultural practices. The traces of the skilled practice of movement are obfuscating in a manner which is akin to Gell's technology of enchantment. The particularities of an unknown wearer's movements are unknowable to the

Opposite
Figure 8.9 Cloth 36, *2015. Ellen Sampson.*

viewer: the viewer may understand someone has walked in these shoes, but quite how and where is lost to them. The outputs of this 'skilled work', of our gestures, are the marks of wear upon our clothes. Wearing transforms the garment from mass-produced to unique; in the processes of wearing, the garment becomes original. In the performance of dressing and the practice of everyday life, we are marking and altering our clothes.

Just as the line of a pen or paintbrush is fundamentally gestural, informed by the techniques of the body, the marks upon our clothes are the output of our gestures. Lines are the outcome of gesture. Walking creates lines in two ways: in the line of the body (as Mauss suggested) and in the tracks that are left by our feet, the cartographies of our lives. These lines, our tracks and traces, present an opportunity for retrospective abduction, the retracing of steps. Retracing steps, following a line back to its origin, is the root of many kinds of historical practice: an attempt through recapturing movements (of peoples, objects, land masses or armies) to understand what came to be. Lines of enquiry are just that, after all: steps forward into the unknown or diligent retracings of the past.[7] Lines are the result of movement and, as such, are always a form of record.

Marks and lines are the records of our everyday experience: so that worn and used clothes are maps of experience. However, for the viewer the desire to retrace a line back to its origin, to understand the movements that are made manifest in the object, cannot always be realized. Though one may address one's own clothes with a knowledge of how some (if not all) of the marks were made, or even recognize the gestures of a friend or relative in the creases of a jacket sleeve or the wear of a lapel, the movements of strangers are, for the most part, lost to us. Wearing clothes is a form of mark making, a language we cannot necessarily decode.

Cognitive stickiness

For Gell, the artwork's 'indecipherability' (1998: 71) was at the root of its affective qualities, its captivism. Gell terms these incomprehensible artefacts 'mind traps' (Gell 1998: 80), stating that the impossibility of reconstructing the movements which produced them makes them 'cognitively sticky'. They 'use formal complexity and technical virtuosity to create "a certain cognitive indecipherability" (Gell 1998, p.95) which may tantalize and frustrate the viewer in trying to recognize wholes and parts, continuity and discontinuity, synchrony and succession' (Hoskins 2006: 78). The viewer is captivated not simply by the magnitude of the skill, but also by their inability to retrospectively abduct from them:

> We cannot retrace fully the process whereby the design came into the world, by the agency of this woman, because we cannot reconstruct her skilled movements (and the intentions guiding them) from the design which has resulted from them. I attribute the cognitive stickiness of patterns to this blockage in the cognitive process of reconstructing the intentionality embodied in artefacts.
>
> (Gell 1998: 86)

This obfuscating nature of pattern and marks is useful when exploring the affective power of used clothing. The patterns of wear, cartographies of gesture and experience, present an unreadable map of the past. The marks of wear are both the result of skilled work (the techniques of the body) and a form of pattern. The person and the garment become intermingled so that the garment remains a distributed aspect of the person, even when no longer worn. The records of this intermingling remain on the garment as creases, stains, abrasions and tears. These cartographies of gesture are the root of the affective experience of viewing the worn and used – markings, which act upon us not as symbols, but as distributed personhoods, people and things entwined.

The affect of the worn garment is located in this unknowing; the experience of the artefact we are unable to 'read'. The used garment is simultaneously recognizable and unrecognizable; one may accurately place it within our network of things and yet the gestures which have marked it cannot be recollected or regained. There is, I think, a difference between the affect and nostalgia of the worn and used. Nostalgia is rooted in knowing, in being able to locate an artefact both within our network of things and narrative: to know or imagine where it came from: to be able to abduct a narrative from it. Nostalgia takes one on a journey back to a real or imagined past – a retracing of steps. Nostalgia allows, however briefly, a return. This return is reliant upon two things: the presence of a pathway, and knowledge of where one must go; there must be both a route into the memory (the artefact as trigger), and a guide through it. Our memories, the stories that we tell ourselves, are the maps we use to navigate the nostalgic journey. This navigability relies upon a narrative. Our own worn clothes often, though not always, present us with this experience – a chance through reminiscences to retrace our steps. Though nostalgia is frequently presented as a positive or at least wistful longing, the experience of one's own garments is not always comfortable. The recollections one may abduct from the worn object may not be pleasant, and the garment imbued with our past bodily selves may be a trigger of shame.

The experience of the unknown garment is quite other to this. Though the artefact itself may be the same, what one abducts from it is not so much akin to a retracing of steps but rather to being lost. Rather than offering a pathway to the past, it highlights places that you may never go. Though the trigger is present (in the garment's material form), there is no path to follow. Instead, the viewer experiences the worn garment as a dead end, an experience unbounded by words. This affect is a blockage, a path that, however apparent, however visible, may not be followed. As discussed in the previous chapter the marks of use may make explicit how a garment was worn and used, but for the unfamiliar viewer it is difficult to translate those mark into a narrative. Excluded from a verbally mediated experience, the garment and the viewer meet in a visceral and bodily manner. If known objects engage the viewer by asking them a question which they may answer, the affect of the unknown is a question to which there is no response. If nostalgia is a route into the past, then the affect of a used garment is a door slammed shut.

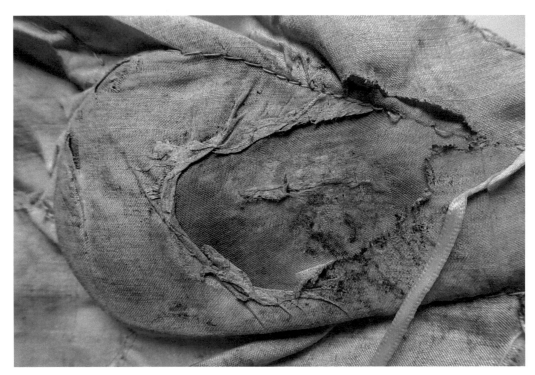

Figure 8.10 Cloth 39, *2015. Ellen Sampson.*

Knowing and unknowing: Dissonance and the affective power of the worn

> I continue to take photographs of scars. I cannot stop because they are so much like a photograph. More than like, they have almost the same quality as a photograph. They are visible events in the past and recorded days. Both the scars and the photographs are the manifestation of sorrow for the many things that can never be retrieved and love for a life that is a remembered present.
>
> (Ishiuchi Miyako, quoted in Gibbons 2009: 41)

There is a dissonance between the experience of knowing what (the capacity to comprehend and locate a garment within our network of things) and knowing how (the ability to abduct a specific narrative from it). The affect of the worn garment lies in the space between these two forms of knowledge, the gap of the unknown. One may recognize a used garment and yet never fully comprehend the gestures, movements and encounters it embodies. The intermingling that occurs through wear alters the shoe, so that parts of the wearer remain within it. Central to this research has been the concept of intermingling, that person and artefact become entwined and intermixed through touch and use. Clothes and their wearers are always in the process of cleaving, joining

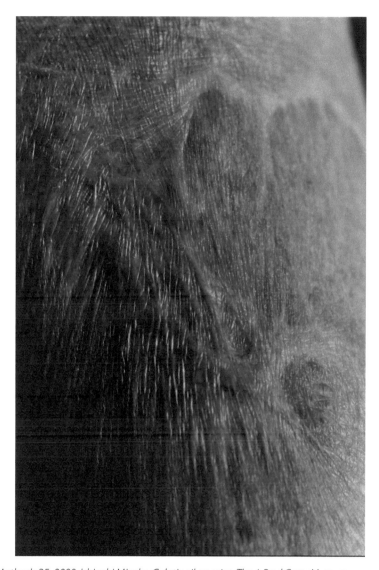

Figure 8.11 Mother's 25, *2000. Ishiuchi Miyako. Gelatin silver print. The J. Paul Getty Museum.*

together and splitting apart. These objects become layerings of agencies, both material and human. The bounding of the self is complex; wear and touch induce attachment, but also blur the edges of what is and is not us. This ambiguity is present in all habitual and bodily objects, an ambiguity as to where user and used begin and end. Gibbons, writing of the work of photographer Ishiuchi Miyako, describes the artefacts in her photographs as 'objects that might be seen as contiguous with and carriers of traces of her mother's body [...] clothes, underwear, shoes, hairbrush (still with hairs), used lipsticks etc.' (2009: 39). This entanglement (a word resonant with our complex encounters with clothing) is both material and psychic. As the garment and body meet, the garment is incorporated into the wearer's psychic and emotional self, and simultaneously the wearer's experiences are embedded in its material form – meeting and transferring matter through touch and wear. So that there is not just one instance of intermingling but many; each time the garment and the body meet the self and the garment mix.

Attachment is both cumulative and tactile, a process of touch and of repetition. Through these incorporations, the garment becomes part of the wearer (or maker) and the wearer (or maker) becomes part of the garment. These agencies remain even when they are separated; the self is distributed through its presence in these worn and habitual things. These distributed parts of the self remain within the garment even away from the body so that they may act upon the viewer or next user. So that the worn garment has the power (a power invested through use rather than manufacture, design or cultural signification) to act as an emissary of the absent body: to act for the absent body in different and distant locations.

This book has argued that the particular affective power of the worn garment, and in particular the worn shoe, is located in its ability to make present an absent body, not as a coherent narrative but as a trace. These traces, the marks of use and wear, are the manifestations of our intermingling with the things we wear – traces embody experience. This research suggests that the marks of wear upon our shoes, the scuffs and creases, the smoothing of soles and stretching of toes, are cartographies of our lives: maps of gestures and affordances. These maps of gestures, the temporary and unrepeatable made material, produce a 'cognitive stickiness' for the viewer; they work as 'mind traps' in a similar way to the art object. The marks of wear upon the worn shoe, traces of the agencies with which it is intermingled, form patterns which are obfuscating for the viewer. The viewer may comprehend the processes through which these marks were made, but is unable to know where the shoes have walked or what tasks they have performed. Thus these marks take on an obfuscating, pattern-like quality – engaging, yet impossible to decode.

Wearing Diary 9

At times this project was a painful one. To make objects with care that I knew later I would destroy. To feel an object once beautiful tipping over the edge from cleanliness to abjection. Feeling the weight of my body obliterate the fruits of my labour.

This research made me more conscious of my body. Of the weight of it, its capacity to crush or break my shoes. It made me acutely aware of the ways I walk, the rhythm of my steps, my right-handed and thus left-footedness. The shoes made to be symmetrical did not wear evenly; they are records of the asymmetry of my body postures and movements.

As I broke my shoes I felt loss, the sorrow of my creations destroyed. Simultaneously I was glad; the shoes which had caused me blisters and cuts were no more, my work with them was done.

(Wearing Diary, December 2015)

Afterword

I ask you to pause and look down at what you are wearing, to inspect the reality of your clothes. Look closely at the creases in the sleeves of your shirt where you have sat hunched and typing; the scuff on your shoe where you kicked your heels as you waited for the bus; the stain where you ate your breakfast too quickly or leant to hug your sticky-handed child. You are dressed in the things you have done today and the things you have done before. You are enveloped in material memories.

This book starts from the position that imperfect garments are prevalent and ubiquitous, not an exception but the norm. The majority of clothes are neither new in shops or pristine examples in museums: neither are they damaged beyond repair – the majority of our clothes remain in the liminal state that is wornness. So that this in-between state is the condition of most of our clothes. Garments are rarely in stasis (a word used so eloquently by Museum of London curator, Beatrice Belhen (2018) to describe garments in archives) but instead in a continuous state of change – as we wear, launder and store them they are transformed. Thus the garment is always in the process of becoming, located somewhere between the lost and the new. In the reciprocal tactile encounter which is wearing, the body is continuously if minutely altering the garment so that, with each wear, launder or repair, it is gradually remade. The worn garment, caught in an iterative cycle of change, is not static, but instead mutable and bodily. The things we wear are active agents, mediate both internal and external experience and in turn alter through use.

This research set out through practice and writing to examine our attachment to shoes, to presence the often unspoken relationships we have with the things we wear in images, objects and words. Through the process of making and writing, the paired practices of research *into* and research *through* wearing, new questions arose: how is the self constituted through material culture, what are the relationships between making and wearing clothes and how is memory embodied in the objects we wear? However, the central question of this research has been: what is the value and impact of the worn and used? It suggests that, through wear, both the handmade and the mass-produced (the anonymized commodity, so often separate from its maker in our culture) become powerful. This power is the result of an intermingling between wearer and worn: the shoe (or garment) as an indexical record of the wearer's gestures, of the performance of a life. The patterns of our lives are manifest in the wornness of our clothes.

This book suggests that the power of a worn garment is its capacity to embody experience; the tactile and social encounters of the body in the world. Our clothes more directly than almost any other form of material culture embody histories that cannot or have not been put into words. The mass-produced is re-appropriated and made powerful through wear. As such, this book suggests a reinterpretation of wearing; much in the way that Barthes (1977) suggested a reinterpretation of reading in 'Death of the Author'. Wearers, as well as designers and makers, are the authors of their clothes. The wearer makes the garment unique not simply through dressing and styling but through the alteration of its material form: wear renders the mass-produced auratic.

Overleaf

Figure 9.1 *Black sandal – unworn. Polaroid 1, 2015. Ellen Sampson.*
Figure 9.2 *Black sandal – wear 1. Polaroids 3 and 6, 2015. Ellen Sampson.*

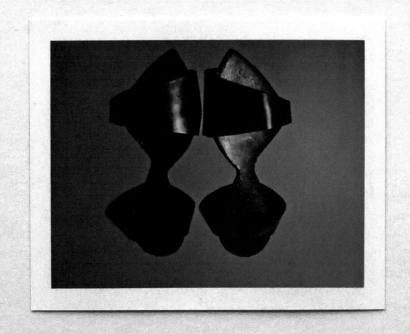

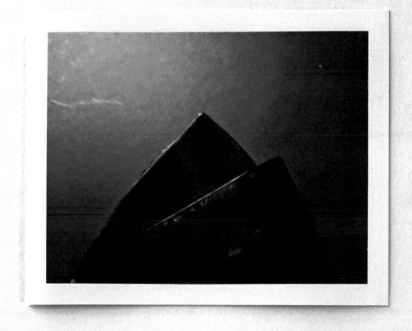

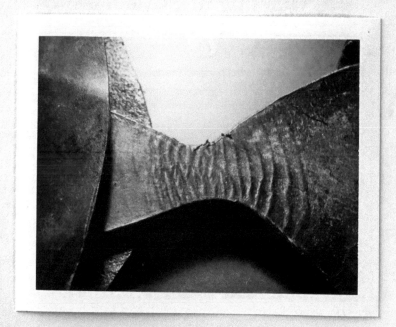

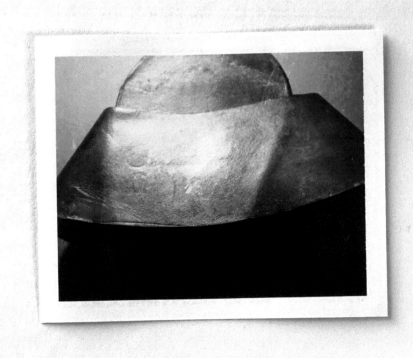

There were many potential approaches and methodologies to interrogate this research question and multiple ways the research could be presented. My choices were based on the belief that at times artefacts could speak more clearly than words – that in emphasizing the materiality of these often overlooked objects I could enhance and highlight their capacity to affect us deeply, and that this affect could generate new forms of knowing. My role as researcher was threefold: to create (through wearing and walking), record and interpret (through writing and image making) the marks of wear. By making shoes which functioned as art objects, by wearing them in performances and recording the marks of wear, I aimed to create an encounter for the viewer, to lead them towards the questions that I as a researcher had explored. In doing so and in bringing these worn and dirtied objects into the gallery space, I sought to examine and highlight their affects – their power as objects which embody experience. The artworks, as an embodiment of the knowledges that I have developed, are dependent upon this encounter, on the relationship between the viewer and the shoes (or the images of shoes) I have made and worn. So that making, wearing and recording became communicative tools just as writing and editing were. The text and the images in this book are thus intended to work as paired: as complementary but differing expressions of the same research process, answering the same questions but in different ways. I made work from the standpoint that there were (and are) aspects of our relationships to clothes which were not only unarticulated but in fact unarticulable – that aspects of this tactile and tacit experience could not readily be expressed through words.

As a maker, the decision to make objects that I would damage over time, and in some cases destroy, was complex. Though my shoes were made to alter through wear, at times I would panic as they became ugly or abject, unsure whether to carry on. The process often felt risky and uncomfortable and made me aware of how rarely makers see their products change over time. These risks, however, were rewarding; as the marks of my experience built up on the shoes, they were transformed into something new, not flawless or beautiful but bodily and strange. Similarly, wearing them was not always a comfortable or easy process; the shoes were not always what I would have chosen to wear. Putting on these shoes represented for me a shift, a change in role from artist to performer, to researcher, to being in the world. It was often during the performance of wearing that the ideas which underlie this thesis emerged, in walking and wandering, my feet and shoes touching, changing, becoming cleaved. In performing research these ideas were made. It was through wear and through the experience of my worn and dirty shoes that my ideas developed, were tested and explored. In making and wearing as research practice, I drew upon a phenomenological approach to material: culture – one that seeks to understand the relationship between bodies and things as sensory and subjective: as existing only in the context of our abilities to perceive them and locate them within our networks of things. This book has emphasized the ways that material culture exists outside the body but becomes part of it; that we as makers and users internalize these external things, so that over time they become integral parts of our selves.

Opposite

Figure 9.3 *Black sandal – wear 1. Polaroid 4, 2015. Ellen Sampson.*

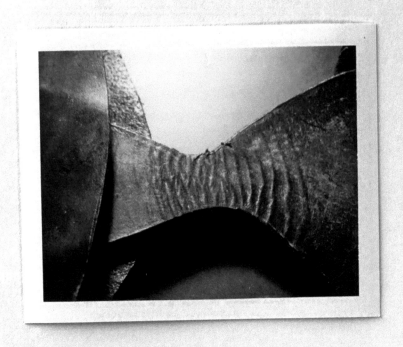

The product of this research is two distinct manifestations of knowledge, which may complement each other but are nonetheless different. The words do not attempt to describe the meanings embodied in the artefacts and images, or record the experiences that made them through wear and nor do the artefacts and images illustrate the words. It is my hope that the artworks, imprinted and bodily, speak for themselves as auto-ethnographic objects, objects which aim to induce an affect for the viewer. The encounter with artefacts, with images and with text is always different for the viewer/reader; textual and material meanings may never move seamlessly into one another. While the writing and material outputs relate to each other as closely as they can, they are not, and cannot be, the same thing. They are instead like two parallel lines, close but never meeting. They are akin to the childhood mirror game, a game in which both players try to mimic each other precisely, each new gesture demanding the other reconfigure themselves to match. In the mirror game, there is always a dissonance, a delay between seeing and responding. There will always be disjunctures and dissonances, things which in one form or another cannot be said. It is in these dissonances, the spaces between writing and making, between what can be seen and what can be said, that I hope new knowledge will unfurl.

This book started with a new pair of shoes, everyday yet over-determined objects. It explored ways that shoes are understood as cultural artefacts – as bearers of symbolic meaning, cultural capital and markers of absence and loss. In turn it addressed the tactile and bodily experience of wearing: the embodied experience of wear and the intimate and at times ambivalent relationships we have with the things we place closest to our bodily selves. It presents the dressed body as a body in motion – a body which is constantly meeting and being affected by other agencies, so that clothing is a mediating surface between the self and the world. It explored the process of cleaving, the way that through the tactile encounters of making and wearing garments become an aspect of the self: a part that can be distributed beyond the boundaries of the body: a self which remains entangled in the things we wear. It explored the outcomes of that intermingling, the marks of use: creases, crumples and stains. Presenting them not only as symbols of an absent body but as parts of it, materially as well as psychically entangled. The final chapters address the affects of this entanglement, the ways that a used garment acts upon us when the wearer is gone from it.

Opposite
Figure 9.4 *Black sandal – wear 1. Polaroid 6, 2015. Ellen Sampson.*

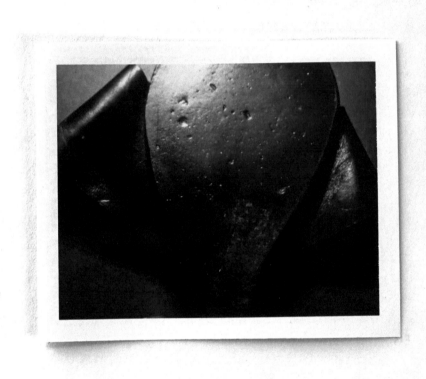

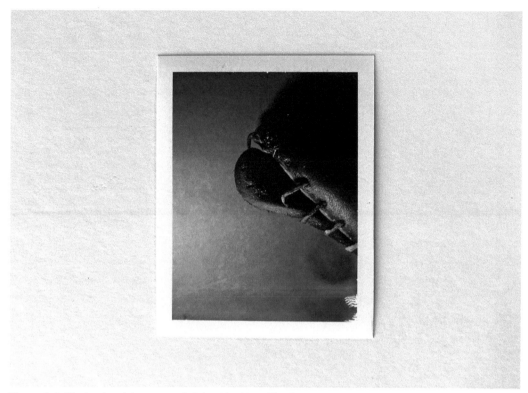

Figure 9.6 *Black pointed shoe – wear 2. Polaroid 5, 2015. Ellen Sampson.*

This book has taken a journey though both our collective and my individual relationship with the things we wear: mixing personal and cultural; practice and theory. It has sought to approach wearing, and the outcomes of wear, not from a historical or sociological position but instead from a phenomenological and psychoanalytic one: to examine the experience of things, their sensory and emotional affects. In doing so, it perhaps moved outside the realm of traditional fashion scholarship towards a more embodied approach to dress research which encompasses multiple practices and processes: auto-ethnography, performance and the practices of writing, image and object making. In creating this work, the paired writings and images, I sought to highlight these relationships as intimate and important, and in so doing to suggest a reframing of our relationships to clothes as lived, tactile and bodily, as a relationship which often sits outside or beyond the fashion system. It suggests that there is merit in a broader phenomenology of dress, of approaching our garments as experiences rather than things. Equally, that using a psychoanalytic approach to the interrogation of the material culture of dress might help us to understand dressing as a psychic as well as a bodily encounter: the ways that garments impact upon and reside within both our internal

Opposite

Figure 9.5 *Black sandal – wear 1. Polaroid 5, 2015. Ellen Sampson.*

and external worlds. In consequence, this research does not present a single unified understanding of our attachment to footwear or of the affect of the worn. Instead, it invites us to look closely at those things we wear, to acknowledge the complexity of our relationships with them and their capacity to affect us deeply. This research set out to highlight the qualities of the worn and the process of wearing; to start a dialogue, which positions the worn as an important category in our understanding of the things we wear. That garments are not finished when they are first constructed but, through use, are in a constant state of becoming. They are 'made' with each and every wear. It highlights the importance and the power of these garments within our networks of things, seeking to act as a counterpoint to the dominant discourse that focuses upon the value of the garment as a signifier. In a culture where the maintenance and care of clothes have been largely superseded by fast-fashion and the disposable garment, this research asks the viewer to engage with the worn, and, through this privileging of the worn, it presents a different perspective on our relationship with garments.[1] It raises the potential for the worn and used to act as disruptive objects; as counterpoints to commodity culture. It suggests that these artefacts might become subversive, the explicitness of wear allowing them to act as a voice outside of the prevalent fetishization of the new. Like any piece of research, this is the start of a conversation – a conversation which asks to be continued and developed – to paraphrase Bloch: a conversation as 'a curve', that asks to be 'extended into the future' (Bloch 1946: 118).

Opposite
Figure 9.7 *Black pointed shoe – wear 2. Polaroids 8 and 9, 2015. Ellen Sampson.*

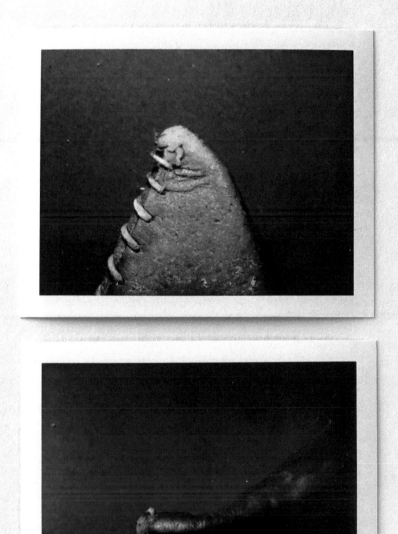

Notes

Introduction

1 There is an unacknowledged violence in wearing which, I think, unsettles us; in wearing, we destroy our clothes.

2 This shift, from the subjectivity of desire to the subjectivity of experience, is one which, I suggest, makes a considerable difference to the understanding of the things we wear.

3 See Miller 2005; Ingold 2013; Connor 2011; Hodder 2012; and Sennett 2008.

4 The art nexus was for Gell (1998) a means of mapping the ways that artworks act upon us (their affect or aura) and the agencies which those artworks embodied. Taking the viewer as the 'patient' upon which the artwork's agency is enacted, Gell maps the relationships between the different agents and agencies that went into the artefact's production.

5 Fetish shoes (Steele & Hill 2013), hip-hop trainers (Heard 2008; Turner 2019) and fairy-tale shoes (Davidson 2006, 2015; Sampson 2016) have all been examined for their symbolic function and cultural capital.

6 Clearly not all garments enfold the body; a garment that is too tight, too loose or cut wrongly for the body upon which it is placed will constantly remind (and discipline) the wearer. Though traditionally undergarments have served as disciplining garments (bras, girdles, corsets and the like), stiff materials like denim may have a similar effect. Eco, in the essay 'Lumbar Thought', writes of the bodily experience of being gripped by his jeans:

> As a result, I lived in the knowledge that I had jeans on, whereas normally we live forgetting that we're wearing undershorts or trousers. I lived for my jeans, and as a result I assumed the exterior behaviour of one who wears jeans. In any case, I assumed a demeanour. It's strange that the traditionally most informal and anti-etiquette garment should be the one that so strongly imposes an etiquette. As a rule I am boisterous, I sprawl in a chair, I slump wherever I please, with no claim to elegance: my blue jeans checked these actions, made me more polite and mature. I discussed it at length, especially with consultants, of the opposite sex, from whom I learned what, for that matter, I had already suspected: that for women experiences of this kind are familiar because all their garments are conceived to impose a demeanour – high heels, girdles, brassieres, pantyhose, tight sweaters. (Eco 1986: 192)

7 Over the course of this research, image making emerged as an integral aspect of my research practice. Initially the images were documentary, their aim being to record or highlight aspects of wear. The intimate and enlarged images serve to highlight the marks of wear in a manner that was affective: taking photographs as a means of looking closely. The image making became a process of uncovering the intimate and hidden parts of the shoe, making these spaces unavoidably present.

8 An earlier version of this chapter was published in *International Journal of Fashion Studies*, see Sampson 2018a.

9 An earlier version of this chapter was published in *Fashion Theory*, see Sampson 2017b.

10 Aspects of this chapter were published as Sampson 2017b.

Chapter 1

1 Within this research these wearing diaries functioned as field notes and often embodied that tri-part approach which this work took: making, wearing and writing as iterative and circular practices, each informing and building on the next.

2 For Ellis and Bochner (2000) auto-ethnography is successful when it provides affective experience for the reader/viewer. Similarly, for Richardson successful auto-ethnography must be 'substantive, aesthetic, reflexive, impactful and expressive' (1994: 527).

3 It could be said that 'The Gift' (Mauss [1928] 1954) and 'gift theory' underlies much material culture research into, for example, *Cloth and Human Experience* (Weiner and Schneider 1989).

Chapter 2

1 So embedded is the shoe as a symbol of desire and success in popular women's fiction ('chick lit') that a guide to becoming a successful author in the genre is called *Will Write for Shoes: How to Write a Chick Lit Novel* (Yardley 2007). Shoe symbolism has become a particular trope in women's fiction and a plethora of books use the shoe in their titles: *The Other Woman's Shoes* (Parks 2012), *Her Sister's Shoes* (Farley 2015), *If the Shoes Fit* (Lawless 2010), to name but a few.

2 'Limo shoes' are so called because the wearer must be driven from kerb to kerb in order to avoid walking in them (for example).

3 In fiction, Carrie Bradshaw, the lead character in HBO's *Sex and the City* (HBO 1998), is presented as having accidentally spent $40,000 on shoes rather than saving to buy herself an apartment (Sex and the City, 1998, episode 64).

4 Not all scholars view the self-indulgence as a negative. Gamman (2001) writes that women's shoe-shopping may be seen as a form of narcissistic pleasure and embracing of commodity fetishism, presenting this experience both as a site of self-involvement and as rebellion against and freedom from the self-sacrificing domestic and corporate spheres to which women are tied.

5 See Olivier (2012). 'Imelda Marcos' famous collection of 3,000 shoes partly destroyed by termites and floods after lying in storage in the Philippines for 26 years since she was exiled'. *The Daily Mail*. [Online] 23 September. Available from: www.dailymail.co.uk/news/article-2207353/Imelda-Marcos-legendary-3-000-plus-shoe-collection-destroyed-termites-floods-neglect.html. [Accessed: 30 August 2013].

6 Perhaps the most marked intersection between status and footwear is discussed by Ko (2008) in her book *Cinderella's Sisters*. Ko examines the history of Chinese foot-binding and lotus shoes in relation to status and embodied experience. Stating that there was not one but multiple foot-binding cultures in China which evolved and changed over centuries, Ko examines foot binding as an embodied practice, which made manifest both male and female desires. Ko examines foot binding as a form of skilled women's work that was highly valued and technically complex. The intersections between this skill and the status afforded to small and neatly bound feet created a complex hierarchy of desire, hegemony, class, empowerment and bodily experience, one which requires a nuanced interpretation.

7 See Serres (2008) for a more detailed discussion of the possible mistranslation from fur to glass. On this subject, Hill states: 'While many elements of fairy tales require a strong suspension of disbelief, the glass slipper has sparked a special debate among fairy tale historians and enthusiasts. One frequently repeated theory is that Perrault erred in his transcription of the oral tale, writing verre (glass) rather than vair (variegated fur). Others believe that the word was simply mistranslated from French into English' (2016: 46).

8 In this film it is the character Vicky Price's professional and romantic ambitions which lead to her demise, the uncontrolled and uncontrollable desire both triggered and symbolized by the red shoes. Similarly, Dorothy's 'ruby slippers' in *The Wizard of Oz* (Fleming & Langley 1939) become a literal agent of life and death.

9 Freud's writing on shoes in dreams is not the only psychoanalytic interpretation of footwear. Abraham examines shoes as a fetish object. For Abraham (1910), the shoe was a site of great conflict and desire. In his 1910 paper on shoe and corset fetishism Abraham describes how, through the process of binding the shoe to the foot, its slimness, delicacy and restraint become qualities of desire for the patient. Here, rather than the shoe being simply a sexual symbol, the act of putting the shoe on the foot becomes sexualized.

10 Similarly, Thomas's (1999) interpretation of 'The Worn-Out Dancing Shoes' views the princess's trips to the underground world each night as a metaphor for the awakening of the adolescent princess's desire.

11 The ESRC-funded project by Hockey et al. (2013) 'If The Shoe Fits: Footwear, Identity and Transition' at Sheffield University looked at the symbolic meanings afforded to shoe shopping. In particular they examined how buying shoes and keeping them when they are not worn might be linked to the maintenance of past or fantasy identities. A summary of the research can be read at www.socresonline.org.uk/18/1/20.html.

12 This is also true of our hands and their adornments such as nail polish, gloves or jewellery.

13 Fashion is predominately a gaze-based medium; it is a practice of looking and of being seen. It is a process of looking (at other wearers or at fashion media), then mirroring and adapting what one has seen and then finally presenting oneself for the gaze.

14 For Freud (1917) narcissistic identification is an attempt to regain the lost object; this 'served to establish an identification of the ego with the abandoned object' (Freud 1917: 249).

15 Lyon (2001) addresses the ways in which the bare foot was conceptualized as healthier by footwear reformers, nudists and dancers. She links the fetishization of the bare foot to Modernism's simultaneous fixation with ideas of both progress and of the primitive.

16 The phrase 'barefoot and pregnant' alludes to a woman deprived of social and financial agency, either through the stigma of being an unmarried mother or as a result of subjugation by her husband.

17 *The Soldier's Foot And The Military Shoe; A Handbook For Officers And Noncommissioned Officers Of The Line*, an American guide to shoe care for soldiers stipulates:

> It is highly important, in preventing foot injuries, that a good, well-fitting shoe, once secured, shall be kept in good condition. This can be accomplished with a little attention. The leather of shoes which are put away without use in dry weather tends to become hard and wrinkled. Shoes which are being kept for marching should therefore be worn now and then; and if not sufficiently supple, lightly rubbed over with the neatsfoot oil supplied by the Quartermaster's Department. (Munson 1912: n.p.)

18 Conversely, for the upper classes, the need to keep up appearances was either delegated to others (butlers and valets wearing-in shoes, for example) or avoided entirely; the capacity to present as a little down at heel both belying and reaffirming social status. In embracing the patina of wear (see Charpy 2013), the upper classes were able to denote both their history (old families equal old things) and place themselves in opposition to the conspicuously consuming merchant classes (see Veblen 1899).

Chapter 3

1 Because of their necessity as everyday objects, in becoming impractical, shoes make excellent Veblen goods.

2 Cf. Steele & Hill 2013 for a discussion of the role of very high heels as fetish shoes.

3 This abjection was particularly present for me during the final year of my doctoral research. Making and wearing twenty-four pairs of shoes over the course of a year meant that my studio and house were often full of dirty and used shoes. Often, despite the fact that they were an aspect of my practice, I found the worn shoes shameful and rushed to tidy them away when visitors arrived.

4 Representations of worn shoes feature in discussions of race, class and status (Barthelemy 2001; Nahshon 2008; Jones 2012) and, notably in the case of Van Gogh's boot paintings, they have formed a strand of twentieth-century philosophical discussion. The Heidegger/Meyer Schapiro argument concerned Heidegger's interpretation of a van Gogh painting of a pair of empty boots in 'The Origin of the Work of Art' (1936). Of these boots Heidegger states:

> Truth happens in van Gogh's painting. This does not mean that something is rightly portrayed, but rather that in the revelation of the equipmental being of the shoes that which is as a whole world and earth in their counter-play – attains to un-concealment […]The more simply and essentially the shoes appear in their essence […] the more directly and fascinatingly does all that is attain to a greater degree of being. (1936: 680)

Meyer Schapiro counters this argument in his 1968 essay 'The Still Life as a Personal Object: A Note on Heidegger and Van Gogh' by stating that:

> They are not less objectively rendered for being seen as if endowed with his feelings and reverie about himself. In isolating his own old, worn shoes on a canvas, he turns them to the spectator; he makes of them a piece from a self-portrait, that part of the costume with which we tread the earth and in which we locate strains of movement, fatigue, pressure, heaviness – the burden of the erect body in its contact with the ground. They mark our inescapable position on the earth. To "be in someone's shoes" is to be in his predicament or his station in life. For an artist to isolate his worn shoes as the subject of a picture is for him to convey a concern with the fatalities of his social being. Not only the shoes as an instrument of use, though the landscape painter as a worker in the fields shares something of the peasant's life outdoors, but the shoes as "a portion of the self" (in Hamsun's words) are van Gogh's revealing theme. (1968: 140)

It is worth noting that this is really an argument about the nature of art, of representations and of being rather than a discussion of shoes themselves. Representations of footwear and shoes themselves should not be confused.

5 Bataille (1929) in 'The Big Toe' suggests that feet are considered 'base' in direct opposition to the 'elevated' upper body and head. That is to say, Bataille believed that a central aspect of the human condition is the struggle to elevate oneself out of the dirt. The foot, unable to do this, is therefore considered abject and unclean.

6 In an essay on spectacles, Steven Connor writes of the ways that 'Glasses are never simply used or worn; they are to use Jean-Paul Sartre's expression existed – both lived out and brought into active and magical existence' (2011: 89).

7 Even in the case of bespoke shoemaking, where lasts are made to the measurements of the client's foot, the last, and thus the shoe, cannot correspond precisely to the shape of the foot. The last is always a compromise between the desired style of the shoe and the form of the foot.

8 Kula exchange, by the Trobriand Islanders of Papua New Guinea, involves the exchange of jewellery, shells and other items between different families on the islands. Rather than exchange between two individuals, the debt is 'paid forward' so that the material artefacts and thus the obligations cross the sea. Of this process Malinowski asked: 'why would men risk life and limb to travel across huge expanses of dangerous ocean to give away what appear to be worthless trinkets?' (attributed to Malinowski 1922). For Mauss, exchange created a gift economy, one where social ties were sealed not through written contracts and financial exchanges, but through the obligation to repay a gift. Whether through direct exchanges, such as potlatch, or circular exchange such as Kula, each gift received requires reciprocation in an ongoing cycle: gifting begets gifting. Thus obligation creates or seals social ties; indebtedness produces attachment.

Chapter 4

1   The mistrust of the dressed body and its capacity to conceal the true nature of the wearer is a recurrent theme in post-Enlightenment writing. The idea of the 'natural human', so dominant in Enlightenment discourse, presents the naked body and the bare foot as simpler, healthier and more moral. The bare foot is often perceived as more liberated than the shod foot. The naked foot, like the shod one, is often fetishized.

2   For example McNeil (in McNeil & Karaminas 2009) explores how the extravagant dress of the macaronis was interpreted by the British press as indicative of moral and sexual ambiguity. He examines how the macaroni's artifice in dress and mannerisms was perceived as indicative of social climbing, profligacy and being of ambiguous origins; that in this case the flamboyant dressed body in fact revealed the true nature of the wearer rather than concealing it.

3   Walking exclusively on two feet is a uniquely human trait: that we are upright mammals defines us. Bataille in 'The Big Toe' writes of the big toe (non-opposable) as 'the most human part of the human body' (1929: 1), the most differentiated from other apes. He suggests that uprightness or verticality is the defining feature of being human; presenting the foot as an object of shame, the part of us closest to the ground from which we have been elevated.

4   Nowhere is the public nature of walking as evident as it is in the contrast between the mannequin and the flâneur. The cat-walker, the mannequin, walks only to be observed, their walk being designed to court the eye. Evans (2013) writes of the ways that the walks of models (the intersections of their bodily and social selves) were developed and reproduced in accordance with the fashions of the time, the posing of the body as a socially mediated construction. In contrast the flâneur, wandering the streets, highlights walking as an act of looking, of observing the multiple modes of city life. The flâneur may preen or pose, but his motive is to remain unobserved, a voyeur in the midst of a crowd. It is also worth highlighting the gendered natured of these forms of walking, women on display to the 'male gaze' and available, men hidden and looking.

5   Schmid writes of the differing perception of the same space in a way that could equally be extended to affect: 'Perception is a central concept of phenomenology. How does a subject perceive an image, a landscape, a monument? Evidently perception depends upon the subject: a peasant does not see "his" landscape in the same way as a city-dweller enjoying a walk there' (2008: 38).

6   Or indeed Merleau Ponty who states:

   The things of the world are not simply neutral objects that stand before us for our contemplation. Each one of them symbolizes or recalls a particular way of behaving, provoking in us reactions that are either favourable or unfavourable. This is why people's tastes, character, and the attitude they adopt to the world and to particular things can be deciphered from the objects with which they choose to surround themselves, their preferences for certain colours or the places where they like to go for walks. (Merleau-Ponty 2004: 63)

7   Of the mediating and transformative nature of footwear in fairy tales, Sampson writes:

   In fairy tales, as in the real world, clothing is often viewed as an agent of change; alter egos and true selves are mediated and produced through clothes. Shoes, with their ability to help or hinder movement and to elevate their wearers, are literal and metaphorical causes of transformation. In fairy tales, the acquisition of shoes is often linked to a shift in a wearer's status or morality; new shoes enable the production of a new self. (2016: 237)

Chapter 5

1   In 'Fashion and Anxiety' Clarke and Miller (2002) present an interesting discussion of the way clothes are understood and articulated as correct or appropriate.

2   Lemma (2010) suggests that one function of marking the skin's surface (through tattooing, scarification and self-harm) is to strengthen it, while also to allow oneself to break through to the unconscious below. The skin integrates inks and makes signs to society about our emotional self. The skin, a receptive surface, is altered as it protects our interior space. Similarly the garment, as a protective surface, both mediates our bodily experience and protects our bodies from harm.

3   Ingold (2013), Hodder (2012) and Miller (2005, 2008, 2010) explore the complex relationships between making and using. Similarly Sennett (2008) and Chapman (2005) look at how knowledge of material and materiality may inform the end product and the life cycle of an artefact. The relationship between wearers and garments is beautifully described in many publications, including De la Haye (2005), Stallybrass (1993) and Entwistle (2001), and the relationship between the maker and garment in Lee's (2015) exploration of seams and seamlessness.

4   In this research I am both the maker and the wearer of my shoes; doubly cleaved with them. Though making one's own clothing used to be very common (and is still the norm in some cultures), shoes, as garments which need to be highly durable and require particular and non-transferable making skills, are less frequently homemade. Though there have been certain instances of home shoemaking (a fashion in eighteenth-century Britain for middle-class women to make their own slippers (cf. McGuire 2014)) or home shoe repair as a necessity in times of poverty or war, shoes are usually acquired new or second-hand.

5   It could be said that *The Gift* (Mauss 1928) is the basis of most modern material culture studies and as such has informed a great deal of research on clothing and fashion.

6   In fact, often clothes are no longer wanted, a rejection which is at the heart of the fashion cycle. The reasons why they are no longer wanted, despite their material durability, are interesting. Like Winnicott's transitional object, the unwanted garment appears to 'lose its meaning' and become dispersed.

7   Layton defines the patient thus: 'People and things are only agents if there is a recipient (a "patient") for them to act upon. Patients enter into a social relationship with the index, the art object' (2003: 10).

8   The art nexus for Gell was a means of mapping the ways that artworks act upon us (their affect or aura), and the agencies which those artworks embodied. He examines the magical or auratic qualities that allow artworks to function. Taking the viewer as the 'patient' upon which the artwork's agency is enacted, Gell maps the relationships between the different agents and agencies that went into the artefact's production.

9   Layton writes of the term 'abduction': 'In order to avoid treating art as a medium of communication, Gell introduces the term abduction. "Art-like situations can be discriminated as those in which the material 'index' (the visible, physical, 'thing') permits a particular cognitive operation which I identify as the abduction of agency … Abductions are inferential schemes, and we infer the same type of agency in a real and a depicted person's smile" (Gell 1998: 13–15).' (Layton 2003: 15).

10 Sometimes making is not an actualization of an idea or fantasy but a giving into the agency of the materials one works with: letting the material agency, the body, the rhythm of process take over. Making like this may become a surprise; unexpected outcomes may lead the maker to somewhere quite other than their initial idea. Rosenberg writes about action painting and the 'chance' mark upon the canvas:

> With regard to the tensions it is capable of setting up in our bodies the medium of any art is an extension of the physical world; a stroke of pigment, for example, works within us in the same way as a bridge across the Hudson. For the unseen universe that inhabits us an accidental blot or splash of paint may thus assume an equivalence to the profoundest happening. (1952: 22)

11 It is often considered important that marks of making are not visible to the user, that the means of production is occluded through skill. Though contemporary craft may embrace and even fetishize the marks of making, smoothness and seamlessness are still highly valued. It is as though Gell's (1998) 'mind traps' are perceived as most effective when the means of production is not just complex but completely hidden from the viewer.

12 Though this research does not deal directly with second-hand clothing (particularly because shoes for a range of reasons, such as size specificity, difficulty in cleaning and modifying, are less likely to be traded and reused than other garments), it is worth noting that second-hand clothing is particularly interesting as a site of intermingling or cleaving. Second-hand garments often contain physical traces of their previous users, whether that is bodily trace, such as sweat stains or stretched elbows, or modifications of the garment's form, such as shortening a hem or letting out a seam. In these modifications, the new wearer is brought into direct bodily relationship with the traces of the previous wearer's agencies. One must either seek to overcome these interminglings (washing the garment or letting down the hem) or feel the previous user's agencies upon one's body in the form of slightly too short sleeves, or a perfume you would not yourself have chosen. In this vein DeLong et al. write that vintage clothes shopping 'is about fitting the body from clothing that fitted a person of another era […] reconfiguring the current body proportions with different foundational structures' (DeLong, Heinemann & Reiley 2005: 13).

Chapter 6

1 An absent presence so liminal in the case of the Turin Shroud that Didi-Huberman ends the essay questioning if the stain exists at all.

2 In my own practice the shoes are often constructed specifically in order to be destroyed through wear. They are then 'made' through the twin processes of construction and destruction; erasure as a form of making. In the practice of carefully constructing then wearing these fragile shoes, I linked these two modes of making. For Gell (1998) 'cognitive stickiness' is produced through 'the enchantment of technology', through the maker's virtuosity and intentionality. In contrast, the imprints left on worn shoes are unintentional, habitual, unavoidable traces. My role as the maker, wearer and researcher allowed me to connect these two contrasting processes and to highlight the ways that use may become a form of 'making': altering artefacts and rendering them unique.

3 In many ways my own practice is concerned with this duality, the simultaneous making resonant and erasure of the garment through wear. I make objects which are designed to be more receptive to the marks of wear than usual; they either break down more readily or show damage more clearly than an everyday shoe. There is something poignant for the artist about making artefacts that will inevitably be destroyed. Their material frailty and the inevitability of their loss cause you to attend to them more closely; each use both binds and separates you. This fragility is resonant of Boltanski's comments (see Chapter 2) on impermanent monuments which 'require a continuous engagement' (Boltanski, quoted in Solomon-Godeau 1998: 1).

Chapter 7

1 In an introduction to 'Between Memory and History: Les Lieux De Mémoire', Nora (1989) writes of memory 'places' and the intersection between the material, symbolic and functional in these sites. He states that all memory places are a confluence of these categories: real, imagined and archival.

It could be said that 'memory objects' function in a similar way: all memory objects mediate a space between the material and immaterial, the cultural and personal, and the real and the imaginary.

2 The passage is as follows: 'I raised to my lips a spoonful of the tea in which I had soaked a morsel of the cake. No sooner had the warm liquid mixed with the crumbs touched my palate than a shudder ran through me and I stopped, intent upon the extraordinary thing that was happening to me. An exquisite pleasure had invaded my senses, something isolated, detached, with no suggestion of its origin' (Proust 1913: 48).

3 In his work on unwanted memory and trauma, Van der Kolk writes: 'research into the nature of traumatic memories indicates that trauma interferes with declarative memory, i.e. conscious recall of experience, but does not inhibit implicit, or non-declarative memory, the memory system that controls conditioned emotional responses, skills and habits, and sensorimotor sensations related to experience' (Van der Kolk 1999: 258). Hence, though the recollection of a narrative may be inhibited, the experience is retained as sensorimotor sensations and emotion.

4 There is much written on the relationship between memory and truth, and though I do not want to stray too far into what constitutes true or real memory, it is worth acknowledging that artefacts and memory objects are one of the key places where the ambiguities of memory, history and truth come to intersect. Landsberg (2004) writing on 'Prosthetic Memory' suggests that broadcast media, and new media in particular, allows for the layering of and confusion between private and public memory. As artefacts often cross the boundaries between personal and cultural memory, multiple discourses come to reside in or surround these particular artefacts. What we 'should' or 'wish' to remember may become as closely affixed to the artefact as what we ourselves have experienced or learnt.

5 Diana's wedding dress became so symbolically loaded that it functioned more like a relic at a site of mass worship than a memory object. During the years after her death the dress toured in an exhibition, Diana: A Celebration. And it became a central part of what has since been referred to as the cult of Diana. Taking on an almost relic-like quality, the dress was housed in the old stable block of her family home of Althorp. The exhibition which remained at Althorp until 2013 was frequently referred to as a shrine. The wedding dress, already heavily loaded with the symbolism of a virgin bride, came to stand in for Diana's perceived innocence and the wrongs which had befallen her. It became a metonymic garment, representative of the qualities the dead princess was said to embody: 'What is also intriguing is what happens when a symbolic object dies. Diana, since entering the public stage in the early 1980s, had already been mythologized. The wedding with Charles was commonly referred to as a "fairytale wedding" of a Prince and Princess. Her public activities of a humanitarian nature since her divorce as well as the fashion impact she had throughout public life, had already become part of the Diana mythos. Yet with her death she was venerated almost instantaneously as something even greater – an irreproachable exemplar of the good, the true, and the beautiful: Our symbol has died, and thus we feel a need to transform this symbol into something even greater' (Tite 1998: 27).

Chapter 8

1 For Derrida, trace was the 'mark of the absence of a presence, an always-already absent present' (Spivak 1976: xv–11); trace is a lack. Though Derrida's use of the word 'trace' may have some commonalities with my own, his work is largely absent from this research. Derrida's trace is a linguistic or semiotic concept, one located in language; by contrast, my use of the word is grounded in the material, in matter and movement. Trace is, in the terminology of this research, the tangible or intangible aspect of a thing left behind when its source or origin is gone.

2   Just as the 'material turn' shifted our thinking towards the body, the environment and the sensory, the 'affective turn' demands a renewed focus upon experience beyond or outside language. In fashion, as in much of the humanities and social sciences, there has been an affective turn: a move towards studies of the things we wear and the images we make of them in the context of the affects they produce. Affect studies in fashion and dress research rely upon a phenomenological approach to the dressed body, as exemplified by the work of Lucia Ruggerone (2016).

3   In the work of psychiatrist Van der Kolk on the nature of traumatic memory, certain experiences are retained differently from 'normal' experiences. Thus 'the very nature of traumatic memory is to be stored initially as sensory fragments that have no linguistic components. They only came to develop a narrative of their trauma over time' (Van der Kolk 1999: 289) and 'research shows that in contrast to the way that people seem to process ordinary information, traumatic experiences are initially imprinted as sensations or feeling states, and are not collated or transcribed into personal narratives' (ibid.: 296). Events that produce high levels of affect create non-representational 'memories'. Similarly, LeDoux (1999) writes that affective experience engages very early our innate responses, responses which, though we may learn to control them, we cannot alter or rewrite.

4   Massumi's definition of the body does not exclude the mind, but instead views it as part of the whole.

5   So much so that in the act of looking the stain 'appears' on the shroud for the viewers. Didi-Huberman ends the article by implying that in fact there may be no such stain.

6   Shoes, in particular, are often used as talismans or magical objects. Swann writes: 'there is much recorded on other shoe superstitions, which are rife wherever shoes are traditionally worn. They are symbols of authority, as in the Old Testament. They are linked with fertility: we still tie them on the back of wedding cars. And they are generally associated with good luck (witness all the holiday souvenirs in the shape of shoes). But most of all they stand in for the person: it has been a common practice from at least the sixteenth century to at least 1966 to throw an old shoe after people "for luck"' (1996: 56).

7   Anthropologist Tim Ingold writes of his own research on lines: 'In doing so I have joined the ranks of draughtsmen, calligraphers, hand writers, storytellers, walkers, thinkers, observers – indeed of practically everyone who has ever lived. For people inhabit, in the first place a world that is made not of things but of lines. After all what is a thing, or indeed a person, if not a tying together of lines' (2007: 5).

Afterword

1   More broadly there is potential to widen this study beyond shoes and to look at our attachment to other garments and other forms of material culture in a similar way. In particular, garments which bear traces of our engagement with them, such as leather jackets, jeans and hats, but also those artefacts worn against the body for long periods of time like watches, wedding rings and glasses – garments which through tactile engagement and emotional attachment become simultaneously part of the self and other to it.

References

Abrego, S. (2018), 'Cone Mills Denim: An investigation into Fabrication, Tradition, and Quality', *Fashion Theory*, 22: 1–16.

Abraham, K. ([1910] 1988), 'Remarks on the Psychoanalysis of a Case of Foot and Corset Fetishism', in K. Abraham, *Selected Papers on Psychoanalysis*, London: Karnac Books.

Adamson, G. (2009), *The Craft Reader*, London: Berg.

Ahmed, S. (2006), *Queer Phenomenology: Orientations, Objects and Others*, Durham, NC: Duke University Press.

Ahmed, S. (2010), 'Happy Objects', in M. Gregg and G. J. Seigworth (eds), *The Affect Theory Reader*, 29–51, Durham, NC: Duke University Press.

Ahmed, S. and J. Stacey (2001), *Thinking Through the Skin*, London: Routledge.

Andersen, H. C. ([1845] 1997), 'The Red Shoes', in *The Complete Fairytales*, London: Wordsworth Editions.

Anzieu, D. (1989), *The Skin Ego*, trans. C. Turner, New Haven: Yale University Press.

Appadurai, A. (1988), *The Social Life of Things: Commodities in Cultural Perspective*, Cambridge: Cambridge University Press.

Armstrong, L. and F. McDowell (2018), *Fashioning Professionals: Identity and Representation at Work in the Creative Industries*, London: Bloomsbury.

Arnold, R. (2008), 'Movement and Modernity: New York Sportswear, Dance, and Exercise in the 1930s and 1940s', *Fashion Theory*, 12 (3).

Ash, J. (1996) 'Memory and Objects', in P. Kirkham (ed.), *The Gendered Object*, Manchester: Manchester University Press.

Bachelard, G. ([1964] 1992), *The Poetics of Space*, London: Beacon Press.

Baert, B. (2017), 'Stains. Trace – Cloth – Symptom', *Textile*, 15 (3): 270–91.

Barthelemy, A. (2001), 'Brogans', in S. Benstock and S. Ferriss (eds), *Footnotes on Shoes*, New Brunswick, NJ: Rutgers University Press.

Barthes, R. (1967), *The Fashion System*, New York: Hill & Wang.

Barthes, R. (1977), 'Death of the Author', in *Image-Music-Text*, New York: Hill & Wang.

Barthes, R. (1980), *Camera Lucida*, trans. R. Howard, New York: Hill & Wang.

Bataille, G. ([1929] 1985), 'The Big Toe', trans. A. Stoekl with C. Lovitt and D. Leslie, in G. Bataille, *Visions of Excess: Selected Writings, 1927–1939*, Minneapolis: University of Minnesota Press.

Benjamin, W. ([1936] 1968), 'The Work of Art in the Age of Mechanical Reproduction', in H. Arendt (ed.), *Illuminations: Selected Writings*, London: Fontana.

Benstock, S. and S. Ferriss, eds (2001), *Footnotes on Shoes*, New Brunswick, NJ: Rutgers University Press.

Benthien, C. (2002), *Skin – On the Cultural Borders between Self and the World*, New York: Columbia University Press.

Berger, J. (1972), *Ways of Seeing*, London: Penguin Modern Classics.

Bettelheim, B. (1976), *The Uses of Enchantment*, London: Penguin Books.

Bick, E. (1968), 'The Experience of Skin in Early Object Relations', *International Journal of Psychoanalysis*, 49: 484–6.

Bide, B. (2017), 'Signs of Wear: Encountering Memory in the Worn Materiality of a Museum Fashion Collection', *Fashion Theory*, 21: 449–76.

Bloch, M. ([1946] 1999), *Strange Defeat*, New York: Norton.

Bollas, C. (1979), 'The Transformational Object', *International Journal of Psychoanalysis*, 60 (1): 97–107.

Borges, J. (1962), *Ficcones*, New York: Grove Press.

Bourdieu, P. (1977), *Outline of a Theory of Practice*, Cambridge: Cambridge University Press.

Bourdieu, P. ([1977] 1987), *Distinction: A Social Critique of the Judgement of Taste*, trans. R. Nice, Cambridge, MA: Harvard University Press.

Bratu-Hansen, M. (2008), 'Benjamin's Aura', *Critical Enquiry*, 34 (2): 336–75.

Brazelton, T., B. Koslowski and M. Main (1974), 'The Origins of Reciprocity: The Early Mother-infant Interaction', in M. Lewis and L. Rosenblum (eds), *The Effect of the Infant on Its Caregiver*, New York: John Wiley & Sons.

Breward, C. (2006), 'Fashioning Masculinity: Men's Footwear and Modernity', in G. Riello and P. McNeil, *Shoes: A History from Sandals to Sneakers*, Oxford: Berg.

Buick, Nadia (2010), 'Framing Fashion Curation: A Theoretical, Historical and Practical Perspective', PhD thesis, Queensland University of Technology.

Callard, F. and C. Papoulias (2010), 'Affect and Embodiment', in S. Radstone and B. Schwarz (eds), *Memory: Histories, Theories, Debates*, 246–62, New York: Fordham University Press.

Campbell, V. (2015), 'Red Pashmina', in R. Gibson (ed.), *The Memory of Clothes*, Rotterdam: SensePublishers.

Candlin, F. (2000), 'Practice-based Doctorates and Questions of Academic Legitimacy', *Journal of Art & Design Education*, 19 (1): 96–101.

Carol-Jones (2001), 'Empty Shoes', in S. Benstock and S. Ferriss (eds), *Footnotes on Shoes*, New Brunswick, NJ: Rutgers University Press.

Carter, M. (2012), 'Stuff and Nonsense: The Limits of the Linguistic Model of Clothing', *Fashion Theory*, 16 (3): 343–53.

Certeau, M. de ([1980] 1984), *The Practice of Everyday Life*, Berkeley: University of California Press (original ed.: *L'invention du quotidien*, Paris: Union Générale d'Editions).

Chaiklin, M. (2006), 'Purity, Pollution and Place in Traditional Japanese Footwear', in G. Riello and P. McNeil (eds), *Shoes: A History from Sandals to Sneakers*, Oxford: Berg.

Chapman, J. (2005), *Emotionally Durable Design*, London: Routledge.

Charpy, M. (2013), 'Patina and Bourgeoisie: Appearances of the Past in Nineteenth-Century Paris', in G. Adamson and V. Kelley (eds), *Surface, Finish and the Meaning of Objects*, 45–59, Manchester: Manchester University Press.

Chauvet, E. (2009–13), *Zapatos Rojos*. Available online: https://zapatosrojosartepublico.wordpress.com/elina-chauvet/elina/ (accessed 2 October 2015).

Chong-Kwan, S. (2012), 'Drawing on Jules Prown's Material Culture Method of Object Analysis to Investigate Sensory Engagement with Everyday Dress', in R. Lifte (ed.), *Working Papers in Fashion Studies*, vol. 2, 1–6, London: London College of Fashion.

Chong-Kwan, S. (2017), 'Making Sense of Everyday Dress: Integrating Multi-sensory Experience within our Understanding of Contemporary Dress in UK', PhD thesis, London College of Fashion.

Clarke, A. and D. Miller (2002), 'Fashion and Anxiety', *Fashion Theory*, 6 (2): 191–214.

Clements, N. (2011), 'Revival: The Aesthetics of Revival Subcultures and Re-enactment Groups Explored Through Fashion Image-making', PhD thesis, Royal College of Art, London.

Connor, S. (2003), *The Book of Skin*, London: Reaktion.

Connor, S. (2011), *Paraphernalia: The Curious Lives of Magical Things*, London: Profile Books.

Crooke, E. (2012), 'The Material Culture of Conflict', in S. Dudley et al. (eds), *Narrating Objects, Collecting Stories: Essays in Honour of Professor Susan M. Pearce*, 25–35, London: Routledge.

Davidson, H. (2006), 'Sex and Sin: The Magic of Red Shoes', in G. Riello and P. McNeil, *Shoes: A History from Sandals to Sneakers*, Oxford: Berg.

Davidson, H. (2008), 'The Red Shoes [Bunhongsin]', in M. Uhlirova (ed.), *If Looks Could Kill: Cinema's Images of Fashion, Crime and Violence*, 143–51, London: Koenig Books.

Davidson, H. (2013), 'Grave Emotions: Textiles and Clothing from 19th Century London Cemeteries'. Available online: www.academia.edu/4888930/Grave_Emotions_Textiles_and_Clothing_from_19th_Century_London_Cemeteries (accessed 22 September 2015).

Davidson, H. (2015), 'Shoes as Magical Objects', in H. Persson (ed.), *Shoes: Pleasure and Pain*, London: V&A Publishing.

De Certeau, M. (1984), *The Practice of Everyday Life*, Berkeley: University of California Press.

De la Haye, A. (2006), "Vogue and the V&A Vitrine," *Fashion Theory*, 10 (1–2): 136.

De la Haye, A. (2018), 'Four Short Papers: Introduction by Amy de la Haye', *Fashion Theory*, 22 (4–5): 507–8.

De la Haye, A., L. Taylor and E. Thompson (2005), *A Family of Fashion: The Messel Dress Collection*, London: Philip Wilson Publishers.

Dean, S. E. (2012), 'Somatic Movement and Costume: A Practical, Investigative Project', *Journal of Dance & Somatic Practices*, 3 (1–2): 167–82.

Deleuze, G. and F. Guattari (1987), *A Thousand Plateaus: Capitalism and Schizophrenia*, trans. R. Massumi, London: Continuum.

DeLong, M., B. Heinemann and K. Reiley (2005), 'Hooked on Vintage!' *Fashion Theory*, 9 (1): 23–42.

DeMello, M. (2009), *Feet and Footwear: A Cultural Encyclopedia*, Santa Barbara, CA: Greenwood Press.

Didi-Huberman, G. (1984), 'The Index of the Absent Wound (Monograph on a Stain)', *October*, 29: 63–81.

Dilnot, C. (1993), 'The Gift', *Design Issues*, 9 (2): 51–63.

Dolphijn, R. and I. van der Tuin (eds) (2012), *New Materialism: Interviews & Cartographies*, Ann Arbor: Open Humanities Press.

Douglas, M. (1966), *Purity and Danger*, London: Routledge.

Du Maurier, D. ([1938] 2003), *Rebecca*, London: Virago.

Eco, U. (1986), 'Lumbar Thought', in *Travels in Hyperreality*, 191–5, London: Picador.

Ellis, C. and A. Bochner (2000), 'Autoethnography, Personal Narrative, Reflexivity: Research as Subject', in N. Denzin (ed.), *The Handbook of Qualitative Research*, 733–67, Beverly Hills, CA: Sage.

Entwistle, J. (2000), *The Fashioned Body: Fashion, Dress and Modern Social Theory*, Cambridge: Polity.

Entwistle, J. and E. Wilson, eds (2001), *Body Dressing*, Oxford: Berg.

Evans, C. (2001), 'The Enchanted Spectacle', *Fashion Theory*, 5: 271–310.

Evans, C. (2013), *The Mechanical Smile: Modernism and the First Fashion Shows in France and America, 1900–1929*, New Haven: Yale University Press.

Evans, C. (2014), 'Materiality, Memory and History: Adventures in the Archive', in C. Evans, A. O'Neill et al., *Isabella Blow: Fashion Galore!* New York: Rizzoli.

Farley, A. (2015), *Her Sister's Shoes*, AHF Publishing.

Feldman, J. (2006), 'Contact Points: Museums and the Lost Body Problem', in E. Edwards, C. Gosden and R. Phillips (eds), *Sensible Objects*, 245–68, Oxford: Berg.

Fenichel, O. ([1937] 1987), 'The Scopophilic Instinct and Identification', in *The Collected Papers of Otto Fenichel*, New York: Norton.

Forster, P. (2011), *Peirce and the Threat of Nominalism*, Cambridge: Cambridge University Press.

Forty, A. and S. Küchler (1999), *The Art of Forgetting*, Oxford: Berg.

Foucault, M. (1975), *Discipline and Punish: The Birth of the Prison*, London: Vintage Books.

Frayling, C. (1993), 'Research in Art & Design', *Royal College of Art Research Papers*, 1 (1): 1–5.

Freud, S. ([1900] 1991), 'The Interpretation of Dreams', in *Penguin Freud Library*, Vol. 4, London: Penguin Books.

Freud, S. ([1905] 1991), 'Three Essays on the Theory of Sexuality', in *Penguin Freud Library*, Vol. 7, London: Penguin Books.

Freud, S. ([1909] 1986), 'Analysis of a Phobia in a Five-Year-Old Boy', in *The Standard Edition of the Complete Psychological Works of Sigmund Freud*, Vol. 10, 1–150, London: Hogarth Press.

Freud, S. ([1910] 1986), 'On the Antithetical Meanings of Primal Words', in Five Lectures on Psycho-Analysis, Leonardo da Vinci and Other Works, in *The Standard Edition of the Complete Psychological Works of Sigmund Freud*, Vol. 11, London: Hogarth Press.

Freud, S. (1917), 'Mourning and Melancholia', in *The Standard Edition of the Complete Psychological Works of Sigmund Freud*, Vol. 14, 237–58, London: Hogarth Press.

Freud, S. ([1919] 2003), *The Uncanny*, London: Penguin Books.

Freud, S. ([1925] 1961), 'A Note upon the "Mystic Writing Pad"', in *The Standard Edition of the Complete Psychological Works of Sigmund Freud*, Vol. 19, 225–32, London: Hogarth Press.

Freud, S. ([1937] 1961), 'Constructions', in *The Standard Edition of the Complete Psychological Works of Sigmund Freud*, Vol. 23, 257–69, London: Hogarth Press.

Gamman, L. (2001), 'What's at Stake – Female Fetishism or Narcissism?' in S. Benstock and S. Ferriss (eds), *Footnotes on Shoes*, New Brunswick, NJ: Rutgers University Press.

Geisbusch, J. (2007), 'For Your Eyes Only? The Magic Touch of Relics', in E. Pye, *The Power of Touch: Handling Objects in Museum and Heritage Contexts*, Walnut Creek, CA: Left Coast Press.

Gell, A. (1998), *Art and Agency: An Anthropological Theory*, Oxford: Clarendon Press.

Gibbons, J. (2009), *Contemporary Art and Memory: Images of Recollection and Remembrance*, London: I. B. Tauris.

Gibeault, A. (2006), *Symbolization Process*. Available online: http://nosubject.com/Symbolization (accessed 16 June 2018).

Gibson, J. (1979), *The Ecological Approach to Visual Perception*, Boston, MA: Houghton Mifflin.

Goett, S. (2009), 'The Textile Self Re/collected: Materials, Metaphors, Memories, Methods and Making. Crossing Conceptual Boundaries', *PhD Annual Yearbook*, New Series 1: 78.

Goett, S. (2015), 'Materials, Memories and Metaphors', in J. Jefferies, D. Wood Conroy and H. Clark (eds), *The Handbook of Textile Culture*, London: Bloomsbury.

Goldsmith, S. (2018), 'Looking Beyond the Warp and Weft: Unpicking Latent Narratives in Clothing,' *Textile: Cloth and Culture* 16 (3): 320–32.

Granata, F. (2012), 'Fashion Studies In-between: A Methodological Case Study and an Inquiry into the State of Fashion Studies', *Fashion Theory*, 16 (1): 67–82.

Greg, M. and G. Seigworth (2010), *The Affect Theory Reader*, Durham, NC: Duke University Press.

Grew, F. and M. de Neergaard (1988), *Shoes and Pattens*, London: Museum of London.

Grimm Brothers ([1812a] 2014), 'Cinderella', in *The Original Folk Tales of the Brothers Grimm: The Complete First Edition*, Princeton: Princeton University Press.

Grimm Brothers ([1812b] 2014), 'Little Snow White', in *The Original Folk Tales of the Brothers Grimm: The Complete First Edition*, Princeton: Princeton University Press.

Grimm Brothers ([1812c] 2014), 'The Twelve Dancing Princesses', in *The Original Folk Tales of the Brothers Grimm: The Complete First Edition*, Princeton: Princeton University Press.

Gros, F. (2014), *A Philosophy of Walking*, London: Verso.

Harrod, T. (2015), *The Real Thing: Essays on Making in the Modern World*, London: Hyphen Press.

Hauser, K. (2004), 'A Garment in the Dock; or, How the FBI Illuminated the Prehistory of A Pair of Denim Jeans', *Journal of Material Culture*, 9 (3): 293–313.

Heard, N. (2008), *Sneakers*, London: Carlton Books.

Heidegger, M. ([1936] 2002), 'The Origin of the Work of Art', in *Off the Beaten Track*, trans. J. Young and K. Haynes, Cambridge: Cambridge University Press.

Heidegger, M. (1962), *Being and Time*, trans. John Macquarrie and Edward Robinson, New York: Harper & Row.

Heidegger, M. (1968), *What is a Thing?* trans. W. Barton and V. Deutsch, London: Gateway Editions.

Henare, A., M. Holbraad and S. Wastell, eds (2006), *Thinking Through Things: Theorising Artefacts Ethnographically*, London: Routledge.

Hicks, D. (2010), 'The Material-Cultural Turn', in D. Hicks and M. C. Beaudry (eds), *The Oxford Handbook of Material Culture Studies*, Oxford: Oxford University Press.

Hicks, D. and M. C. Beaudry (2010), 'Introduction. Material Culture Studies: A Reactionary View', in D. Hicks and M. C. Beaudry (eds), *The Oxford Handbook of Material Culture Studies*, Oxford: Oxford University Press.

Hill, K. (2012), 'Collecting and the Body in Late Victorian and Edwardian Museums', in K. Boehm, *Bodies and Things in Nineteenth-Century Literature and Culture*, London: Palgrave Macmillan.

Hill, S. (2016), *Fairy Tale Fashion*, New Haven: Yale University Press.

Hockey, J., V. Dilley, D. Robinson and A. Sherlock (2013), 'Worn Shoes: Identity, Memory and Footwear', *Sociological Research Online*, 18 (1): 20. Available online: www.socresonline.org.uk/18/1/20.html.

Hockey, J. et al. (2010–13), *If The Shoe Fits: Footwear, Identity and Transition*. Available online: www.Sheffield.av.uk/iftheshoefits (accessed 5 September 2015).

Hodder, I. (2012), *Entangled*, Chichester: Wiley Blackwell.

Hoskins, J. (2006), 'Agency, Biography and Objects', in C. Tilley et al. (eds), *Handbook of Material Culture*, London: Sage.

Hovey, J. (2001) 'Rebecca's Shoes: Lesbian Fetishism in Daphne Du Maurier's Rebecca,' in S. Benstock and S. Ferriss (eds), *Footnotes on Shoes*, New Brunswick, NJ: Rutgers University Press.

Hunt, C. (2014), 'Worn Clothes and Textiles as Archives of Memory', *Critical Studies in Fashion & Beauty*, 5 (2): 207–32.

Igoe, E. (2010), 'The Tacit-turn: Textile Design in Design Research', *Journal for Research in Textiles and Textile Design*, 1 (1): 1–11.

Ingold, T. (2007), *Lines: A Brief History*, Oxford: Routledge.

Ingold. T (2008), 'Bringing Things to Life: Creative Entanglements in a World of Materials'. Available online: www.reallifemethods.ac.uk/events/vitalsigns/programme/documents/vital-signs-ingold-bringing-things-to-life.pdf (accessed 6 March 2013).

Ingold, T. (2011b), *Being Alive*, London: Routledge.

Ingold, T. (2011a), 'Worlds of Sense and Sensing the World: A Response to Sarah Pink and David Howes', *Social Anthropology*, 19 (3): 313–17.

Ingold, T. (2013), *Making*, London: Routledge.

Ingold, T. (2014), 'That's Enough about Ethnography!', *Hau: Journal of Ethnographic Theory*, 4 (1): 383–95.

Jones, O. (2012), *Chavs: The Demonization of the Working Class*, London: Verso.

Kahn, N. (2012), 'Cutting the Fashion Body: Why the Fashion Image Is No Longer Still', *Fashion Theory*, 16 (2).

Kelley, V. (2015), 'Time, Wear and Maintenance: The Afterlife of Things', in A. Gerritsen and G. Riello (eds), *Writing Material Culture History*, London: Bloomsbury Academic.

Ko, D. (2008), *Cinderella's Sisters: A Revisionist History of Footbinding*, San Francisco: University of California Press.

Kristeva, J. (1982), *Powers of Horror*, New York: Columbia University Press.

Landsberg, A. (2004), *Prosthetic Memory: The Transformation of American Remembrance in the Age of Mass Culture*. New York: Columbia University Press.

Laplanche, J. (1998), *Essays on Otherness*, London: Routledge.

Latour, B. (2005), *Reassembling the Social*, Oxford: Oxford University Press.

Latour, B. ([2005] 2009), 'From Realpolitik to Dingpolitik or How to Make Things Public', in F. Candlin and R. Guins (eds), *The Object Reader*, 153–64, London: Routledge.

Latour, B. (2009), 'Where are the Missing Masses? The Sociology of a Few Mundane Artifacts', in F. Candlin and R. Guins (eds), *The Object Reader*, London: Routledge.

Lawless, P. (2010), *If the Shoes Fit*, Dublin: Poolbeg Press.

Layton, R. H. (2003), 'Art and Agency: A Reassessment', *Journal of the Royal Anthropological Institute*, 9 (3): 447–63.

LeDoux, J. (1999), *The Emotional Brain*, New York: Weidenfeld & Nicolson.

Lee, Y. (2016), *Seamlessness: Making and (Un)knowing in Fashion Practice*, London: Intellect.

Lefebvre, H. (1991), *The Critique of Everyday Life*, Vol. 1, trans. John Moore, London: Verso.

Lemma, A. (2010), *Under the Skin*, London: Routledge.

Leroi-Gourhan, A. (1993), *Gesture and Speech*, Cambridge, MA: MIT Press.

Luria, A. (1987), *The Mind of a Mnemonist*, Cambridge, MA: Harvard University Press.

Luvaas, B. (2016), 'Urban Field Notes: An Auto-ethnography of Street Styleblogging', in H. Jenss (ed.), *Fashion Studies: Research Methods, Sites, and Practices*, 83–100, London: Bloomsbury.

Lyon, J. (2001), 'The Modern Foot', in S. Benstock and S. Ferriss (eds), *Footnotes on Shoes*, New Brunswick, NJ: Rutgers University Press.

Macfarlane, R. (2012), *The Old Ways: A Journey on Foot*, London: Viking.

MacLeod, K. (2000), 'The Functions of the Written Text in Practice-based PhD Submissions', in *Working Papers in Art and Design*, 1, ISSN 1466–4917.

Malinowski, B. ([1922] 1984), *Argonauts of the Western Pacific*, London: Routledge.

Marchand, T. (2015), *Craftwork as Problem Solving: Ethnographic Studies of Design and Making*, London: Routledge.

Marks, L. (2000), The *Skin of the Film: Intercultural Cinema, Embodiment, and the Senses*, Durham: Duke University Press.

Mason, J. and Davies, K. (2009), 'Coming to our Senses? A Critical Approach to Sensory Methodology', *Qualitative Research*, 9 (5): 587–603.

Massumi, R. (1987), 'Introduction', in G. Deleuze and F. Guattari, *A Thousand Plateaus: Capitalism and Schizophrenia*, trans. R. Massumi, London: Continuum.

Matthews, S. (2005), 'The Materiality of Gesture: Intimacy, Emotion and Technique in the Archaeological Study of Bodily Communication', paper presented at 11th Annual Meeting of the European Association of Archaeologists, 5–11 September, Cork (Ireland). Available online: https://semioticon.com/virtuals/archaeology/materiality.pdf.

Matthews David, A. (2015), *Fashion Victims: The Dangers of Dress Past and Present*, London: Bloomsbury.

Mauss, M. ([1928] 1954), *The Gift: Forms and Functions of Exchange in Archaic Societies*, trans. I. Gunnison, New York: W. W. Norton.

Mauss, M. ([1935] 2006), 'Techniques of the Body', in *Techniques, Technology and Civilisation*, Oxford: Durkheim Press.

McGuire (2014), 'The Genteel Craft of Subversion: Amateur Female Shoemaking in the Late Eighteenth and Early Nineteenth Centuries', in A. Moran and S. O'Brien (eds), *Love Objects: Emotion, Design and Material Culture*, London: Bloomsbury.

McNeil, P. (2009), 'Macaroni Masculinities', in P. McNeil and V. Karaminas (eds), *The Men's Fashion Reader*, Oxford and New York: Berg.

McNeil, P. & G. Riello (2006), 'Walking the Streets of London and Paris: Shoes in the Enlightenment', in G. Riello and P. McNeil, *Shoes: A History from Sandals to Sneakers*, 94–115, Oxford: Berg.

Merleau-Ponty, M. (1962), *The Phenomenology of Perception*, London: Routledge.

Merleau-Ponty, M. (2004), *The World of Perception*, London: Routledge.

Metzl, J. and A. Kirkland (2010), *Against Health: How Health Became the New Morality*, New York: NYU Press.

Meyer, K. (2008), 'Rhythms, Streets, Cities', in K. Goonewardena, S. Kipfer, R. Milgrom and C. Schmid (eds), *Space, Difference, Everyday Life: Reading Henri Lefebvre*, London: Routledge.

Mida, I. (2016), *The Dress Detective*, London: Bloomsbury.

Miller, D., ed. (2005), *Materiality*, Durham, NC: Duke University Press.

Miller, D. (2008), *The Comfort of Things*, London: Polity Press.

Miller, D. (2010), *Stuff*, Cambridge: Polity Press.

Miller, D. and S. Woodward, eds (2010), *Global Denim*, London: Berg.

Morin, V. (1969), 'L'Objet Biographique', *Communications*, 13: 131–9.

Munson, E. L. (1912), *The Soldier's Foot and the Military Shoe; a Handbook for Officers and Noncommissioned Officers of the Line*. Available online: https://archive.org/details/soldiersfootmili00munsrich (accessed 20 September 2015).

Nahshon, E. (2008), *Jews and Shoes*, Oxford: Berg.

Nora, P. (1989), 'Between Memory and History: Les Lieux de Mémoire', *Representations*, 26: 7–24.

Olivier, A. (2012), 'Imelda Marcos' Famous Collection of 3,000 Shoes Partly Destroyed by Termites and Floods After Lying in Storage in the Philippines for 26 Years Since She was Exiled', *Daily Mail*, 23 September. Available online: www.dailymail.co.uk/news/article-2207353/Imelda-Marcos-legendary-3-000-plus-shoe-collection-destroyed-termites-floods-neglect.html (accessed 30 August 2013).

Parkins, I. (2008), 'Building a Feminist Theory of Fashion', *Australian Feminist Studies*, 23 (58): 501–15.

Parks, A. (2012), *The Other Woman's Shoes*, London: Penguin.

Perrault, C. ([1697] 1989), 'Cendrillon', in M. Sorano (ed.), *Charles Perrault, Contes*, Paris: Flammarion.

Petreca, B., N. Bianchi-Bertouze, S. Baurley, P. Watkins and D. Atkinson (2013), 'An Embodiment Perspective of Affective Touch Behaviour in Experiencing Digital Textiles', Proceedings of the 6th Biannual Humaine Association Conference on Affective Computing and Intelligent Interaction, Geneva, 2–5 September.

Pietz, W. (1985), 'The Problem of the Fetish, I', *RES: Anthropology and Aesthetics*, 9 (16).

Pink, S. (2005), *The Future of Visual Anthropology: Engaging the Senses*, London: Routledge.

Pink, S. (2015), *Doing Sensory Ethnography*, 2nd ed., London: Sage Publications.

Polanyi, M. (1967), *The Tacit Dimension*, New York: Anchor Books.

Prown, J. (1982), 'Mind in Matter: An Introduction to Material Culture Theory and Method', *Winterthur Portfolio*, 17 (1): 1–9.

Prown, J. (2002), *Art as Evidence: Writings on Art and Material Culture*, New Haven, CT: Yale University Press.

Pinney, C. (2005), 'Things Happen: or from Which Moment Does That Object Come?', in D. Miller (ed.) *Materiality*, London: Duke University Press.

Pollak, S. (2007), 'The Rolling Pin', in S. Turkle (ed.), *Evocative Objects: Things We Think With*, 224–31, Cambridge, MA: MIT Press.

Ponsonby, M. (2014), 'Textiles and Time: Conservation and Public Response', in V. Kelly and G. Adamson (eds), *Surface Tensions: Surface, Finish and the Meanings of Objects*, Manchester: Manchester University Press.

Proust, M. ([1913] 2003), *A la Recherche du Temps Perdu*, London: Penguin Classics.

Ratcliffe, M. (2018), 'Perception, Exploration, and the Primacy of Touch', in *Handbook on Enactive Cognition*, Oxford: Oxford University Press.

Rebecca (1940), [film] Dir. A. Hitchcock, USA: United Artists.

Richardson, L. (1994), 'Writing: A Method of Inquiry', in N. K. Denzin and Y. S. Lincoln (eds), *Handbook of Qualitative Research*, 516–29, Thousand Oaks, CA: Sage.

Riello, G. and P. McNeil (2006), *Shoes: A History from Sandals to Sneakers*, Oxford: Berg.

Rosenberg, H. (1952), 'The American Action Painters', *Art News*, 51 (8): 22.

Rossi-Camus, J. (2019*)*, 'Curating the Fashion Victim: Establishing Strategies for Exhibition Making Towards the Presentation of Fashion and Humour in Museums and Galleries', PhD thesis, London College of Fashion.

Rousseau, J. ([1763] 1979), *Emile, or On Education*, trans. A. Bloom, New York: Basic Books.

Ruggerone, L. (2016), 'The Feeling of Being Dressed: Affect Studies and the Clothed Body', *Fashion Theory*, 21 (5): 573–93.

Salcedo, D. (1992–93) *Atrabilious*. See online: www.moma.org/collection/works/134303?locale=en (accessed 2 October 2015).

Sampson, E. (2003), 'Dancing Shoes and Fairy Feet: Footwear Power and Sexuality in the Western European Fairytale', Dissertation, University College London.

Sampson, E. (2016), 'Dancing, Desire and Death: The Fairy Tale Shoe', in S. Hill (ed.), *Fairy Tale Fashion*, New Haven: Yale University Press.

Sampson, E. (2017a), 'The Cleaved Garment: The Maker, The Wearer and the "Me and Not Me" of Fashion Practice', *Fashion Theory*, 22 (6): 1–20, https://doi.org/10.1080/1362704X.2017.1366187.

Sampson, E. (2017b) 'Creases, Crumples, and Folds', *Fashion Studies Journal*, 3, http://www.fashionstudiesjournal.org/2-visual-essays-2/2017/4/2/creases-crumples-and-folds-maps-of-experience-and-manifestations-of-wear.

Sampson, E. (2018a), 'Entanglement, Affect and Experience: Walking and Wearing (Shoes) as Experimental Research Methodology', *International Journal of Fashion Studies*, 5 (1): 55–76. https://doi.org/10.1386/infs.5.1.55_1.

Sampson, E. (2018b), 'The Lens, the Mirror and the Frame: Glasses, Good Taste and the Material Culture of Looking', *Luxury Journal*, 5: 129–50.

Schapiro, M. ([1968] 1998), 'The Still Life as a Personal Object – A Note on Heidegger and van Gogh; Further Notes on Heidegger and van Gogh', in *Theory and Philosophy of Art: Style, Artist, and Society, Selected Papers 4*, 135–51, New York: George Braziller.

Schilder, P. (1935), *The Image and Appearance of the Human Body*, New York: International Universities Press.

Schmid, C. (2008), 'Henri Lefebvre's Theory of a Production of Space', in K. Goonewardena, S. Kipfer, R. Milgrom and C. Schmid (eds), *Space, Difference, Everyday Life: Reading Henri Lefebvre*, London: Routledge.

Scrivener, S. (2000), 'Reflection In and On Action and Practice in Creative-production Doctoral Projects in Art and Design', Working Papers in Art and Design, 1, https://goo.gl/U8x9RR. (accessed 4 March 2018).

Scrivener, S. (2002), 'The Art Object Does Not Embody a Form of Knowledge', Working Papers in Art and Design, 2, https://goo.gl/68UVdk. (accessed 4 March 2018).

Sennett, R. (2008), *The Craftsman*, New Haven: Yale University Press.

Serres, M. (2008), *The Five Senses: A Philosophy of Mingled Bodies*, New York: Continuum.

Serres, M. with B. Latour (1995), *Conversations on Science, Culture and Time*, trans. R. Lapidus, Ann Arbor: University of Michigan Press.

Sex and the City (2003), Season 4, Episode 64, [TV series] Home Box Office.

Shklovskij, V. ([1917] 1998), 'Art as Technique', in J. Rivkin and M. Ryan (eds), *Literary Theory: An Anthology*, 8–14, London: Blackwell.

Solnit, R. (2001), *Wanderlust: A History of Walking*, New York: Penguin Books.

Solomon-Godeau, A. (1998), 'Mourning or Melancholia: Christian Boltanski's "Missing House"', *Oxford Art Journal*, 21 (2): 3–20.

Spinoza, B. ([1677] 2012), *Ethics*, trans. R. Elwes, New York: Courier Books.

Spivak, E (2014), *Worn Stories*, New York: Princeton Architectural Press.

Spivak, G. C. (1976), 'Introduction', in J. Derrida, *Of Grammatology*, Baltimore: Johns Hopkins University Press.

Stallybrass, P. (1993), 'Worn Worlds: Clothes, Mourning and the Life of Things', *The Yale Review*, 81 (2): 35–50.

Stallybrass, P. (1998), 'Marx's Coat', in P. Spyer (ed.), *Border Fetishisms: Material Objects in Unstable Spaces*, New York: Routledge.

Stallybrass, P. (2014), 'The Value of Culture and the Disavowal of Things', in H. Turner (ed.), *The Culture of Capital: Property, Cities, and Knowledge in Early Modern England*, London: Routledge.

Stallybrass, P. and A. Jones (2001a), *Renaissance Clothing and the Materials of Memory*, Cambridge: Cambridge University Press.

Stallybrass, P. and A. Jones (2001b), 'Fetishizing the Glove in Renaissance Europe', *Critical Inquiry*, 28 (1): 114–32.

Steele, V. (1996), *Fetish: Fashion, Sex & Power*, Oxford University Press.

Steele, V. and C. Hill (2013), *Shoe Obsession*, New Haven: Yale University Press.

Stewart, S. (1993), *On Longing*, Durham, NC and London: Duke University Press.

Strathern, M. (1988), *The Gender of the Gift*, Berkeley: University of California Press.

Swann, J. (1996), 'Shoes Concealed in Buildings', *Costume*, 30: 56–69.

Taussig, M. (1983), *The Devil and Commodity Fetishism in South America*, Rpt ed., Chapel Hill: University of North Carolina Press.

The Red Shoes (1945), [film] Dirs M. Powell and E. Pressburger, Rank.

The Red Shoes (2005), [film] Dir. Kim Yong-gyun, Korea.

The Wizard of Oz (1939), [film] Dir. V. Flemming, Metro Goldwyn and Meyer.

Thomas, H. (1999), 'Undermining a Grimm Tale: A Feminist Reading of "The Worn out dancing shoes"', *Marvels and Tales. Journal of Fairytale Studies*, 13 (2): 170–83.

Thrift, N. (2008), 'Understanding the Material Practices of Glamour', *Journal of Cultural Economy*, 1 (1): 9–23. DOI: 10.1080/17530350801913577.

Tilley, C. (2006), *The Handbook of Material Culture*, London: Sage.

Tite, P. (1998), 'Princess Diana, Mythmaking and the Academic Study of Religion', *Council of Societies for the Study of Religion Bulletin*, 27 (2): 27–30.

Torres, L. (2018), 'Towards a Practice of Unmaking: A Strategy for Critical Fashion Practices', PhD thesis, London College of Fashion.

Turkle, S., ed. (2007), *Evocative Objects: Things We Think With*, Cambridge, MA: MIT Press.

Turner, T. (2019), *The Sports Shoe: A History from Field to Fashion*, London: Bloomsbury.

Valle-Noronha, J. (2017), 'On the Agency of Clothes: Surprise as a Tool Towards Stronger Engagements', *Proceedings of the 3rd Biennial Research Through Design Conference*, Edinburgh, 22–24 March, 518–34 (Article 33).

Van der Kolk, B. et al. (1999), *Traumatic Stress: The Effects of Overwhelming Experience on Mind, Body and Society*, New York: Guilford Press.

Veblen, T. ([1899] 2009), *The Theory of the Leisure Class*, Oxford: Oxford University Press.

Vianello, A. (2006), 'Courtly Lady or Courtesan? The Venetian Chopine in the Renaissance', in G. Riello and P. McNeil, *Shoes: A History from Sandals to Sneakers*, Oxford: Berg.

Weiner, A. (1992), *Inalienable Possessions*, Berkeley, CA: University of California Press.

Weiner, A. B. and J. Schneider (eds) (1989), *Cloth and Human Experience*, Washington: Smithsonian Institution Press.

Winnicott, D. W. (1953), 'Transitional Artefacts and Transitional Phenomena – A Study of the First Not-Me Possession', *International Journal of Psycho-Analysis*, 34: 89–97.

Winnicott, D. W. (1971), 'Transitional Objects and Transitional Phenomena', in *Playing and Reality*, London: Routledge.

Wolfe, F. (1938) 'Choosing Shoes', in M. Barrows (ed.), *200 Best Poems For Boys And Girls*, Racine: Whitman Publishing Company.

Woodward, S. (2005), 'Looking Good, Feeling Right: Aesthetics of the Self', in S. Woodward, D. Miller and S. Küchler (eds), *Clothing as Material Culture*, 21–40, Oxford: Berg.

Woodward, S. (2007), *Why Women Wear What They Wear*, Oxford: Berg.

Woodward, S. (2008), 'Digital Photography and Research Relationships: Capturing the Fashion Moment', *Sociology*, 42 (5): 857–72.

Woodward, S. (2015), 'Object Interviews, Material Imaginings and "unsettling" Methods: Interdisciplinary Approaches to Understanding Materials and Material Culture', *Qualitative Research*, 16 (4): 357–74.

Woodward, S. and T. Fisher (2014), 'Fashioning Through Materials: Material Culture, Materiality and Processes of Materialization', *Critical Studies in Fashion & Beauty*, 5 (1): 3–22.

Woolf, V. (1928) *Orlando*, London: Penguin Classics.

Yardley, C. (2007), *Will Write for Shoes: How to Write a Chick Lit Novel*, London: St Martin's Griffin.

Index

Index